MARK CLATTENBURG

WHISTLE BLOWER

MY AUTOBIOGRAPHY

with Craig Hope

HEADLINE

First published in 2021
by HEADLINE PUBLISHING GROUP

2

Cataloguing in Publication Data is available from the British Library

Hardback ISBN 978 1 4722 8203 3

Typeset in Warnock Pro by CC Book Production

Printed and bound in Great Britain by Clays Ltd, Elcograf S.p.A.

HEADLINE PUBLISHING GROUP
An Hachette UK Company
Carmelite House
50 Victoria Embankment
London EC4Y 0DZ

www.headline.co.uk
www.hachette.co.uk

To Claire, Nathan and Mia, and Thomas and Anne Lindley.

CONTENTS

PREFACE

I AM Mark Clattenburg. To some of you, I will be an arrogant prick. To even more of you, I'm the bloke who has cost
your team points. You might be right on that score. But I am
rarely anything other than the fella in black who was up his
own backside. That was me. The world knew exactly what
I was.

Yet, I got to forty-two years of age and had never spoken
publicly. If you asked any of those who returned judgement,
'What does his accent sound like?', they would not have a clue.
Surely, it is not possible to make a balanced character appraisal
without hearing from the subject himself?

That is why I am here now, committing my story to print. I
hope, in part, it is why you are here. Will you finish this book
and think, 'He's not an arrogant prick after all'? I hope so. But
I also hope you come to understand why you thought that in
the first place.

I know why a certain picture of me was portrayed in the
press. I accept how I was perceived. On the evidence available,
it was probably fair. But no one ever heard my side. Opinions

were based on what I did in my place of work for an hour and a half once or twice a week.

Only when I quit the Premier League in 2017 was I able to present myself in the media. Since then, I would like to think that people have seen a different side. I do not expect everyone to say, 'Oh, isn't he a great guy.' Not at all. You might still dislike me, just for different reasons. That is fine. But dislike me for who I really am.

I have not varnished my story to shine an unnatural light on it. These are my words and my feelings. I have told it how I saw it, and I have not held back. There is a lot of conflict, it is the theme that underpins my career. I have fallen out with a lot of people and there is a lot of me believing I am right. Maybe the others involved would tell a different version.

I am aware that I often portray myself as the wronged party in my various clashes with authority. I hope you will realise why I felt like that – I was a football-mad kid from a council estate who found himself in a world of former public schoolboys, geeks and back-stabbing bullies. I was different to them. I did not conform and they did not like it. But being different was my biggest strength.

What you saw on the pitch was, in many ways, an act. I was not being false. I was simply adopting a character to survive. I needed to don this cloak of supreme confidence to mask my insecurities. I became a different person. At least different from the one you would find at home or in the pub.

I will always refute the 'arrogant' tag, because anyone close to me will tell you that is not true. That is not to say you misread my refereeing persona. A brash exterior was my thing. It was why, I believe, players generally liked me. Over time, and with more success, I slipped into that role with absolute ease.

Of course, it was not a person alien to myself, I had the skills within me. Hell, that brash exterior is something I make no apology for. But, as a referee, it was always with the motivation of creating an aura that won me respect and allowed me to control a football match.

Away from the pitch, I have made mistakes and found myself in situations that could have been avoided. So much for newspapers being 'fish and chip paper' the following day; those stories from the past now reside online forever. None of them, though, are ever accompanied by my version, and people tend to believe what they read.

The *Daily Mail* ran a headline in 2014: 'Controversial Clattenburg is drawn to both the high life and the headlines.' I know why it was written. I was a referee, not a footballer, and I left myself open to such accusations with the expensive cars, private number plates, tattoos, a hair weave. Some of those things I look back on and think, 'What a dick.' Others, I will defend fiercely – I had to get the hair replacement, I was starting to look like Friar Tuck, especially on those elevated tactical cams!

So maybe there are two Mark Clattenburgs. The dad, the husband and the friend. And then the referee. I hope you come to understand both of them.

Oh, and by the way, it is a Geordie accent.

1

END GAME

'You know what, I don't give a fuck any more'

Wednesday 15 February 2017.
Gibraltar International Airport.

There is no turning back once I get on this flight. I can see the Rock of Gibraltar, just beyond the runway. I suppose that's fitting. I feel like I have been staring at a rock face for the past few weeks, grappling with the decision in front of me. I cannot eat. I cannot drink. At the other end of this journey is a piece of paper that will change my life. Financially, I will be made. But it comes at a cost. I will be giving up everything I have worked for, everything I have fought so hard to keep. Last call for the flight to Jeddah.

HERE I am in the summer of 2016, the number one referee in Europe. I have just taken charge of the FA Cup, Champions League and European Championship finals, yet I am only thinking about one thing – quitting the Premier League.

I know that to do so will risk losing my Champions League and international matches. But I feel empty. I have achieved almost everything I wanted to. What else is there for me now?

The World Cup Final? Absolutely, that would be a dream come true. I know I will be going to Russia 2018, but there is close to zero chance of getting the final. Politics will make sure of that. No one has ever refereed the finals of the European Championship and World Cup. That would make me the most successful referee in history. The powers-that-be among the refereeing hierarchy at FIFA would not allow that to happen, no way.

I still have the Champions League, and those nights under the lights at the likes of the Bernabeu and San Siro are magic. But again, I will not be getting another final. I have no goals in front of me. And I am sick of the abuse. I want out.

I started what would turn out to be my final season in the Premier League in August, a goalless draw between champions Leicester and Arsenal. I was bored. I had done every big fixture in this country several times over. What was I working towards? It was starting to feel like a job, and that was never me, I was driven by being the best. Like a lot of things in life, the journey and not the destination is perhaps the most enjoyable part. I was beginning to realise that.

I also knew I could not stay at the same level of performance forever. I was forty-one years old. David Elleray had retired at forty-nine, Dermot Gallagher at fifty and Mark Halsey at forty-five. They did not finish their careers as bad referees, but I think even they would accept their standard was not what it once was. I was worried people would start to criticise me if I was making mistakes, because I did not retire when the time was right. Your brain slows down while the game gets faster, and I would never allow that to be me, an old fella dragging himself around the pitch guessing at decisions. Not that I felt on the decline just yet, but I always had it in my head that I wanted to finish at the top.

Then there were the insults, the constant scrutiny and fear of ridicule and threats made against me and my family. Be it TV, radio, newspapers, social media, managers, players or supporters, they all took aim as if you were some inanimate object – a punchbag would be the most appropriate description. You need a thick skin to be a professional referee, for without that you risk becoming consumed by the negativity. I felt robust in that regard. But are you immune to it? Absolutely not.

Social media took the hate to another level. It went beyond criticism of a decision. There were death threats, and there still are. I have social media accounts now and I don't even have to check the TV listings to know when one of my games is being replayed – a stream of vitriol in my notifications tells me that.

As a referee, you are never going to be popular. I get that. I chose this path with my eyes open, which is ironic given the number of times I have been accused of being blind. But you have to accept there are maybe only traffic wardens who get more stick than you for simply doing their job. Then again, traffic wardens probably say the same about referees.

There comes a point when the abuse makes something as huge as quitting the Premier League easier to contemplate. The thought of removing that anxiety, the feeling of always being public enemy number one, the fear of being mocked in front of your children – it's as enticing as any pay cheque that may be on offer elsewhere. For all of that, wanting to quit and having the opportunity to do so are very different things.

In November 2016, I took a call from Pierluigi Collina, my boss at UEFA. He said I had been shortlisted for best referee at the Global Soccer Awards. It was a prestigious prize. The ceremony was in Dubai between Christmas and New Year and the Premier League gave me permission to go.

I won the award – which was mind blowing, to be considered the best referee in the world – collecting my trophy on the same night as Cristiano Ronaldo was named the world's best player. It was the perfect end to the perfect year, and I felt at the peak of my powers.

But in that environment, chatting to people involved in the world game, you realise there is a life beyond the Premier League. I had options, China being one of them. I flew back home with so many thoughts populating my head, none of which involved me staying in the Premier League. My agent, Rob Segal, started talking to Chinese agents but nothing materialised. But by initiating that, my mind was now elsewhere.

One thing I had noted in the press was that Howard Webb, the former Premier League and World Cup Final referee, was leaving his position in Saudi Arabia, where he was head of refereeing. He was set for a new job in the United States. I gave him a call at the end of January and asked if Saudi would be interested in me. He could not hide his delight; this was ideal for him. He could nominate a successor and leave quietly for the States.

In one phone conversation this idea that had been with me for months, an improbable thought that would not go away, suddenly became something real. That chance call had left me trembling when I hung up, and I did not know if it was excitement or fear.

I knew the money in Saudi could set me up for life. This would not be about leaving for a better league or furthering my career on the pitch, I realised that. This, now, was about securing my family's financial future at a time when I felt ready to do so.

It started to move quickly. The Saudis arranged a flight and I met with Howard and the president of their football federation in Riyadh. I never told anyone beyond my wife, Claire, and my agent. In that one meeting, we were close to agreeing a deal.

The money, as I suspected, was life-changing – £525,000 a year, tax free. In the Premier League I was earning £100,000 plus bonuses, which came to around £30,000, all of which went into my pension. To put that into context, one year in Saudi would be the equivalent of around eight in the Premier League. I would defy anyone with a wife and two children to resist that temptation.

The arrangement suited me – three weeks in Saudi, one week back home. I would still be refereeing but would also be responsible for the development of Saudi referees. This would get a management role on my CV and that is where I saw my future. I left Riyadh and landed back in the UK with my head battered amid a storm of conflicting emotions.

I returned to referee Arsenal 2 Hull 0 on 11 February, in which Sam Clucas would become my last Premier League red card. I had VAR training at Stockley Park the following day, where I told Mike Riley, my boss at the Professional Game Match Officials Limited (PGMOL), about the Saudi offer for the first time. I told him I was giving it serious consideration. I saw in his face that there was genuine shock. Good. Not having to answer to him anymore was definitely a tick in the Saudi column.

But sitting there in Stockley Park's VAR headquarters wasting my weekend, it did not interest me at all. This could be the future – refereeing on a Saturday then staying down south to spend Sunday in a studio surrounded by television screens. I am a big advocate of VAR – it will, with time, prove for the betterment of the game – but this just was not for me. I always wanted to be in the thick of the action, not fiddling about with buttons in a darkened room.

I told Riley that, even if I did take the Saudi role, I still wanted to referee at the 2018 World Cup. I asked him if it would be possible to do some Premier League games the following season, leading up to the tournament. Saudi were happy for me to do a total of ten matches and that would have been enough to keep me involved with the Champions League and on track for the World Cup.

Collina, my mentor and the one person in authority who I trusted, was also the chairman of FIFA's Referees Committee, and I was sure he would be happy with this arrangement. Everyone seemed on the same page. I should have known that would change.

I flew out to Spain with Claire for a short break that same week. It was one last chance to think things over. Nothing had been signed and I was still undecided. I needed Claire during those few days – someone to listen, someone to challenge me, someone who cared. My dad had passed away twenty years earlier and I had not spoken to my mam for five years. Any advice from Riley and some of the others at the Premier League would have been laced with self-interest. Claire had to deal with it all, and I was throwing a lot at her.

The euphoria after the initial offer from Saudi had now made way for trepidation. I was on the verge of sacrificing the career I knew so well, the job that defined me. My head was saying yes, go and secure your future, escape the hate. My heart, in many ways, was telling me to stay – you are a referee in the best league in the world, you would be crazy to give that up.

I was torn to the point of insomnia, although the more thought I gave it, the less sure I became. But then I would consider all of the shit that went with the job. Driving four hours from Seaham down to St George's Park every fortnight for our referees' meetings that lasted an hour. We would then train for a couple of hours before coming inside to build paper fucking castles. Seriously, this was the crap they made you do. I was bored, it was mind-numbing. You weren't allowed to be your own person. You were in this bubble where it was a case of, 'Do as you're told and wear what we tell you.' It felt like a religious cult at times.

Claire and I met up with my agent in Spain. We talked through every angle. I would be giving up my Premier League career. It was everything I had worked for since the age of sixteen, when I first refereed my dad's junior team on a park in Newcastle. It was everything I had fought so hard to keep when I was suspended and sacked by the PGMOL in 2008, and later in 2012 when I was wrongly accused of racism by Chelsea. I will detail both of those periods later.

But the fact I was here, giving such serious consideration to walking away, that told me something. Bang. I'm doing it. That's it. I'm signing with Saudi.

I got a flight from Gibraltar to Jeddah that same night. Once the plane took off, the decision that I was about to commit to felt bigger than it had done at any stage. My gaze was locked on the flight map – Jeddah, my life changes there. It was like my body was being carried along by someone else. Every noise and sight beyond my own head was a blur.

I landed in Jeddah and began to think more clearly. Being on the move was a welcome distraction, rather than trapped in a window seat. I had agreed to tell Riley and Collina at the same time if, and when, I signed. I thought that was fair and I wanted to keep them both on-side. I still thought I could go to the World Cup in sixteen months' time.

And there it was, the contract in front of me. There was no going back now and nor did I want to. I scribbled my name, trying to disguise my tremor. How did I feel? Relief, that was my overriding emotion. Total and utter relief that I no longer had to wrestle with the decision. Relief that I was leaving an organisation, the PGMOL, that I no longer enjoyed working for. Relief that I had taken care of my family.

It was announced the same day, 16 February 2017, that I would be leaving the Premier League for Saudi Arabia. Career-wise, a lot of people said I was making a mistake. They could not fathom why I would do such a thing while still in my prime. If I had quit twelve months earlier – before the three finals – then yes, I would agree. But not now. Once I signed the contract, it felt so right. I felt free.

Offers from elsewhere started flooding in. Suddenly, I had a voice. Over the course of the next year I signed with TV2 in Norway, there was TV work in the United States, a column with the *Daily Mail*, a podcast deal with Paddy Power. It was liberating. I'm Mark and I'm a Geordie! No one had ever heard me speak before.

First of all, though, I told Riley I would see out the final few months of my Premier League contract, taking me up to the end of the 2016/17 season. He appointed me to West Bromwich Albion versus Bournemouth on 25 February. Bloody hell, he could not have made it any more obvious, a crap game as punishment for leaving.

I later sat down with him to negotiate the ten games I thought I would be refereeing during the following season, as we had discussed previously. Little did I know what was already going on behind my back. The PGMOL had been sharpening their knives. Riley said the ten games would not be happening, they just wanted me to leave. I was gutted, angry and upset. Riley knew this would cause me problems with regards to the World Cup. I should have seen it coming.

I still thought FIFA and Collina would find a way to get me there. I was already one of fifty-three pre-selected officials for Russia 2018, and the only one from England.

In early April, I flew to Florence for a FIFA course to prepare for the World Cup, which was now fourteen months away. I did not like the vibe I was picking up. I could not get much out of Collina at all, and that was unusual. I considered him a father figure, I wanted him to reassure me that I would still be going to Russia. I expected FIFA to tweak the rules so that I could be registered in Saudi but still be England's representative. Why shouldn't a referee be based abroad? Players are. I honestly thought they would find a way.

I was starting to feel anxious. I could sense a change in their mood. It felt like I was being shut out, as if they thought, 'How dare you leave the Premier League and leave Europe.' I finished the course and, as I headed for the airport, I knew then that the World Cup would not be happening for me.

Maybe I had been naive and presumptuous to want my cake and eat it. I don't know. But I do know how sad I felt during that journey home. It felt like a vindictive and needless act from all of those who did not help me get to Russia.

My relationship with Collina changed after that, a man who

had invested so much time in me and made me the best referee in the world. But he was different with me in Florence. I knew him well enough to know when those eyes were staring straight through you. I had mistakenly thought he would respect my decision. He had done things in his career to look after his family, I had to do right by mine. The price I paid was missing out on a World Cup. Collina either could not or did not want to find a solution for me.

Even now, I cannot get over the pettiness of the PGMOL and Football Association in not pushing to get me there. I was their one and only nominee. But instead of me, they thought they could try putting forward Martin Atkinson, who had always been their preferred choice – a square, like them. But Atkinson was too old to be selected. It was brainless what they did, it backfired and we ended up with no English officials at the 2018 World Cup. That was a crying shame – for me, for them, for English refereeing.

Politics and backstabbing were never more obvious than within the PGMOL and FA, only this proved to be an act of self-harm. To think, people could not understand why I was walking away from it all.

★　★　★

Mike Riley asked where I would like to referee my last Premier League match. 'I would love it to be at Spurs, at White Hart Lane,' I told him. My family could go, we could get a nice box and have a weekend in London.

That happened for every referee, they always chose their last game. After the service I had given to the Premier League, I assumed my request would be granted. What a stupid assumption to make.

I ended up back at West Brom, where your guests are stuck on the far side of the ground. It is not the best experience for them compared to the hospitality elsewhere. But that was Riley in a nutshell in my experience. He had no respect. To do that to me was snide, it was insulting.

So after thirteen years in the Premier League, my family were not even there for my last game. After all that time – the lost weekends, the trials and tribulations and the good times – I am refereeing my final match with my family 200 miles away.

There was one positive to take from it. The whole episode made my decision to quit even easier to live with. It served as justification. I knew I had made the right call when I was given that match.

So Saturday 29 April 2017 was my final game as a Premier League referee. West Brom 0 Leicester 1. Richard Scudamore, the Premier League chairman, called beforehand and thanked me for my service. I have a lot of respect for Scudamore, especially how he supported me when others tried to get rid of me in 2008. I owe him a lot, and it was kind of him to call.

Riley was there before the game at The Hawthorns but there was no sign of him afterwards. It was sad that he did not have the decency to thank me. But you know what, fuck you. Every incident like this was making me feel better about myself, not worse.

I then discovered that David Elleray – the former Premier League referee and now technical director of the International Football Association Board – was trying to get my international badge stopped with immediate effect. Other referees, in the same situation, had been allowed to carry on longer. Elleray was slippery, a sly toff. He just could not help himself.

The Australian FA had been in touch to ask if I could referee their friendly against Brazil in Melbourne in June. Absolutely, I said, and I was searching for flights before the end of the call. But because of Elleray, this dream fixture had turned into a nightmare to organise. I had to negotiate a way to do it. I am so glad I did not give in to him and that I pushed to make it happen. What a way to finish your international career, refereeing Brazil in a 4–0 win in front of 50,000 at the famous MCG.

I blew for full-time and could not get a handle on how I felt, I did not know if I was happy or sad. Was this the end or the beginning? I regained my focus and emailed 'Lord Elleray' after the match to tell him that I had quit the international panel. Better to jump than allow that prick to push me.

There were a couple of other examples during this period of how shoddily I was treated. There was an FA initiative in which referees who took charge of international matches received a velvet cap when they retired, much like the caps given to England players. It had the year that you started and the year you finished embroidered on the peak. It was a nice gesture. Only it would have been had I not been forced to chase mine.

Elleray, who was also chairman of the FA's referees

committee, did not reply to my messages on the matter. I went above him to Martin Glenn, the FA chairman, and he sorted it. He asked me to come to Wembley and presented me with it. But why did they have to make it such an ordeal?

The PGMOL then held their annual conference. I was not invited, not that I was bothered about that, it was a lucky escape. But they introduced a new PGMOL Hall of Fame. My two assistant referees and two additional assistant referees from the Champions League and Euro 2016 finals were inducted – but there was no mention of me. That was an embarrassing error of judgement, it was pathetic. Without me, those officials would not have been in those finals in the first place. But that's Riley, his bitterness blinded him to the bigger picture. Those who were there on the night could not believe it, and it was no surprise when the newspapers pounced on it and made a mockery of the situation.

So when people ask, 'Do you regret quitting the Premier League?' I can honestly say, 'Absolutely not'. I have made a career out of making decisions, and that was the best one I ever made. Howard Webb told me it would be.

'Mark, it feels strange at first. But after a few months, it feels like the best thing ever,' he said.

He was right, but he was also wrong – I felt wonderful straight away. I started to enjoy life again, spending time with my family without my mind replaying a penalty decision from the previous day. I started sleeping properly. I sacrificed a World Cup, but it was worth it.

I worked for BT Sport for the first time and I had to laugh at the reaction on social media to my accent. My favourite was, 'Mark Clattenburg has the voice of a fourteen-year-old extra from Byker Grove.' But the fact that 'Clattenburg voice' was trending on Twitter tells you everything about the existence of a referee – seen, abused and ridiculed, but never heard.

I hope my decision to leave the Premier League gives others the confidence to do the same if they are feeling like I did. You can feel trapped, I have been there. But there are opportunities, if you have the will and the want to look for them.

And England did end up having a referee at the World Cup in Russia. Me. I went as a pundit for ITV and I loved every minute. Even my ITV colleague Roy Keane was nice to me, and that was a first. I felt on top of the world.

$\star$ $\star$ $\star$

I am often asked if there was one particular match that persuaded me to quit the Premier League. What follows is as close as I can remember to a definitive moment when I thought, 'You know what, I don't give a fuck anymore.'

It was Stoke versus Manchester United on 21 January 2017. Being sent to Stoke can make you feel like that at the best of times, let alone when you are at breaking point. It is no myth, Stoke is always freezing and it is always windy. It is noisy and you get loads of stick.

For all of that, on this particular day, I thought I had a good game. I came off and was pleased with my performance. The tunnel in the corner of the pitch at the Britannia Stadium can be brutal, with home fans on one side and away supporters on the other. This time I wandered towards it without any fuss. Wayne Rooney had just broken Sir Bobby Charlton's Manchester United scoring record with a late free-kick for a 1–1 draw. The focus would be on him.

It was not long after full-time when there was a knock at my dressing-room door and United manager Jose Mourinho came in. I was just taking my boots off.

'You must be happy this time,' I said. 'You can't blame me for that draw, can you?'

'I can,' he said.

He started going on about a handball in the penalty area by Stoke defender Ryan Shawcross.

'What you on about?' I said. 'I got that right, I know I did.'

'No. I've seen the video. You were wrong.'

He was going on and on. Shut up man, will you? I picked up my boot and launched it against the wall next to him.

'Fucking get out of my dressing-room. Get out!'

Mourinho froze. I lost it with him. I did not give a shit anymore. I knew I wanted to quit the Premier League, not that I had even spoken to Saudi at this point.

'Tell you what,' I said. 'If I'm wrong, I'll quit. I'll wrap up tomorrow. I'm sick of this.'

He did not know what to say. I was so fed up with all of the ridiculous mind games. What he said had got inside my head. I drove home while going over and over the Shawcross incident.

I watched it on *Match of the Day* and I was right, the ball hit him flush on the chest. So why was Mourinho playing funny buggers with me? Why did he say he had seen a handball on the video?

I went to bed that night and I knew I'd had enough. 'You know what,' I thought, 'I can't be bothered with idiots like that anymore.' I had worked so hard to get to a position where I thought I would command more respect. But no, don't be daft, you are still the referee. You are still only there to be abused. I was done with this rubbish. I just needed the right opportunity.

I woke up the next day and scrolled down through the contacts in my mobile phone. There he was . . . Howard Webb. Maybe Saudi Arabia could be my ticket out of here.

2

SURVIVAL INSTINCT

'I can't take this home, my mam and dad will kill me'

1993. St James' Park, Newcastle.

I need a piss. Will Newcastle ever stop attacking? I'm gonna have to go. I squeeze through the mass of black-and-white shirts and take the steps three at a time down the back of the Gallowgate End. The stand is being renovated. There's a queue for the portable toilet. I'm finally in. Ah, the relief. The crowd are getting louder. Newcastle must be back on the attack. There's the roar, they've scored! Get in! But wait a second, what the fuck? I'm upside down. Someone has tipped the toilet over – and there's no toilet seat! Arrghh! I'm drenched, and I stink. I would have been better off pissing myself on the terrace. I shove open the door and crawl out. Everyone is bent over laughing. But you know what? I couldn't be happier.

WITHOUT me ever realising, my childhood prepared me for being a referee. I was always fighting to survive. And trust me, without survival instinct you will not last long as the fella who is screamed at and hounded for ninety minutes.

I did not know it but growing up as the middle of five children in council houses with little-to-no money was, all the while, shaping the person and referee I would become. When you wear crap trainers, a raggy uniform and everyone knows you live in the poorest part of town, it does not take long to become a target for the school bullies.

I had to learn pretty quickly how to avoid conflict. Walking home from school should be a happy time for most children. For me, it was a daily battle of wits. I had five different routes, each of them dependent on who had threatened to 'get me' that day. That sharpens your instincts. I was trained, unknowingly, to spot danger, to think on my feet and find a way out of trouble. It was a grounding in the life skills needed to be a referee, even if that was the last thing I thought I would become at the time.

I wanted to be a footballer. I wanted to play for Newcastle United. I had posters of Paul Gascoigne and Chris Waddle on my bedroom wall. Later, it was Micky Quinn and Lee Clark. Bob Cass, the sports journalist, had a weekly local radio show called *It's A Goal* and I would not miss it. I lived for football.

My dad came home from work one day – he drove the team bus for Sunderland, would you believe – and he'd somehow got me Kevin Keegan's match-worn football boots, as well as my first Newcastle shirt, the one with the iconic blue star on the front. Kevin didn't have big feet but these boots were like boats on a nine-year-old. That didn't stop me wearing them and, for years, I had newspaper stuffed inside to fill the gap at the toe.

The fact I was also quite good at playing football was my

way of being accepted at school. I played above my age for a good few years. That won me respect from some, but there was jealousy from others. For them, it was another reason to hit you.

Sport was in my genes. The Clattenburg family name only came to the UK when my granddad, Larry Clattenburg, arrived from Canada. He was a professional ice-hockey player, a net-minder, and came over to play for Durham Wasps. I never met my granddad and we were told he had died back in Canada from a brain haemorrhage. It was only years later that Claire and I received a book tracing the history of the family name as a gift, and that said he had died in Gateshead. I guess I will never know what really happened. All I have is an old Durham Wasps programme with a picture of him inside.

My dad, David, was born in Durham. He met my mam, Janet, through the bus company for which they both worked and I was born in Consett, County Durham on 13 March 1975. I am often referred to as 'Consett's Mark Clattenburg', even though I have little recollection of living there. There are a number of other famous names given the same tag, the actor Rowan Atkinson and cricketer Paul Collingwood among them. So I am happy enough to stick with it.

We moved to Blyth in Northumberland when I was very young, to a council estate behind the Kitty Brewster pub. We had an outside toilet with the coal house next door for the fire. It was bloody freezing in our bedrooms, even in the summer.

But we were happy, five kids always playing together – my older brother and sister, David and Vicky, and my younger brother and sister, Richard and Jill. We were hardly ever in the house. We played in the street until it was too cold or too dark, and I was forever in and out of the pub trying to steal beer mats so we could play with them.

We later moved to Cramlington and another council estate, although this was an upgrade – we had a toilet inside the house this time! But it was still in the rough end of town.

I started at Eastlea Primary School, where my job was to put the letters on the board so everyone knew what choices we had for lunch – a fourth official in the making! I also began to realise that I had a talent for sport when I lost my plimsoll and managed to get it back on and still win the race during our summer sports day.

I moved to Brockwell Middle School at nine years old, and this is when life became more difficult. You start to notice other children have more money than you. They have better clothes and shoes and go on holiday. It is sad, but that becomes a thing for them to tease you about. Football was my saviour, my escape. I was usually first picked in the playground and that gave me a bit of status and self-esteem.

It was around this age, though, that the bullying began, and it did not stop. We always walked to and from school by ourselves. I was terrified of one underpass in particular, where one of the bullies would wait for me. I would enter the darkness praying that I had picked the right route home. I did not always get lucky. He would push me, goad me, throw my bag to the floor. It was humiliating. It got to the point where I would rather take my chances with the traffic on the road above. You try not to cry but inside it is tearing you to pieces. I always left that underpass and thought, 'Why me?'. My mam tried to warn him off, but it did not work. So those years, going from middle school up into high school, they were all about damage limitation, just getting through.

I was twelve when I joined Cramlington High School, still with no idea of what I wanted to be in life beyond a professional footballer, although I later refused to play for the school team. I was playing on a Sunday morning for local teams Cramlington Blue Star and later Wideopen Juniors, where my dad was a coach, but school football did not feel as competitive. The teacher in charge was not a proper coach and I thought the standard was poor.

It was the intervention of another teacher named Mr Reach which, not only got me back involved with school football, but would also lead me into refereeing. I was placed on report for being cheeky to a teacher. School report was a slip that recorded my behaviour every day and I had to take it home for my mam and dad to sign. I will never forget the look of fury on their faces. I can still hear that slipper now.

I came off report but was soon back on it. It was over nothing, I was not a bad lad at all. I spoke to Mr Reach.

'I can't do it, I can't take this home, my mam and dad will kill me,' I told him.

I knew he wanted to get me on the school team, so I used that to my advantage.

'If my parents know I'm on report they won't ever let me play football,' I said.

'Okay, we'll keep this between us,' he said. 'But you'll play for the school?'

'Deal.'

I have laughed about that since with Mr Reach, but I also have a lot for which to thank him.

I had a trial match down at Millwall which came to nothing. I knew then I was not good enough to make it. But it was Mr Reach who took me to one side during my last year of high school.

'Mark, you're not going to be a footballer, why not try refereeing?' he said.

He was right about the football. I knew that myself. But refereeing could be another avenue for making a bit of pocket money, and our family needed every penny we could get.

★   ★   ★

Money had always been a struggle with five children. My dad was a bus driver for the company that ran between Northumberland and Newcastle. Before that, for Moordale Coaches, he had driven Sunderland's first team all over the country. He quit after the boss let his own son drive the coach for the 1985 League Cup Final at Wembley, which they lost 1–0 to Norwich. My dad had done every game that season, so he wasn't standing for that.

He used to take my older brother, David, to watch

Sunderland. He was even the matchday mascot once. That was never for me – I would rather face the slipper! Newcastle was my team.

My dad took me to my first match against Leicester City, a midweek game in 1985. It was my tenth birthday. The anticipation of walking into St James' Park for the first time is a feeling I will never forget. It was a place I had only seen on TV and in the newspapers. When it becomes something real, it becomes a part of you. Saying that, we were beaten 4–1, so at least it was a fitting introduction to life as a Newcastle United supporter. But I was hooked.

My dad only took me to that one game. After that I went with my friends. Every home match we would head into town on the bus for twenty pence, pay around £3 on the turnstile of the Gallowgate End and stand beneath the scoreboard.

One match, when the new stand was being built, I went to the toilet, one of those blue Portaloo types. Rob Lee scored and someone pushed it over. I was lying on my side with the contents of this toilet coming towards me. I came out covered in piss. My mates thought it was hilarious. Happy days.

But I needed money to go to the match. From twelve years old, I had three paper rounds. Some of what I earned went to my mam and I once had to work eight weeks for free, delivering papers for the Happy Shopper, just to clear the tab she had built up. There were some hard times.

We had a slot meter on the back of the television where you dropped fifty pence into a box to top up the time and keep it working. The rentals man collected the money every week. Only we would put fifty pence in and somehow get fifty pence back out. You had to leave enough in to avoid being rumbled, and I will never know how we got away with that for so many years. But we survived and it was a loving family. It was only later in life that we went in different directions after my dad passed away.

There were some crazy moments growing up. Like most of our neighbours in what was a deprived area, money was tight, yet gambling was a huge part of our upbringing. For people of lesser wealth, it is often a pastime born out of escapism or desperation. A win was celebrated by the whole family, but we did not hear about the losses until there was a knock at the door. We could not afford to lose huge sums but we were often left short, meaning my paper rounds became a source of family income.

Me and my siblings also gambled, although, the money involved was not much, twenty-five pence on a placepot at the weekend for a bit of fun. We would pick the horses from the newspaper and our parents would put the bet on. I was playing football in the park one day when I heard my dad shouting down the street.

'Son, son, you've got five horses placed, you're going into the last leg!'

A placepot requires you to have a horse placed – usually first, second or third depending on the number of runners – in the first six races at one meeting. I ran back to the house.

In those days, you followed the racing results on Teletext.

The runners and their odds came up on the screen before the race was off. My dad started shouting at me.

'You've backed a 16/1 shot, you stupid idiot!'

'Why you being like that?' I said.

'A 16/1 shot won't be placed, will it?' he said.

Teletext took an eternity to show the result. The winner eventually flashed up, at 25/1. The page came around again and the second-placed horse was there on the screen – it was mine! We were jumping up and down like lunatics, everyone hugging each other. But we also knew that another horse at long odds in third place would increase the payout. We settled down and waited. Finally, the page reloaded. The third horse was in – at 33/1! My mam and dad were dancing around the coffee table, it was like *Charlie and the Chocolate Factory* when they find the Golden Ticket. We won about £1,000. It was big money for us, not that I saw much of it. My reward was a chocolate bar and staying up late that night to watch television, which was still spitting out fifty-pence pieces despite our new-found wealth.

My mam did eventually take me to JD Sports in Newcastle for some new Troop trainers. The biggest thrill was getting the JD Sports plastic bag, with the drawstring. I had the bag longer than I did the trainers. I thought I was so cool with it swinging over my shoulder. Something as daft as a plastic bag felt like a treat and, because of that, I was an entrepreneur from a young age out of necessity, always trying to make a few quid.

I started pulling rank at the newspaper shop because I was

the longest-serving paper boy. I made sure the posh new estate in Cramlington was mine, if only for the tips at Christmas.

I was always knackered by the time I came to play football on a Sunday morning because I had been up since 6 a.m. delivering papers with the supplements inside. Now, when I see a *Sunday Times*, I still shudder at the size and weight of it.

I sold *The Football Pink* on a Saturday night. Even if customers were out, I always delivered the paper and got the money later, because I knew how much people loved it. I did too, checking the football scores and studying the league tables between houses. My customers usually looked after me with an extra five pence on top of the twenty-five it cost. I only had to pay the paper shop fifteen pence per copy, so that round was my best earner, and I got to read Newcastle's match reports while working.

There was one fella who always gave me the flat twenty-five pence. He used to wait for his five pence change. Really? Tight git. I once played a little game with him.

'Next time the weather is bad, I won't be able to make it, sorry,' I said.

He got the message. I was always thinking of ways to make a few extra pennies.

We could have done more as a family, if it wasn't for the gambling. My dad fought hard most of his working life. But his health started to deteriorate after we moved back to Blyth when I was sixteen. For years he had coached the football team at Wideopen, he was fit and active. Then he was diagnosed with angina and went downhill rapidly. He needed a walking stick to get around come the end.

My mam went out and got a job as a legal secretary. We had to fend for ourselves during the day but my mam was then getting home from work and looking after all of us. It was not easy for her, I see that now.

My dad passed away aged forty-nine in 1997. I was twenty-two years old. I fell out with him before he died. It was stupid. I wanted to move out and live on my own, I wanted my freedom. My parents needed my board money because my dad was ill and unable to work. We rowed about it and he swung for me. He wasn't strong enough at the time to make a fight of it, but him going for me like that caused a divide. My mam took his side. I know why she had to do that, but I felt it was them against me. I moved out and I got what I wanted, but it came at a cost.

My dad was a tough father but I respected him. He thought nothing of giving you a whack as a kid, and that was the way with a lot of parents of that era. I knew right from wrong because of him. I never smoked, I never took drugs, I was never in trouble with the police. The fear of reprisal from him meant I was scared to step out of line. My brothers and sisters were the same.

He was in hospital the week before he died. I went to see him. There was still a little bit of tension but we talked and buried the hatchet. I realised that I was being selfish. But in no way did I think it would be the last time I saw him.

He was released from hospital on a Wednesday but, on the Thursday evening, he complained of pains in his legs. He had blood clots, not that we realised. They travelled up his body and he died at home the next day. I still feel regret and anger, because it could have been avoided with something as simple as a tablet. He was alone in the house with our dog, a black labrador called Digger. The dog was so traumatised that he eventually had to be put down.

I will never forget the phone call to say my dad had died, the shock of it. It is a moment in life that acts as a page break – you remember things before he died, and you remember things after he died. It is like they are two different universes. At different points in my life and my career, I have caught myself thinking, 'I wish Dad had been here for this, what would he have thought? What would he have said?'

Yes, he had a short fuse and so did my mam – there was not even a good cop you could run to – but we got through. My childhood and our years together as a family were happy and, all the while, I was oblivious to it shaping the character needed for the career I would one day pursue.

I had a job as an apprentice electrician lined up as I prepared to leave Cramlington High School at sixteen. But Mr Reach had also mentioned refereeing. 'I'll give it a try,' I thought . . . 'but I can't really see it going anywhere.'

3

CARDS MARKED

'Half of them were still pissed from the night before'

1993. Morpeth Sunday League.

He's swung for him, that's a red card. My first-ever red card. Am I ready for this? Yes, he's got to go, you can't do that. I'm eighteen, this lad is probably a couple of years older than me. Off you go. Ah shit, he's fuming, I've upset the wrong fella here. 'I'll be waiting for you after the game,' he snarls. He's just missed with one punch, maybe that was a range-finder. He ain't gonna miss with me. Where's my support? There isn't any, is there? The linesmen are just some of the subs. Is this really worth it?

I WAS sixteen years old when I first stepped onto a football pitch wearing a black kit and gripping my whistle like a panic alarm. I did not have a clue.

Thankfully, it was a match involving one of the teams that my dad coached at Wideopen Juniors in Newcastle, so the parents were pretty forgiving with me.

I had gained the refereeing qualification as part of The Duke of Edinburgh's Award scheme. Mr Reach, my teacher at

Cramlington High School, suggested that I do it and the school paid for the eight-week course, during which I learned the *Laws of the Game*. After that, you had to pass an exam. You would have to be a fool to fail, you had the *Laws of the Game* with you and the answer to every question was in there. I wish my GCSEs had been that easy, they did not go so well.

So I passed, I was now a qualified referee. I had to buy my kit, my whistle and my red and yellow cards. Ah, those cards. My first match was a junior game so the chances were I was not going to need them, but I still had them ready in my top pocket. I was secretly hoping someone would throw a punch.

I walked off after that first game and thought, 'It's definitely not my last'. I was losing my enjoyment for playing but still wanted to be involved in football. Straight away I got more of a buzz from refereeing. I wanted to get every decision right; it stayed with me for days when I got one wrong. I was running further than I ever had as a player and I got such a kick from being constantly involved in the game. The satisfaction of leaving the pitch knowing that everyone was happy – it gave me a feeling of pride that I had lost as a player.

I had been moved to right-back by the age of sixteen after playing as a striker, so the glory days were long gone. I was still playing for Wideopen Juniors and maybe I could have carried on into the Northern League. But my mind was made up one Sunday morning when the manager dropped me.

'Mark, do you mind being linesman?' he said.

Piss off. I stormed out. I stopped playing after that and dedicated everything to refereeing.

As a player, I was not going to improve much. I knew what I was and what I wasn't. But, as a referee, I was getting better every week. I became addicted to charting that development within myself. I wanted more and more matches. My dad was supportive and most of those early games that I refereed were for his team. I was soon doing three matches every Sunday and that could mean as much as £30. I was going to Newcastle United reserves games just to watch the referee and pick up tips. I was taking it more seriously than I ever did schoolwork, and the *Laws of the Game* was my new favourite textbook.

I left school at sixteen and began work as an apprentice electrician. Even if I was going to make it as a referee in the Football League – and I had that ambition very quickly – referees were not employed professionally at the time, so I needed a career to support me.

I have written about my childhood preparing me for being a referee but as a teenage kid fresh out of school among senior tradesmen, that toughened me up. They used to send me for a 'long stand' or 'glass nails'. The fella in the store would just laugh at me. But it gave me the skills needed for dealing with men, for dealing with ridicule and humiliation.

I still speak to some of the guys I worked with back then. They all say, 'We knew you wouldn't hang around with us.' They could see the desire I had and the sacrifices I was making to push myself as a referee.

Overtime at weekends paid well, but I missed out on that to do games. I still progressed at work and eventually moved into a management job as an electrical estimator. But those teenage years were about learning my trade, be that as an electrician or referee. They both had their fair share of shocks.

I was soon refereeing men's football on a Sunday morning. I was a boy, really. I would be in the dressing-room before the game, looking at my watch, wishing it would stop ticking. Shit, I've got to go and referee adults now. They would try to eat me alive. My parents were worried about me; my dad knew what football was like at that level.

Once I got into the game, I was usually okay, I could handle them. Half of them were still so pissed from the night before that they would abuse you no matter what, but I felt that others started to respect me. It was the same as beating the bullies at school. I had the tools to deal with these arseholes. I knew how to get out of conflict and how to defuse situations. But there was still the odd scary moment.

My first sending-off in the Morpeth Sunday League was up at Ellington in Northumberland. The recipient of the red card said he was going to wait for me in the car park, he was threatening to break my legs. I was petrified. You feel alone. It's not as if you've got ten team-mates backing you up. I did not even bother getting changed or showered after the game, and I certainly did not have the nerve to go into his team's dressing-room to ask for my match fee. I ran straight to my car and got the hell out of there.

You should not be made to feel like that and part of me wanted to pack it in. But it's like falling off a bike – you get back on and forget about the pain and the bits that aren't very nice. The only difference with refereeing is that it does not matter how good a rider you become, you're always going to fly over the handlebars again at some point.

It was not just on the pitch where they tried to intimidate you. I was eighteen when I was out drinking in Whitley Bay with my friends. I went to the toilet and this lad started shouting at me.

'You refereed me last Sunday. You were shit.'

What do you do? I couldn't book him, could I? You just have to make light of it and not react. My man-management skills were coming on, even if it was for the wrong reasons at times.

I felt far more safe in the High Pit Social Club in Cramlington. That was my favourite haunt. I was still giving a lot of my wages to my mam, but the cash from refereeing I had for pocket money. Or, to be more precise, beer money.

Every Friday night me and my mates would head to the club, queuing up to get in no matter the weather. It was not old fellas sat having a game of cards, either. Every eighteen-to-thirty year old in Cramlington wanted to be in there for the disco. It closed at 11 p.m. and you would get some fish and chips and the bus home. They were good times.

Not that it impacted on my refereeing. I started out as a 'Class 3' referee with the Northumberland FA at sixteen. By eighteen I was applying for 'Class 1', which was unheard of for someone so young. But they did it, no hesitation, promoted me straight away. It meant I could run the line in the Northern League, the ninth tier of the football pyramid. Thankfully, those kick-offs were not until a Saturday afternoon, so I had all morning to pull myself around after the joys of the High Pit Social.

My first game as a Northern League linesman was Alnwick Town versus Morpeth Town. Just arriving at the ground for the first time you feel part of it, the occasion, the sense of it meaning something to a lot of people. It was a special league to be around.

The clubs were so hospitable and you always had a beer after the game. One Saturday night at Bedlington Terriers we did not leave until 2 a.m. In fact, you would spend most of your match fee in the clubhouse. I hardly made a penny. At least I got my pie and peas for free.

Non-League Day over a Bank Holiday weekend was the best day of the year. The league would stagger the kick-off times so the anoraks could do four matches in a day. I was one of them, I would referee my game and then go to watch the others. I miss the people at that level, they are the fabric of their football club. For me, it is the heart and soul of the game.

I used to get some abuse as a referee, particularly at places like Tow Law, where it was fierce but funny at the same time.

'Referee, you're shite,' one voice would pipe up.

'Aye, and this is one of his better games,' another would add.

They weren't laughing one day at Tow Law when the

floodlights went out at the start of the second half. They were calling the Northern Powergrid trying to get to the bottom of it. They eventually checked the referee's room, where there was a switch connected to the lights. I had been leaning against the wall before going out for the second half and must have knocked it off! We were nearly ready to go home when they realised, and I would still have got my match fee because we had already played forty-five minutes. Instead, it was back out in the freezing cold.

I was running the line a lot during those early days. It was never for me, it was boring. I was refereeing in the Northern Alliance, the eleventh tier, and I started doing the youth teams of Newcastle and Sunderland. That was good for me, because I was dealing with young professional footballers who were drilled to pass and move. It was like refereeing a different game compared to non-league, where it was blood, studs and thunder. The two of them combined gave me a rounded exposure. I was learning fast.

By twenty-two, I was promoted to Northern League referee. I was still getting out of bed before the milkman and working on building sites being battered by wind and rain – it can be like that up here in the summer – but I felt my refereeing was going places.

I was so fortunate to have the Northern League as a grounding. I was refereeing big matches in front of big crowds. For me, it is the best non-league division in the country for its standard of player and level of competition. It is with good reason that Northern League clubs have dominated the FA Vase at Wembley for many years. I am proud to have been part of it.

But my career changed one Saturday in January 1999, when I was twenty-three years old. I was linesman in the Conference by now and we had a game at Barrow, who were playing Rushden & Diamonds. Clive Oliver, Michael Oliver's dad, was referee. He picked up myself and the other linesman, Don McCloud, and we drove across to Cumbria, three hours away.

There was a lot of attention on the game because Rushden had drawn 0–0 at home to Leeds United, of the Premier League, in the FA Cup Third Round the previous weekend. Their replay at Elland Road was in a few days' time. All the TV cameras were at Barrow's Holker Street and every national newspaper had reporters there.

As we were driving across, Don turned to me.

'Mark, you go senior linesman today,' he said. 'You've got more chance of progressing in your career than I have.'

It was nice of him, but it meant nothing really. If the referee got injured then the senior linesman replaced him, and that never happened. Only this day it did.

Ten minutes into the game and Clive pulled a muscle. Christ, I'm going on here. It took me five minutes to get the cards into my top pocket, my hand was shaking so much. From nowhere I was thrust into this match, and I felt like the world was watching.

After just a few minutes, a defender flew into a challenge. Yellow card. Thank you. It calmed me down. I felt like the rest of the game went well. At least I got to full-time and no one was threatening to wait for me in the car park. Rushden won 2–0.

We were in the bar afterwards and this big guy, a Barrow

fan, starts walking towards me. His team have lost, remember. Oh God, I could get chinned after all.

'Son, you're the best referee we've ever had at Barrow,' he said, and shook my hand.

I couldn't stop smiling all the way home.

The referees' assessor was at the game and gave me ten out of ten. I refereed Sheffield Wednesday reserves a short while later and Keith Hackett, the former Premier League referee, also gave me top marks. People were starting to talk in refereeing circles of this young lad from the North-East who was making a name for himself. And with a name like Clattenburg, few forgot it.

★   ★   ★

I have to mention another special day from that same season, a few months earlier in October 1998.

In those days, fourth officials for Premier League matches were often provided by the local FA, allegiance to any specific team did not come into it. It was not what it's like now, when the fourth official is a Premier League referee.

I got a call from the Northumberland FA to say I would be fourth official for Newcastle United versus West Ham. I played it cool on the phone, but when I hung up I started dancing around the room. Let's not forget, I was still only a Northern League referee at the time.

I have refereed hundreds of matches since, but I remember this day better than nearly all of them. I parked over the road from St James' Park and walked into the iconic Milburn Stand entrance. Yes, I had always wanted this moment to be as a player, but I floated up those steps. We had a sandwich before the game and I met the other officials. Graham Poll was the referee and he was the best in the country. I was starstruck.

We walked onto the pitch an hour or so before kick-off and Graham turned to me. I was just a kid he had never heard of before.

'Come on then, Mark, who do you support?' he said.

I can't tell him the truth, can I? We are literally stood on the grass at St James' Park.

'I don't support any team,' I said.

'Rubbish. Everyone supports someone.'

He could tell I was embarrassed.

'Okay then,' he said. 'Which result do you look for first in the newspaper?'

'Sunderland,' I said.

'So you're a Sunderland fan?'

'No. I just like to see if the fuckers got beat.'

It broke the ice. The rest of the day I was in awe of everything around me. Just standing on the touchline at St James' was a dream. Newcastle lost 3–0 and Graham sent off Stuart Pearce. But on that occasion, I did not care about Newcastle getting beaten. I left the ground and thought to myself, 'You know what, this will be me one day, refereeing in the Premier League.' It gave me a burning desire to make that happen.

By the start of the following season, 1999/2000, I had been promoted to Football League linesman and was refereeing in the

Conference. Running the line was tedious. I was doing a game at Sheffield United, 27,000 supporters there, and I was daydreaming. I was thinking about meeting my friends on Newcastle's Quayside later that night. Next thing, this big scream goes up for an offside from the home fans. I just threw my flag up in the air. It was only later that I was told it was nowhere near offside. I remember that because it made me realise I was a useless linesman. I just did not have the concentration. I did not want to be stuck out there waving a flag around, I wanted the whistle.

Towards the end of that season, I was invited for an interview to get on the National List of Football League referees. This was moving fast, every year it felt like I was up for promotion. I had only done one season in the Conference and no one got moved up that quickly. I travelled down to London for the interview at the FA's Lancaster Gate headquarters.

I sat on a bench in Hyde Park beforehand and the enormity of it all suddenly hit me. I was twenty-four, I could be the youngest Football League referee since World War II. I had been told by others not to get too disheartened if I did not make it this year. I was young, they said, and my merit marks were good, there was always next year. But I was not having that. I wanted it now.

The interview was strange. Easy, really. They asked me stuff like, 'If there was snow forecast for a Saturday game, what would you do?'

'I would travel down the night before,' I said. It felt like they had already made up their mind, one way or another. The interview itself was a waste of time. I was told a letter would be delivered the following day.

I came out and Colin Webster, another North-East referee, was waiting to go in.

'What's it like?' he said.

'Ah, Colin. It's horrific. They grilled me,' I said.

'Really?'

'Yeah, they were asking me all about referees in the North-East, who was good and who was bad.'

'What did you say?'

'I had to tell them you were terrible.'

'Shut up, man.'

We had a laugh about it. But I was not laughing the next morning back at home as I waited for the postman. I'd had my nose against the glass of the front window for two hours when he finally came into sight. He stopped to talk to my neighbour. For fuck's sake. I was ready to run outside and grab the letter from his bag.

Then it dropped. I ripped it open. 'Congratulations, you are now a Football League referee.' It is funny, but the feeling I had was relief. I realised in that moment how much it meant to me. I was starting to feel a bit of pressure. I was scared of having to tell people that the interview was not successful. I had failed my driving test four times and hated the disappointment in the face of my family and friends every time I told them. For eight years my refereeing career had been all good news, and I was fearful of that first setback.

There was also sadness that my dad was no longer alive to share this with me. He had died two years earlier. I take some comfort from knowing how proud he would have been. He had driven me and my younger brother all over the North-East playing football as kids. He was football mad. For me to achieve this – and everything I did later in my career – he would have loved it. I sometimes think about that. I hope he was looking down on it all with pride and a smile on his face.

Some people used the phrase 'fast tracked' when it came to my progression. I never liked that. It was more that I did well. Yes, they were showing a lot of faith in someone so young, but I felt it was deserved.

I got a booklet that summer with my match appointments ahead of the new season. I kept reading it over and over. I would be getting around £220 per game, plus mileage. My kit was free, too. That felt like a big deal. I tried it on as soon as it arrived. I looked in the mirror at the Football League badge and thought to myself, 'You've made it.'

Saturday 12 August 2000. Chesterfield 3 York City 1.
Football League Division Three.

My first game as a Football League referee, at twenty-five years old. All I had to do was get through it with no major controversy. That would have been nice.

Chesterfield were 3–1 up with fifteen minutes to go when

York captain Peter Swan clashed with an opponent in the penalty area. It was off the ball. No one had seen it, but I had. I sent him off. The incident was not on camera and it caused a hell of a stir afterwards. Even Chesterfield's players said they could not explain the red card. I stood by it and still do.

There was a lot of publicity around me before the game, given my age, and the newspapers had been out to take pictures of me with my wife at the time, Helen. But I could have done without the scrutiny afterwards.

I felt a responsibility, not just for myself but for all young referees. I was not 'fast-tracked', as I have explained, but I did feel like a project. If I failed, it could make the Football Association and Football League think twice about promoting others so soon. But I used to get some stick.

'Have you got a note from your mam to referee this game?'

'Blow your whistle, son, school in the morning.'

There was a bit of scepticism from the older referees, too. I could tell some of them were thinking, 'This kid ain't all that', and they no doubt wanted me to mess it up. But I avoided anything calamitous and managed to get by.

Come the January of my first season, I was refereeing First Division (second tier) matches. It proved that young referees should be backed, if they are good enough. Later, the likes of Stuart Attwell and Michael Oliver broke my record and I was delighted for them. Michael also came through the Northern League, and that was no coincidence.

I would be lying, though, if I said I sailed through that first year. I did not. At best, I survived. If I had a midweek game, because of where I lived in the North-East, I would often be getting home at 1 a.m. or later and then had to get up for work the next morning. Most of my holiday entitlement was also taken up covering those midweek matches. There was no rest, I was worn out.

There were times on the pitch when I was also struggling. I felt a little bit out of my depth and I had to try so hard not to let that show. The second you show weakness as a referee, you have lost control. But players were trying to dominate me. I was apprehensive, nowhere near as decisive as the referee I would become.

What got me through those early years, I believe, was having a personality. I was still working on the tools as an electrician. I was not your stereotypical referee, such as a schoolteacher or a policeman, positions of authority and responsibility. I was getting whacked on the head with conduit every day. If I was holding the cable, they would deliberately turn on the electricity to give me a belt, a little shock. I had to have my wits about me. But it gave me an edge and a bit of cheek.

At the end of my first year in the Football League, it was announced that referees would be turning professional. The Professional Game Match Officials Board – later to become the PGMOL – was established. 'I could make a living out of this,' I thought. No more getting up at 6 a.m. to go and walk on pipe bridges, taking the brunt of the abuse in the bait cabins. I wanted out of that life.

Towards the end of my third year in the Football League, I was convinced I would be promoted to the Premier League. My merit marks were top of the table. So when I got a phone call saying I wasn't going up, I was properly pissed off.

But on reflection it was for the best, and it is not often I praise the PGMOL. It gave me another season with more high-profile matches in the old First Division. It was also the first setback of my career, a little reality check. Over time, I realised that you need such moments, they only make you stronger and more driven.

At the end of the 2003/04 season, it was confirmed I would be promoted to the Premier League. I was twenty-nine. The youngest referee in Premier League history.

Saturday 21 August 2004.
Crystal Palace 1 Everton 3. Premier League.

Four years on from my first game in the Football League, I went into my Premier League debut with the same forlorn hope – get through it without incident. Ninety minutes later and I had awarded a penalty and shown a red card. Decision-wise, at least they were right.

But the biggest lesson learned was this – I needed to be fitter and to pace myself. Because of my nerves, I was charging around like a maniac in the first half. I was so pleased with myself. 'I'm out-running Thomas Gravesen here.' I got in at half-time, sat down and did not want to get back up. I had a bit of excess around my midriff at that stage as well, which did not help. I was later shown my second-half running stats, and they were shocking. From trying to sprint a marathon in the first half, it looked like I had gone for a stroll after half-time.

I sent off Everton's Gary Naysmith for a stupid shirt-tug on Wayne Routledge, a second yellow. The penalty was easy, too. Palace goalkeeper Julian Speroni brought down Kevin Campbell and Gravesen scored. No one complained about me afterwards. Job done.

I was lucky in that Keith Hackett was the new boss of the PGMOL. He wanted referees to let the game flow and manage the players without the need for flashing your cards. It suited me perfectly. Some of the older guys, as good as they were, they were stuck in their ways, too regimented. Me and Howard Webb, who had been promoted a year earlier, were like a breath of fresh air for what the Premier League wanted. Our style aided the product they were trying to sell around the world.

Managers and players responded well to us. You would get comments like, 'We're glad we've got you today.' That would dry up with some over time, as grudges emerged. But my first couple of years in the Premier League went as well as I could have hoped, one or two howlers apart, and I will come back to them.

I turned professional ahead of my first season in the Premier League and I tried to juggle that with my job as an electrical estimator. The company wanted me to stay on but it did not work, not least because Mondays were taken up telling my colleagues all about my match at the weekend.

Being a full-time referee meant a daily fitness programme where you had to wear a heart monitor and send your data to the PGMOL. There was also more time for rest and video work, on top of our fortnightly get-togethers.

As confident as I felt, I still look back and think I was unrecognisable from the referee I became. I would run after the ball, like a kid in the playground. As I got older, everyone used to say I was the fittest referee. I was certainly one of them and pushed myself to the limit, but my approach was as much to do with learning how to read the game and running less. If the full-back had the ball and was shaping to play it downfield, I was already on my way anticipating the next phase. Too many referees – and for several years I was one of them – are like a moth to a flame with the ball. The upshot is you run too many needless yards and tired referees make mistakes.

But I was also discovering that running around and knowing the *Laws of the Game* did not make you a top Premier League referee. This was the home of the big egos. I would need to develop one of my own, if I was going to survive.

4

THE MANAGERS

'Jurgen Klopp. Brilliant manager. Sour loser'

I ALWAYS tried to build a relationship with managers. It was a form of protection. If there was mutual respect, they might be less inclined to take aim for you in the media.

Why does that matter? Refereeing is often about perception. If a narrative emerges in the press whereby you are being criticised every week, then a negative momentum builds. Players take their lead from the manager's comments and, on the pitch, you can feel a change in attitude towards you. Likewise with supporters – once the boss of their team says you're rubbish, the abuse soon follows.

That is why it pays to have managers on side because, when they turn on a referee, it invariably dominates the news agenda. You can see that today more than ever. When a referee has a particularly poor game and managers complain in their post-match interviews, that official is often stood down for the following weekend. The focus now is crazily intense.

If you have a level of trust with a manager then they will understand that mistakes will happen. You could never get too close to them, for that would open you up to accusations of favouritism. But by welcoming dialogue and listening to them, it went a long way to developing a connection that worked for both parties.

I still believe there should be a cooling-off period before managers are allowed to speak to referees after the game. However, I also found those conversations helpful. I was always happy to engage, because it gave you an insight into their thinking – what they wanted and what pissed them off. That knowledge allows you to protect yourself going forward.

I enjoyed occasions like golf days and charity dinners with managers. Most of them are great storytellers and, as a football fan, I could listen to them for hours. But it was also useful in getting to understand their philosophy on the game.

As a referee, you have to arm yourself with as much information as possible. It helps to manage personalities and avoid conflict.

Was this approach guaranteed to quell anger and ensure an easy life? Don't be daft. Read on and you'll understand why.

* * *

It is little wonder my relationship with Sir Alex Ferguson started well, even if it was for entirely the wrong reasons from my perspective.

It was in January 2005 that I took charge of my first Manchester United match, against Tottenham Hotspur at Old Trafford. I had been a Premier League referee for just five months. It was goalless entering the eighty-ninth minute when Pedro Mendes, the Spurs midfielder, scored a goal from the halfway line. The ball was at least a yard over the line before goalkeeper Roy Carroll scooped it back out.

Except, me and my linesman did not see it and did not award the goal. It was not our fault – I will revisit why I believe that to be the case – but it saved United a point and cost Spurs victory. Fergie certainly had no issue with me that day and he was always very pleasant when our paths crossed over the next couple of seasons.

At least, that was, until November 2007, when United played Bolton at the Reebok Stadium. Sam Allardyce had left Bolton earlier that year to manage Newcastle, but the team still had his stamp on it. They were in your face and uncompromising, and this fixture always had an edge.

Bolton striker Nicolas Anelka scored early on and they led 1–0 at half-time. Kevin Davies, the Bolton forward, had targeted Patrice Evra throughout the half and had given him a bit of a battering. It was classic Bolton, using their physicality to unsettle the opposition. I did not mind that, as long as it was within the laws. I respected the way they got the best from themselves.

Coming off at half-time, Ferguson made no attempt to hide his fury as we walked down the tunnel.

'You've given us no fucking protection,' he said, among other profanities and insults. 'You've got no fucking control.'

He was accusing Bolton of bullying them and he took his

anger out on me. He went on and on and would not stop. I'd had enough. I sent him off.

Oh God, I have just sent off Fergie. I'm shaking.

I was still a young referee at thirty-two and trying to make my way in the Premier League. You had to be sure you were right if you were crossing Alex Ferguson. He disappeared into United's dressing-room without saying another word. But Ferguson's body language always betrayed his rage, and I suspected this was not over.

There was a policewoman outside the dressing-room.

'Can you make sure Sir Alex Ferguson does not come back out into the playing area for the second half?' I asked her.

'Me?' she said. 'Why me? I'm not doing it.'

'You're the police!'

She was trembling just as much as me and didn't know what to do. But that was the power of the man. Even the police were terrified of him.

Bolton won 1–0 and I had to laugh at Ferguson's comments afterwards. He claimed that whatever he said to me at half-time must have worked, because I had a much better second half. It was too late for niceties. He was charged by the FA and admitted using abusive and insulting language towards me. He was fined £5,000 and given a two-match touchline ban.

It showed I would not be bullied by him and it did me well in the long run. But it could have gone two ways. Either he holds it against me and tries to get me scratched from the

Premier League – and never underestimate his influence – or he respects me. I think he did the latter.

You sometimes have to remind managers, especially ones like Ferguson, that, ultimately, you are in charge. If players or managers cross the line, like he did here, they have to know they will be punished. He did not abuse me like that ever again. There were cross words, absolutely, but he never repeated the language and aggression of that day at Bolton.

My first little rumbling with him had been in a game at Crystal Palace in March 2005. United were going for the title, but they were poor that day and drew 0–0. That was their chance of winning the league all but gone. I sent off Palace midfielder Vassilis Lakis, but Ferguson still had a moan about me. It was not my fault they could not score against ten men.

That is what Ferguson was like. Over the years, I had plenty of opportunities to see him and his team up close. I am convinced that the players were schooled in Ferguson's tactics for dealing with the officials as much as the opposition.

Ferguson used to blame everyone, from the referee to the catering lady. It was a very deliberate ploy. It was about creating a siege mentality with his players, but also trying to influence future decisions by intimidating officials.

His players would gang up on you in packs. It was like they had a rota system, always a different pair or three or four of them so they would avoid being sent off. Rio Ferdinand, Gary Neville, Roy Keane, Paul Scholes, Wayne Rooney, they would all have a little bite and get in your face. There was the infamous case when United's players hounded referee Andy D'Urso in 2000. That was shocking and exposed how nasty they could be.

You had to be wise to their motivation for targeting you. They were not trying to change the decision that had just gone, they were trying to get inside your head ahead of the next one. Did it work? Not with me. There was no bias towards United from referees, as some supporters of opposition clubs claim.

Yes, there was an aura around them, that was Manchester United. I used to read in the newspapers that referees were influenced by that and gave them favourable decisions. That is absolute rubbish. The same journalists writing that nonsense were shit scared of Fergie themselves. They would have printed things that were very kind just to stay onside with him. That was how he operated. Be it with referees, his own players or the media, it was a climate of fear he created.

You had to be mentally strong going to Old Trafford because they would try everything to influence you. Fergie could turn the crowd against the referee just by jumping up and reacting to a decision on the touchline. It was intimidating, I have no shame in admitting that. I defy anyone in my position not to feel that pressure. It is being able to resist it that makes for a good referee.

It was not just us officials who felt it, I saw it with opposition players. When I left the Premier League, I did some work with TV2 in Norway. I got chatting to Brede Hangeland one day, the former Fulham and Crystal Palace defender, and I asked him what it was like going to Old Trafford. He said that, from the moment you got on the team bus, you knew that a point was a bonus, that you were probably going to get beaten. It was fascinating to hear the impact that club and that stadium had on people during Fergie's era when United were at the top.

As a referee, you would go there not wanting to make a mistake, because it was always a high-profile match and usually on TV. So to go back to my first game at Old Trafford, United versus Spurs in 2005, it could not have gone any worse in that regard.

I blew for full-time and immediately the Sky Sports steady-cam was in my face. Oh shit, that's never a good sign. Instinctively, it told me the Mendes effort was over the line. I had got to eighty-nine minutes and was so close to getting out of there unscathed. Then, from nowhere, Mendes took this audacious shot from the halfway line. I was in the right position, close to the ball, but miles away from the goal. I expected Roy Carroll to catch it, everyone did. But he didn't, he somehow managed to spill the ball towards the goal and dived to claw it back out.

I did not have a clue if it was over the line. How could I? I was fifty yards away, I would be guessing. To award a goal, you have to be sure. This was impossible. My linesman was running to catch up with the ball and, like me, he had no way of being certain. With no goal-line technology, I could not award a goal. I waved play on and looked across to the touchline, where Spurs boss Martin Jol was manhandling Mark Halsey, the fourth official. Oh fuck, this must be close.

When I saw the replay after the game, I was absolutely gutted. The ball was well over the line. So much for getting through my first match at Old Trafford without any major incident, this was headline news.

But I will always maintain that this mistake was not my fault, nor that of my linesman. It is one of the most infamous incorrect decisions in Premier League history, but I was powerless. The human eye did not stand a chance in such a freak circumstance and it highlighted the need for goal-line technology. At least it was a force for good in that regard.

Not that Spurs fans see it that way. They are never shy of reminding me about the 'Mendes goal'. They are right, of course, it was a goal. Of all the decisions in my career, I would go back and change this one above any other. I wish there was a way of me getting it right.

I remember before that game, Rob Styles, a fellow and more experienced referee, sat me down and had a word.

'Mark, Manchester United normally win at Old Trafford. If they're winning, it's straightforward. It gets interesting when they're not winning.'

He was right. Fergie was a bad loser and never more so than the day in October 2011 when Manchester City, by now under Abu Dhabi ownership, came to Old Trafford.

It was one of the biggest and most anticipated Manchester derbies in years. Fergie had recently called them the 'noisy neighbours' and, even in the tunnel before the game, I could tell City were fired up.

They went ahead in the first half through Mario Balotelli, who then revealed his 'Why always me?' T-shirt. I thought it was funny – he had set fire to his apartment that week after lighting fireworks in his bathroom – but I had no choice but to show him a yellow card. I should have asked if he had any spare T-shirts really, given the controversies I would run into in my career.

Early in the second half, I sent off United defender Jonny Evans after he tugged back Balotelli as he went through on goal. It was an easy red, not that it stopped United complaining. Balotelli then got another goal and Sergio Aguero made it 3–0 before Darren Fletcher pulled one back for 3–1.

We were into the eighty-ninth minute when I asked Mike Dean, the fourth official, to prepare the board to indicate the amount of added time. I could hear Fergie down the headset shouting to Mike.

'It's one or two minutes, one or two minutes. No more than that.'

We put up five minutes, which was fair. There was steam coming out of Fergie's ears. He could just about explain a 3–1 defeat down to ten men, but he did not want any more City goals.

I was thinking it was payback for all those years of 'Fergie time', and I was not going to blow up early just to keep him happy. I made sure we played every second of those added minutes. It was subtle and perfectly legitimate, but I was playing a little game with him.

It went 4–1 City, 5–1, 6–1. He was looking at me as if to say, 'You're enjoying this.' Listen, I did not care who won. I just wanted to perform well, which I had done here.

But I did find it amusing, Fergie calling for full-time when United were losing – that was a first! I looked across to the touchline after each of those late City goals. I thought he was going to explode.

Here is something to consider, though. I did not referee another United game that season, which was very unusual. Did Ferguson influence that? I have no idea. But you know what? I enjoyed the peace.

★   ★   ★

Sir Alex Ferguson retired at the top after winning the Premier League in 2013. Arsene Wenger did not and he became more bitter the longer time went on.

That was a shame because I liked Wenger. He was a good man. It was sad to see how far he and Arsenal had fallen when he finally stood down in 2018. He was losing the power to control his players and, for a manager who had been so innovative when he first arrived in England in 1996, the Premier League had left him behind. He did not know how to win the title anymore.

My first season in the Premier League was 2004/05 and Arsenal were the reigning champions, The Invincibles. They were so good that they were a challenge to referee. They would pass, pass, pass, much like Barcelona, and you would often be jumping out of their way. Then, all of a sudden, they would hit this magical ball half the length of the field and you were fifty yards out of position. There were some games I was thinking, 'They've given twelve of us the runaround here.'

But, over the years, they got worse and worse. Come 2016/17, my final season, Wenger had lost his players and was losing his sense of reason.

They got beaten 2–1 at Everton in December 2016 when Ashley Williams headed a late winner from a corner. Wenger came out after the game and criticised me for the award of the corner. But not the one from which Everton scored, it was another directly before that. I mean, come on, it was ridiculous. Even Everton manager Ronald Koeman was laughing at Wenger's comments.

'I am really disappointed in Mr Clattenburg,' Wenger said. 'He is in a really good position to see it and it is not the first time we are really unlucky with his decisions.'

Yes, the ball did clip an Everton player last and should have been a goal-kick. But it was a split-second decision and no one on the pitch complained. Two corners later and Everton scored, yet I got the blame. Marginal decisions like that will happen. Wenger was making excuses and taking it out on an easy target. That's refereeing, you get used to that, even if it is a load of bollocks at times.

There was another game in January 2016 when Arsenal lost 1–0 at home to Chelsea. I sent off Arsenal defender Per Mertesacker in the first half for a clumsy foul on Diego Costa, who was clear on goal. It was an obvious red card, not that Wenger thought so.

To make matters worse, for Arsenal at least, Costa scored the game's only goal five minutes later. He was always winding them up, they just could not handle him.

Wenger then accused me and the Chelsea striker of costing Arsenal points.

'Costa got two players sent off in two games against our side, so he's clever,' he said. 'The referee had a choice. I think it was quick and harsh.'

Again, Wenger was lashing out when everyone else could see it was the right decision.

But for all of that, I respected him. He had a presence about him. You knew when he was not happy, he would just stand on the touchline and fold his arms and stare at you.

Wenger seemed to have power behind the scenes, too. Referee Paul Taylor once crossed him during an incident in the tunnel in 2000 and lost his place on the National Referees List for the following season. The two things may have been unconnected but, from afar, you were wary of just how influential he could be.

On a personal level, I never really fell out with him and I was always well looked after at Arsenal. The club's staff, such as assistant manager Pat Rice and physio Gary Lewin, would take time to have a chat. They were good people. The club mirrored Wenger in that way. He was Mr Arsenal.

I just wish he had left a bit sooner, like Ferguson, because he changed towards the end, always looking for someone else to blame. And who is at the front of the queue when that happens? Yes, that would be the referee.

*   *   *

Jurgen Klopp. Brilliant manager. Sour loser.

I first came across him in April 2014. His Borussia Dortmund side lost 3–0 at Real Madrid in a Champions League quarter-final first leg. Gareth Bale, Isco and Cristiano Ronaldo scored and Real did not even get out of second gear. They had a team full of stars and went on to win the competition, so Klopp could have no complaints.

After the game, I came out of my dressing-room and Real defender Marcelo and his wife asked for a picture. I couldn't say no, that would have come across as arrogant. It was a private picture on their mobile phone so I said yeah, no problem. Klopp walked past just as the photo was being taken.

'Oh, so that's why we got beat, is it?' he said.

He was not being humorous or friendly, he was being sarky.

'You're lucky you only got beat 3–0,' I said.

The fact we were in Madrid probably gave me a bit of bravado to answer back.

It annoyed me when managers could not be gracious in defeat. Klopp never took losing well and that followed him to the Premier League. He had a bit of Fergie about him in that regard, and he would also try to intimidate you.

My first Liverpool match with him was at Chelsea in

October 2015, the same month he arrived from Dortmund. Liverpool won 3–1 and they had played well. Klopp was being interviewed by the media in the tunnel after the game and, as I walked past, he turned over his shoulder and shouted to me.

'Mark, these guys are talking about the top four already!'

'Welcome to England, you'll soon understand the British press,' I said.

We all had a laugh about it. But that was Klopp – when he was winning he was happy, he was good fun. When things were not going his way, he got prickly. That is just the way he was, it does not detract from him being an outstanding manager. His teams had my utmost respect and I witnessed right in front of me just how much his players gave for him.

Saying that, I refereed Liverpool another six times under Klopp and they only won once. After a couple of those, I felt some of his post-match comments were aimed at me. He could also be difficult to manage during the game, but his coaching staff were worse. They would constantly challenge the fourth official, always getting in people's faces. I hated that, they showed no respect. Given how meticulous Klopp was, you would imagine the instruction to do so came from him.

My final game with Klopp was in January 2017 against Chelsea at Anfield. No one knew at the time but I was in the process of leaving the Premier League for Saudi Arabia.

Managers rarely came into my dressing-room for the exchange of team-sheets an hour before kick-off. The likes of Ferguson and Wenger always left it to their assistants to join the captains. On this occasion, Klopp came in with his captain, Jordan Henderson. It was bizarre, he stood and stared at me for about thirty seconds. I just stared back at him. I could see Jordan was a bit like, 'What the hell's going on here?' Did Klopp think I was stupid? I was not going to be bullied by him. He left and all I thought was, 'What a strange bloke.'

Chelsea took a controversial lead when David Luiz scored a twenty-five-yard free-kick while Liverpool goalkeeper Simon Mignolet was still arranging his defenders. I realised Luiz was thinking about a quick shot, so I blew my whistle to indicate play was live. It caused some debate given Mignolet did not appear ready, but I was right to give the goal, Liverpool were sleeping. They later equalised and the game finished 1–1.

I was waiting for Klopp to blame me for the Chelsea goal, but he came out and praised Luiz. He thought it was clever and had no problem with me allowing it to stand. So it was a shame when I quit the Premier League a few weeks later, as it looked like we were just starting to get on!

★   ★   ★

I knew two Jose Mourinhos. The one during his first spell at Chelsea and the one who returned after managing abroad.

I liked the first one. He was a gentleman. I refereed the opening game of the 2005/06 season when Chelsea won 1–0 at Wigan and Mourinho called me a 'great referee' on TV afterwards. Maybe that was mind games. Either way, it was rare for a manager to be nice about you.

Compliments aside, we got on well. I thought he was funny and an entertaining character. The fact Chelsea were also winning most weeks meant nothing was ever an issue.

He left Chelsea in 2007 after two Premier League titles in three seasons and took over at Inter Milan the following year. I was later fourth official for an Inter game and he gave me a cuddle and we had a nice chat. He had charisma. As a football fan, I thought he was good for the game.

Later, when he was manager at Real Madrid, he was banned from the stadium for a Champions League group game against Ajax. He sent me a message via the match delegate wishing me all the best. Real won 3–0 and he came into the stadium afterwards. I saw him and we had a catch-up. Maybe he was playing a game all along, I don't know, but I found him to be a genuinely nice guy. It had no bearing on how I refereed, because just like Fergie's intimidation, you had to block it all out and make decisions in isolation.

But by the time he returned to Chelsea in 2013, Mourinho had changed, and drastically so. This Mourinho was not a nice guy. It was as if he thought the world was against him. He was bitter, always unhappy and did not seem to enjoy it anymore. He had lost his good humour and was no fun to be around.

I refereed Chelsea's game at Leicester in December 2015, after which Mourinho was sacked. They lost 2–1 and were a shambles. They turned up late and their captain, John Terry, was racing to my dressing-room with the team-sheet an hour before the game. Eden Hazard walked off the pitch when he was injured and Mourinho forced him to go back on. They were a mess and deserved to lose. It was no surprise when he lost his job the following day.

But I was shocked when he later suggested it was my fault. He had been moaning about me to the media a few weeks earlier after Chelsea were beaten 3–1 by Liverpool in Klopp's first game. It was a load of rubbish. He was blaming everyone but himself. The reason he got the sack was his own attitude and that of his team, who had stopped playing for him. It was nothing to do with me.

He appeared again as Manchester United manager in 2016. He blanked me before one game, not that I cared. He started buttering up Kevin Friend, my fourth official.

'Don't fall for his crap, Kevin, he's just playing you,' I said.

Maybe that is what he had been doing with me all those years, but I would like to think not. During that first period I saw him be friendly with almost everyone, that was him. Second time around, his pleasantries felt forced and calculated, like he was with Kevin.

Mourinho always had a spy outside my dressing-room to check if anyone from the opposition had been in to see me. During a Manchester derby, City coach Brian Kidd came in. It was nothing untoward, he was only asking how long before I made the signal to leave the dressing-room for the second half. It got back to Mourinho and he went off on one, saying that City were sending in people to manipulate me. I was not standing for spiteful nonsense like that.

'Jose, you're in England now, not Spain or Italy, that doesn't happen here,' I said.

He was paranoid. He was always looking for something or someone to be annoyed about. In the end, as I have written about earlier, he was one of the reasons I decided to quit the Premier League.

Life is too short for putting up with shit from the type of person he became.

★　★　★

Harry Redknapp was a gentleman, a brilliant fella. But one day he pissed me off so badly that it was me waiting outside his dressing-room rather than the other way round.

It was April 2012 and I was refereeing the tea-time kick-off between Queens Park Rangers and Redknapp's Tottenham Hotspur at Loftus Road. Newcastle, who I support, had beaten Stoke 3–0 earlier in the day to go above Spurs and into fourth position in the Premier League. Not that I cared about that once this game started.

Spurs were annoyed when I awarded QPR a free-kick midway through the first half for a Sandro foul on Adel Taarabt. So they were livid when Taarabt then scored from it. We came off at half-time, 1–0 to QPR. I could tell Redknapp had something to say as I approached him, and it was not going to be complimentary.

'You've just given that decision because fucking Newcastle have gone above us,' he said.

'What the fuck are you on about?' I said back to him.

I stormed into my dressing-room, my mind completely distracted by Redknapp's accusation. How dare he say that. I could not let it lie. Maybe I should have done but, in that moment, I could not escape the absurdity of what he'd said. I went and stood outside the Spurs dressing-room. Redknapp came out.

'You were fucking out of order there,' I said. 'You can complain about a decision but never suggest I'm making a decision thinking about Newcastle.'

I did not give a shit about Newcastle when I was refereeing. My reputation was far more important than anything to do with them. But for Redknapp to say that he must have thought it, and that bothered me. In fact, it really bothered me.

To be fair, he apologised.

'Okay, fine,' I said. 'But don't ever say that. Don't ever think that.'

I sent off Taarabt in the second half but Spurs could not find an equaliser and got beaten 1–0.

They finished fourth that season, above Newcastle in fifth, but they lost their Champions League place when Chelsea, who finished sixth, won the competition and qualified instead of them. I felt for Harry when that happened, because he was such a good bloke. He rarely complained about referees and when he moaned, you must have had a bad game. I thought he was a fair person.

Here is a confession, though. In October 2010, I ridiculously allowed a Manchester United goal to stand against Spurs.

Redknapp called my decision 'scandalous' and was warned by the FA about his comments. But I understand why he was angry. It should have been me getting the warning about my decision-making.

United were leading 1–0 with six minutes to play when their winger, Nani, went down in the Spurs area. It was not a penalty and Nani had also handled the ball as he lay on the ground. I waved play on because Spurs goalkeeper Heurelho Gomes had possession. I always preferred to keep the game flowing and I kept the advantage with Spurs because they were losing with not long to go. United also had a man off receiving treatment, so to blow for a free-kick to Spurs would have given that player the chance to come back on.

But then Gomes spun the ball in front of him, as if preparing to take a free-kick for Nani's handball. Nani ran back in and kicked the ball into the empty net. I gave the goal. Spurs were chasing after me, asking what the hell I was thinking. But there had been no whistle, play was live. Under the *Laws of the Game*, I was justified in allowing the goal to stand.

However, I got this wrong, horribly wrong. There was no fairness in scoring that goal. I was applying the laws too literally. I do not know why I did that. Perhaps I was trying to be too clever for my own good. I should have awarded a delayed free-kick to Spurs once Nani had scored. That would have been sensible. United won 2–0.

So, Harry, I am sorry.

★   ★   ★

Sam Allardyce was another manager for whom I had a lot of time. He would be kicking your arse one week but having a laugh and a joke the next. He never held a grudge.

I was fourth official when Bolton drew 2–2 at Chelsea on 28 April 2007. There were stories in the newspapers that he could be going to Newcastle and I was winding him up on the touchline.

'I hear you could be coming to manage my team?' I said.

'You never know, Mark, you never know,' he replied.

'Maybe there was something in it,' I thought. Too right, he resigned as Bolton boss the following day and was appointed Newcastle manager a few weeks later.

I got a message that summer saying Sam needed some whistles for training, could I help? I called into Newcastle's training ground and left a bagful for him. They were top quality ones as well, and he still hasn't paid me!

It did not work out for him at Newcastle, but I respected his Bolton side and the job he did there. They had a plan to make life hard for the opposition but they also had some gifted players, such as Jay-Jay Okocha and Youri Djorkaeff. When you are in the middle of the action you get a feel for teams and I always thought, 'This lot know exactly what they're doing.'

Sam was not scared to upset people but I always thought he was fair. If the referee was crap he would say so, but he wouldn't blame the referee for the sake of it, unlike some. I liked him because he was genuine. When he was angry, he did not hide it.

If you were fourth official at Bolton, the first half was always a doddle because Sam would watch from the directors' box. I used to say to Neil McDonald, his assistant, 'Does he not fancy watching the second half from up there as well?'

Bolton had a reputation as being nasty but they were far more respectful than the players at Manchester United, for example. Gary Speed was a gentleman, one of the best I refereed. Kevin Nolan and Jussi Jaaskelainen were also honest guys who I enjoyed being around. I did not have a problem with them or Sam and I think he liked my style of refereeing. It was a bit like his management in that it was up front and not afraid of confrontation.

We did have a few run-ins when Sam's team started losing, but that was only during those Soccer Aid charity matches he could never win!

★　★　★

Neil Warnock was a real character. I wish there were more like him in the Premier League. But he could also give you hell.

A few of us picked up on an anagram of his name that was doing the rounds – Colin Wanker. When he used to batter me, I would say to him, 'All right, Colin. Calm down.' He did not like that one bit.

He was manager of Sheffield United in 2003 when they played at Nottingham Forest in the first leg of the Championship play-off semi-final. I was twenty-eight, still young to be doing a game of that magnitude. I sent off Forest's Michael Dawson and gave Sheffield United a penalty in a 1–1 draw. They were the correct calls but it was intimidating that night at the City Ground, those play-off games always made for a frenzied atmosphere.

Warnock came into my dressing-room afterwards and shook my hand. He thought I had shown balls.

'I'm going to mark you a zero, son,' he said.

I was taken aback.

'Why are you doing that?' I said. 'They won't promote me to the Premier League.'

'Exactly,' he said. 'I don't want you promoted. It'll ruin you going up there.'

He was joking, I think. But I did not get promoted that year and neither did he – Sheffield United lost to Wolves in the play-off final.

Warnock and I also had some feisty moments. I sent him off once and he was charged by the FA for what he said to me, which was nasty. He was like that, a real Jack in the Box. He could be nice and then just erupt out of nowhere over nothing, like a free-kick in the fourteenth minute that meant bugger all. It was like 'Whoosh', he would just lose it.

But I did like Warnock, even though it was a telephone call from him that led to me getting a one-match suspension for going to an Ed Sheeran concert in October 2014.

I had refereed a 2–2 draw between West Bromwich Albion and Crystal Palace. Warnock was manager of Palace and he wasn't happy with my decision to award West Brom a last-minute penalty, from which they scored.

He also compared a challenge by West Brom's Craig Dawson on his goalkeeper, Julian Speroni, to an incident in the 1956 FA Cup Final when Manchester City keeper Bert Trautmann had his neck broken by an opponent. 'A bit extreme,' I thought, but he blamed me for not seeing it and said I should have sent off Dawson.

He came looking to speak to me after the game but I had already left. I got away a few minutes early because I was going to see Ed Sheeran with my wife and some of my friends back in Newcastle. I had my car at The Hawthorns and wanted to get on the road to make the concert.

PGMOL protocol was that all officials left the stadium together and were driven in a people-carrier back to the hotel to collect our cars. But there was a gentleman's agreement that you could leave by yourself if you had family there, or another genuine reason. Ed Sheeran was my reason.

That would have been fine if Warnock had not rung me from a withheld number while I was driving back to Newcastle. I answered. He wanted a word about the decisions and I listened to him. He thought I did not have my best game and what he said was fair enough.

However, referees are not allowed to take a phone call from a manager. All conversations should be witnessed by the other officials and take place within thirty minutes of full-time. I had left The Hawthorns after twenty-five minutes and that was when Warnock came looking for me, which is why he later called.

I had no choice but to report myself to the PGMOL for

speaking to him and explain why I had left the stadium without the other officials. Mike Riley and the PGMOL took the decision to drop me from all fixtures for the following weekend. It made headline news: 'Clattenburg banned for Ed Sheeran dash'. At least it was accurate.

But I certainly did not tell the press what had happened. The PGMOL must have leaked the reason for my suspension, just to make me look stupid. That would tie in with them trying to derail me ahead of Euro 2016. I suspected they wanted Michael Oliver or Martin Atkinson to go ahead of me.

I got a phone call later that week from Pierluigi Collina, my boss at UEFA.

'Mark, don't let them win,' he said. 'Do what you have to do. Behave yourself. Do not give them any reason to get at you.'

He was right, I had to be twice as careful as any other referee.

But you know what, I made the concert on time, had a few beers and enjoyed a night with my wife and friends on the back of a tough match. Sometimes, there is more to life. Sometimes, you just want to be normal. The PGMOL was all about control, to the point where it intrudes on your life away from refereeing. They never seemed to respect that we had an existence of our own.

So I was banned and had a few days off. I listened to some Ed Sheeran on my iPod and did the garden, which was absolutely immaculate thanks to my free weekend.

★ ★ ★

I had a good relationship with Pep Guardiola from refereeing Bayern Munich in the Champions League.

He spoke well about me after they were beaten by Barcelona in the 2015 semi-final and, when he arrived at Manchester City the following year, I thought we had a mutual respect that would continue.

He called into my dressing-room after his first Manchester derby in September 2016, when City won 2–1 at Old Trafford. He only did that to rile United manager Jose Mourinho, which I found amusing. I'd had enough of Mourinho's sour face by then.

But there was one incident, when I was fourth official for a City game, where Guardiola overstepped the mark. He lost his mind after a decision by referee Anthony Taylor. He grabbed my arm with a fair bit of force and started ranting and raving in my face. I just looked at him and did not flinch. What gave him the right to man-handle me like that? He was frustrated, the game was not going his way, but this was beyond the boundary of even unacceptable behaviour. I grabbed his arm back.

'Do not speak to me like that,' I said. 'I've got bugger all to do with your team. Our relationship is better than that. Don't abuse me.'

He walked away. About twenty seconds later, he came back and apologised. Sometimes you have to remind managers when they are out of order. By this stage I was lucky, I had refereed the three big finals in 2016 and had a bit more respect from the coaches, so I could speak to them more assertively.

Other City managers, such as Roberto Mancini and Manuel Pellegrini, I never got on with. Pellegrini did not speak good English but he could always find the words to criticise the referee. He was a very dour man and was hard to warm to.

I saw the transition of City from what they were to the club they became after the Abu Dhabi investment. But their mentality changed towards referees. They started to expect more decisions to go their way. I never refereed like that and always gave it as I saw it. I upset the big clubs as much as I did the small. That is why I found Mancini and Pellegrini difficult, they would challenge you because they thought City had a right to better treatment from referees. Maybe in their countries it worked like that, but not here.

I did not even give any favours to Rafa Benitez when I refereed Dalian Yifang in China in 2019. I loved Benitez because of the job he had done at Newcastle, but Dalian lost 3–0 that night. At least he did not blame me, because I did not want to fall out with Rafa!

Benitez came to Newcastle in March 2016 after being sacked by Real Madrid in the January. Otherwise he could well have been Real manager when I refereed their Champions League final against Atletico Madrid later that season.

It was Zinedine Zidane who came in and won the first of three straight European titles. Zidane rarely spoke to you and was very respectful, but there was an air of majesty about him, more so because of what he had achieved as a player.

If Zidane was quiet, the opposite could be said of Atletico

boss Diego Simeone. He always used to push his luck on the touchline. You would march over and have a word with him and he would pat you gently on the arm.

'Sorry, don't worry, I won't do it again,' he would say.

Thirty seconds later and he was doing exactly the same, you almost had to laugh. But he never blamed the referee and he was fair with me after the Champions League Final, which Atletico lost on penalties. He pumped his chest and said, 'Well done', which meant a lot.

So it was not all staring competitions, tunnel bust-ups and irate phone calls. I got on well with the majority of managers. They all had their quirks and you had to learn how best to handle them. I always tried to compensate for the pressure they were under. If a manager swears at you, it does not mean you send him off or report him. There has to be tolerance and understanding. There is a limit and, for me, it comes back to human decency. Once that line had been crossed, it was time to punish them.

But there was one thing all managers had in common – you were always a good referee if they had won.

5

THE ACCUSED (PART ONE)

'My career is over . . . my world has fallen apart'

IT was a Friday afternoon in the early part of 2008 when I had an argument with my then-girlfriend, Susan. I walked out of the house we shared in Gateshead. The relationship was over.

That weekend, I was due to spend time with Nathan, my son from my first marriage. I collected him from school and we went to stay with my younger sister in Newcastle.

I had a game at Leeds the following day and I needed to return to the house to collect my kit and equipment. I sent Susan a text message. She made it clear the doors were locked and I was not getting in. I wanted to avoid a scene whereby the police could be called, so I stayed away.

I phoned Keith Hackett, my PGMOL boss, and explained the situation. I had no kit, no equipment and nowhere to live. Keith was great about it. They replaced me at Leeds and arranged for me to stay at the Ramside Hall Hotel in Durham, where myself and Nathan checked in on the Saturday night.

After finally retrieving most of my belongings, I moved into an apartment I owned in Newcastle, which I had been renting out.

I met Claire later in the year and, heading into the summer, I was hopeful that any issues with Susan would soon be behind me. Or so I thought.

Sunday 3 August 2008. Emirates Stadium, London

This doesn't feel right. I have just finished refereeing Arsenal's 1–0 win over Real Madrid in a pre-season friendly. But, as I walk down the tunnel, I am told the chairman and secretary of the PGMOL are waiting for me in a spare dressing-room. What the fuck is going on here? I'm still wearing my kit and boots. I need to know what this is about, I'm not wasting time getting showered. I walk into the dressing-room, where chairman Peter Heard and secretary Graham Noakes are waiting. I do not like the look of this – they've got my contract in front of them. I have no idea what is about to follow. They explain that a series of allegations have been made against me. They have received an anonymous letter. They list the allegations – match-fixing, drug-taking, gambling debts . . . The sender of the letter has used debts connected to my electrical businesses as the reason why I would need money. I deny the allegations in an instant. This is a malicious attempt to cause me trouble. I'm angry. I pull some hair from the top of my head and put it on the table in front of us.

'There you go. Take that. Test it for drugs. That'll be one of the allegations gone.'

I fully expected the PGMOL to support me, for them to help prove that these wild allegations were false, that they were brought by people with ulterior motives. I assumed wrong.

I was scheduled to referee a Champions League qualifier in Hungary three days later, as well as the Community Shield at Wembley the following weekend. It was a huge week in my career – my first game in a European club competition and first at Wembley.

'I'll still be doing those matches, yes?' I asked.

'No, we want you to come off everything while we investigate,' said Heard.

'What? Why should I? I'm innocent. This isn't right, it's a fucking stitch-up.'

Claire was with me in London, it was supposed to be a nice break before the start of the season and the lost weekends. We got the train back to Newcastle in silence. I was stunned, but I also knew I had done nothing wrong, even if I had made some mistakes in business.

I had two electrical companies outside of my employment as a Select Group referee, and that was allowed. One of them had run into trouble. I had taken on a contract at a school in Northumberland and it went badly wrong. The company I used to do some of the work ran up a lot of extra costs. It got out of control and I was losing fortunes. I should have cut my losses and walked away, but my pride made me want to complete the job.

I ended up with debts of around £70,000. I paid £30,000 of that from my own pocket to those who did not have insurance if my firm went into liquidation, which it eventually did.

My business interests took a bit of unravelling, and some details got picked up by the press, including a claim that I had debts of almost £175,000. That was not true at all – that figure was simply fabricated.

Yes, I had made some mistakes in business and I accepted the PGMOL would want more information, but the other allegations listed in the anonymous letter were vicious and untrue.

Later that week, more allegations were sent to the PGMOL, including that I had threatened a business associate called John Hepworth in an email. Only he, I reasoned, could have forwarded that to them.

Graham Noakes called and, immediately, I did not like his tone. I was being suspended on full pay.

I've done nothing wrong! Why am I being punished? They're only allegations, and I haven't been formally pre-sented with them yet. I've explained why I think they've been made. I should be allowed to referee. I'm already missing two big matches, I don't want to miss any more. I've also been ostracised, my colleagues have been told not to speak to me. The PGMOL are making me feel like

THE ACCUSED (PART ONE)

I'm guilty. Where's my support? They should be helping me fight this.

The PGMOL appointed a lawyer from Eversheds in Birmingham. He was instructed to investigate all of the allegations against me, which totalled twenty. Peter Heard was handling everything. That made me uneasy. I always had the feeling he did not like me.

I understood the PGMOL were duty bound to investigate, but were they not also there to support me? I felt alone and exposed.

I provided the investigating lawyer with access to all of my bank accounts and business dealings. Some of the allegations were dismissed on the back of that – things like gambling debts just did not exist. I also handed over a computer that I used for business.

At the end of that first week, my car was vandalised outside of my apartment in Newcastle. My ex-girlfriend Susan was later arrested, a story that was picked up by the newspapers, before she was released without charge.

The Premier League season started and I was still suspended pending the outcome of the investigation. I was struggling to come to terms with my situation. It felt so unjust, but at the same time increasingly serious.

The investigation made me feel like a criminal, despite there being no evidence against me. They were contacting associates, friends and former referees to ask about my personal matters.

It was as if they were digging and digging and finding nothing, so they would go and dig some more.

This went on for four months, but at no stage were the police involved, there was no reason for them to be. The business debts were a civil matter and the other allegations were made-up rubbish with no substance to them.

But the press had jumped on the story and, for the first time and certainly not the last, I found my private life and future being played out on the back pages of the newspapers. I wanted to speak out and set the record straight, be that to the investigators or the press. I needed to tell someone why all of this was nonsense. That frustration builds and I resented being gagged by the PGMOL, it did not feel fair.

Finally, in the first week of December, I was called to London to be interviewed. It was a relief, having the chance to speak about the allegations and give my side. At least I thought that would be the case.

The PGMOL had by now appointed a barrister and he started the meeting by calling me 'Mr Clattenburg'. It was all very formal. It immediately felt like me versus them, we were not on the same side.

Also present were Heard, Hackett and my union representative, Alan Leighton. I did not have a lawyer with me, and that was a mistake I did not make again.

I felt on my own and at no point was I allowed to speak freely. They asked me questions but there was no scope to elaborate, no opportunity to tell my version as to why these spiteful accusations had come about in the first place, leading to us being here.

Most of the allegations relating to things such as drug-taking and gambling had already been dismissed following conversations with Eversheds during the previous months. I was able to prove that some of them were not true. For the others, they had no evidence. Why? Because there was no evidence. I made the point that those false allegations had surely undermined the remainder.

The barrister asked me about one or two of them.

'Can you prove you were not match-fixing?' he said.

'No, not really,' I replied. 'There's nothing to prove. Look at my bank accounts. How can I disprove something that has not happened?'

But the investigation had moved away from the allegations made in the anonymous letter. They were also satisfied with the explanation regarding the business debts. Rather, the hearing was building towards two things.

Firstly, in September, I was playing golf in Seaham when I took a call from an unknown number on my mobile phone. It was a news reporter from the *Daily Mail*. He was asking how I was, saying he was sorry to see what had happened, being very sympathetic. I fell for it. I was frustrated with my situation, with the suspicion that had been cast. I should have hung up but I engaged in conversation, never stopping to think if it was on or off the record.

It was a release, to be honest. I told him that I felt like crap, that my life was in danger of falling apart over these vindictive allegations. He asked me one last question.

'What would you say to everyone out there?'

Naively, I answered.

'The truth will come out. What happens in life is that liars get found out and I'll just sit back until I'm proven innocent and then I'll go back to work, hopefully.'

I was stupid to talk. I had been hoodwinked by his friendly approach and encouraged by my own desperation.

The journalist ran our 'exclusive interview'. I do not know what contact he had with people within the PGMOL before or after our conversation, but I grew concerned about the information and detail he was printing.

The barrister relayed what I had said to the reporter and asked for my thoughts.

'Yes, I said all of that,' I told him. 'But I also referred him to the PGMOL on several occasions.'

The barrister said it was a breach of trust and confidence to have talked to the reporter.

They're accusing me of a breach of trust and confidence? Are they kidding? This journalist has been getting information from somewhere about my situation. I believe it could only have come from people within the PGMOL, so don't talk to me about a breach of trust. This is double standards.

The barrister then produced the email I had sent to my business partner from my Premier League account. He said it was threatening in nature and a misuse of company email.

Part of the email read: 'You are missing the bigger picture. Check you can use our company's money to fund your legal crusade against me. If not, taking me to court might cause your family some pain.'

I understand how that language could be perceived as threatening. But I will swear to my dying day, my intention was not to threaten him. Rather, I was saying that, by taking me to court at the risk of losing the claim, he and his family could be financially worse off.

I believe those who made the allegations knew what I meant by the email, yet they seized upon it and realised it could be used against me. I left myself open to that.

The hearing finished and it was clear that the PGMOL were going to pin me on a breach of trust and confidence and misuse of company email. I did not think they were sackable offences and, while the tone of the interview unsettled me, I firmly believed I would be given a warning and reinstated.

I told the PGMOL that I had arranged to go to New York with Claire, that I needed some time away on the back of the past few months. It felt strange when they sanctioned it with no questions asked. I thought that, if I was going to return to refereeing, they would want me available.

For all of that, I was still convinced my suspension would be lifted when I returned to the UK. I managed to put those worries to the back of my mind and we enjoyed our break in New York, during which we got engaged.

I returned home to County Durham and waited for news of what I genuinely presumed would be my reinstatement. On 5 January 2009, while in the bathroom of the house Claire and I now shared, an email from the PGMOL flashed up on my mobile. I had been sacked.

I am staring at the screen in front of me, locked in a trance. Have I got this right? I read it again. I have been sacked because of the email to my business partner and the phone call with the journalist. They're saying both were a breach of contract. They're also saying I was abrupt in my interview. Are they fucking joking? Of course I was abrupt, I was barely allowed to speak. How has it come to this? My career is over. I'm thirty-three years old, one of the youngest referees in the Premier League. Or at least I was. That's gone. In one email, my world has fallen apart.

I can't believe I even tried to go to bed that night. I was downstairs at 1 a.m. searching for jobs online. I thought that Dubai was my best option. I could not live and work in the UK, not after this.

But I was not thinking straight, I was in a desperate and irrational place. Thankfully, the break of day brought with it some clarity.

Why run away? What have I done wrong, really? I have made some mistakes, but none of them deserve this. If I accept it, that means those who brought the allegations, and those who pursued them, they win. That's wrong. I have to fight for what is right here.

I realised that Heard had suspended, investigated and sacked me. Surely that was contrary to employment law?

But even if it was procedurally incorrect, this was not about building a case for a compensation payment. It was about getting my job back, a career I loved and the one in which I saw my future. I felt robbed of the dreams I had in front of me. I was not going to stand for this bullshit any longer.

I lodged my intention to appeal and the process was supposed to remain confidential. At this point, my sacking had not been made public. Then, in the last week of January, it was revealed exclusively in the *Daily Mail* that I had been sacked. The story was written by the same journalist who had called me on the golf course, and whom I suspected was being fed information from within the PGMOL.

Fuck me. This is one big stitch-up. Who can I trust? So much for confidentiality. This is incredible, I cannot believe these details have been leaked to a newspaper. It feels as if certain people are scared that my appeal will be successful, that they want the world to know I've been sacked, just in case I get my job back. I'm now fighting to

carry on working for an organisation that I want nothing
to do with, and who clearly want nothing to do with me.
But I have to forget that; this is about my career. Fuck
the haters, the lot of them.

In February, I was called to the Premier League offices in London for my appeal hearing. The three-person panel was led by Richard Scudamore, the Premier League chairman.

Scudamore began the meeting by saying, 'Can I call you "Mark"?' I started crying. He looked surprised. For the first time during the process I was being addressed by my Christian name. The tears were born out of relief, comfort, the feeling that someone was going to listen and give me a fair hearing. No one had done that so far. No one had wanted to believe me.

'Okay, Mark,' he said. 'You've got an hour and a half. Tell us everything that has happened.'

I went back to the argument with my ex-girlfriend Susan and the breakdown of our relationship. From there, we walked through everything. I cried on several occasions as I retold the story. It was like therapy, unloading the hurt that had been caused by the hate of others.

I told them what it was like knowing that someone wanted to ruin my life. I did not know who I could trust. I suspected phone calls were being listened to by private investigators, that someone was trying to trick me into incriminating myself. I explained about my car being trashed. Claire's car had also been vandalised. Were these events connected with the spurious allegations that had been reported to the PGMOL? The past six months had been a nightmare, it had felt like harassment.

We went through all of the paperwork relating to my business debts. I did not hide anything. I explained why the email to my business partner was not meant to be threatening. It felt like they understood. It was like a weight being lifted. For the first time, I had a voice in the investigation.

Scudamore had also been through the transcript from the previous hearing. He did not think it was right that I had not been allowed to speak without restriction.

The panel said they would consider all of the evidence and return their verdict within a few days. At least they had listened to me.

On the Monday of the following week, I was sitting in my car at Seaham, overlooking the North Sea, when Alan Leighton called. My dismissal had been reversed, the appeal was successful.

I feel relief, a sense of justice. But also anger. I have lost most of the season because of allegations that were only ever made to harm me. Why could the PGMOL not see that? But I have my career back, that is the most important thing. I should be thankful for that, and thankful that Richard Scudamore saw sense. I have also learnt a lesson – be very careful who you trust in life.

I reached an agreement with the appeal panel whereby I accepted an eight-month suspension, backdated to August.

All of the money owed to me from the period when I was sacked was also paid.

A statement from the PGMOL read: 'Mark Clattenburg has been reminded of his responsibilities and contractual obligations as a Select Group Official, particularly in regard to full disclosure of any outside business interests. PGMOL is confident that he has the ability to regain his position as one of English football's top officials.'

Why did I accept the suspension? Part of me wanted to challenge it. I was not happy about the ban being on my record – I never will be – but I had been fighting for too long. I just wanted to get back on the pitch. When you have lost something that means so much to you, to be given the chance to get it back, you will always be minded to accept a compromise. I also recognised that I had spoken to a journalist when I shouldn't have done.

I arranged to meet Scudamore at Doncaster train station during this period, where we booked a private room. We had a chat and he asked if I needed any help, which I did. I told him I was being sued in two separate cases, one related to my electrical business and the other concerning the ownership of a car I shared with my ex-girlfriend, the vehicle that had been vandalised.

I did not trust the PGMOL with this information, not after what had happened. I wanted to tidy up these outstanding cases before I returned to refereeing. I told Scudamore everything. I trusted him. The Premier League helped me find a good lawyer.

Unbeknown to me, someone then contacted the PGMOL and told them about the outstanding claims against me. It could only have come from the same people in the North-East who, I suspect, had brought the original accusations the previous summer.

But there were also now fresh allegations that I had been going around the North-East bragging about coming back to work, that I was telling everyone I did not care about the PGMOL.

I have since been told that the PGMOL were ready to sack me for a second time in a matter of weeks, although this never materialised. The situation had descended into a farce.

I was advised that the best thing to do was to reach out-of-court settlements on the outstanding cases as soon as possible. That was arranged, even though I wanted to challenge both claims.

But I was done with Heard, it felt like he was all too happy to listen to anything that could bring me down. He also should have known that it was not right for him to be judge, jury and executioner in this case against me.

I returned to referee Manchester City versus Bolton on the final day of the 2008/09 season. It was nice that Keith Hackett had the decency to arrange that. It meant that the media attention around my first game back did not drag on into the following season.

Newcastle were relegated to the Championship that same afternoon, so my return was far from the biggest story in town. I never thought my boyhood team going down would actually do me a favour, but it did that day.

*   *   *

As I reflect on events of that period now, I admit that I made some errors of judgement. In fact, I conceded as much at the time.

The PGMOL were right to remind me about my responsibility to declare outside business interests and any significant debts or legal disputes arising from them. I left myself exposed by trying to sort matters without my employers knowing, and that caused me more problems in the long run. I always thought, 'I can handle this.' Sometimes, you can't. I should have been smarter in protecting myself.

But I did not deserve the scrutiny and suffering caused by false allegations against me, made only worse by the manner in which the PGMOL conducted their investigation. On top of that, I missed an entire season of refereeing, and that should have been avoided.

Someone was out to damage me, and all they cared about was ruining my life. It is frightening to consider how close they came to achieving that.

If it was not for Scudamore, who had the decency to simply listen to me, I would not have refereed again. He was a grown-up who took a fair and level-headed view of everything in front of him. He did not have pre-conceived ideas about the evidence, or lack of it, presented to him. He realised what the PGMOL had done in sacking me was wrong. He saw that their mistake was rectified and my career was allowed to continue. I will always be grateful for that.

But there is one person who helped me rebuild my life more

than any other. Claire could have walked away at any point during our first year together, given the distress caused by a situation that was not of her making. It took a little while for me to trust her, given the scars of what I had been through. But without Claire, I would not have recovered my confidence and enthusiasm for my career.

We got married in 2010 and our daughter, Mia, was born twelve months later. So while 2008 was a horrible year in many ways, it was also the start of something new. It was the start of the rest of my life. The second half, you might say.

6

HAPPY FAMILIES . . .

'A scone bounced off my head'

I NEVER would have met Claire had my flight back to Newcastle from London not somehow avoided a delay amid the chaos inside Heathrow's brand-new Terminal 5.

I had refereed Reading versus Blackburn on 29 March 2008 and had arranged to meet my friend, Neil Saxton, who was going out in Newcastle with two girls. The game was a goalless draw with eight bookings and a red card, so I needed a drink.

But the airport was mayhem. Terminal 5 had been open less than forty-eight hours. I texted Neil and warned him that I probably wouldn't make it. Sliding doors, eh? The flight was one of a handful to take off on time.

I was back home for 10 p.m. and went straight out into town, even though it was absolutely pissing down. I was choking for a beer and intrigued by this mystery blonde called Claire who Neil introduced me to. I must have fancied her from the off because I gave her my coat when we walked from the Bigg Market down to the Quayside. My hair was properly thinning at this stage, so the last thing I needed was a drenching to expose my scalp!

I realised that Claire did not know who I was, so I decided against telling her what I did for a living. I said I was in finance. That was an unfortunate mistake because she was in mortgages. She started asking me questions about my work. I was like, 'Ah, let's just have a drink.' We went to Sea nightclub next to the River Tyne and another fella, a Cockney, started chasing her. He recognised me and was shouting in her ear, 'Don't go with him, he's bad news.' She didn't have a clue what he meant.

It was only the next day that she sent me a text message, 'You're not a financial adviser!' She had been on Google and found out more about me. Thankfully, it did not put her off and we arranged to meet again.

I never liked to tell people that I was a referee straight away, if it could be helped. Back then it was quite easy. I had only been in the Premier League a few years and had not made headlines in the news pages, although that would soon change. I always wanted people to get to know me first, even if it was for a few hours. I was conscious of being pre-judged.

Claire was from Sunderland, so I also had to be careful not to pre-judge her! But I was immediately attracted to her. She was popular, good-looking and smart.

We planned to move in together in September of that same year – which we did – but all of the positivity and happiness building towards that came crashing down in August, when I was suspended from the Premier League. It was a test of a relationship that was barely a few months old. I would not have blamed Claire for walking away. She did not deserve, or expect, any of the scrutiny we were now under.

I was still suspended come December when we arranged a break in New York – which the PGMOL were okay with – and I was expecting to be reinstated when I returned. A few weeks earlier, I'd had an engagement ring delivered to Claire's parents' house and asked her dad, Tom, if I could marry his daughter.

We were ice-skating at the Rockefeller Center in New York, beneath the Christmas tree, and I was getting dragged about all over the place. I was down on my knees more than I was up, which was handy for a man about to propose. It got to the point where I was so wet that I was worried the ring could be water-damaged! I decided this was my time. I pulled out the ring and asked the question right there on the ice. Everyone started cheering and clapping, which made a nice change from the booing I was used to. Claire said yes and everything felt perfect, even if the worries of home were still lurking in the back of my mind.

We went to Gordon Ramsay's restaurant that night to celebrate. I was lucky because they accepted payment on the credit card I had with me. The next day I realised it was maxed out. That would have been embarrassing, washing the dishes to pay the bill hours after getting engaged. We returned home to the North-East and I was happy, I felt optimistic.

Then, in January, came the email that turned my world upside down. I had been sacked by the PGMOL. I felt sick to the pit of my stomach, I was not expecting it.

Just a few weeks after being engaged, Claire said she did not know if she could take anymore. The pressure of the suspension had suffocated us for months, we thought we would be able to breathe in the New Year. But now I was looking for jobs as an electrical estimator in Dubai. What life would there be for us if I had to move abroad? I could not stay in England, not with my sacking public knowledge, it would be too damaging. Even though what the PGMOL had done was wrong on just about every level, I was ready to quit the country and start again. I thought I was about to lose Claire and my career.

Then, as I have already written about, I found a resolve to fight the injustice. By February, I was reinstated as a Premier League referee. There was now a life for me and Claire to build together. It was like this cloak of darkness had been lifted. I was a different person, knowing I would soon be back doing what I loved. It is only when you emerge from those periods that you realise how tormented you really were.

We got married in the summer of 2010 at Seaham Hall in County Durham. The night before we booked an Italian restaurant in Seaham for all of our guests. England were playing Algeria in the World Cup in South Africa and all of the men wanted to watch that, including me. I had to ignore the temptation, although I did not miss much, it was a goalless draw.

The perfect match was waiting for me the following day. Claire and I have been through a lot together, as these pages will testify, but she has always been there for me. Our daughter, Mia, was born in 2011, and she has been my motivation ever since.

But I would not be writing this book without Claire, for the success I enjoyed was only possible because of her support, and boy have I needed it.

★   ★   ★

My first marriage did not last long. I was twenty-five and about to be promoted to the Football League. I met Helen on Newcastle's Quayside and we got married soon after in 2000. We moved to Chester-le-Street, County Durham but were divorced within a couple of years.

My son, Nathan, was born in 2002. The joy and the pride of being a dad made way for sadness after splitting up, for not being able to see my son every day was painful.

I missed out on a lot of things with Nathan, especially at weekends when I was refereeing. That was the time we should have been together, and I regret that. It is not the relationship you imagine with your son. But now that he is older and he can make his own decisions, we see more of each other.

I had always promised him when he passed his driving test that I would buy him his first car. I ended up getting him a Mercedes A-Class, and he pranged it within a fortnight. I know that money does not buy love or make up for lost time, and what I did was probably wrong. But for any father who has not been there to influence his son on a daily basis, you will always feel guilty. The car was me keeping a promise and, maybe selfishly, it felt nice being able to spoil him. Although the repair bill a couple of weeks later did teach him a valuable lesson.

Nathan has taken up refereeing in recent years. I have been to watch him and he has done well. Whether he pursues it as a career does not matter to me, I will not be disappointed if he chooses another path. I just hope he takes from refereeing the development of character that I did. You soon grow up when you're the fella having to look after twenty-two others on a football pitch. It sharpens your instincts.

You might think he has the ideal source of guidance in me, but I cannot help him as much as I would like. I find myself a bit lost trying to offer tips. Grassroots level, where Nathan is at, is about educating and helping the players as much as it is applying the laws. Things like foul throws, for example, you let them take it again and get it right. I have become so used to the top level that I have forgotten what it takes to be a good referee with junior players. Nathan is better than me!

My biggest wish is that he enjoys it and that he finds his own way. If he gets the bug for it, like I did, then great, carry on. If not, give it up, pursue something that interests and excites you. Chase a dream, it might not come off but at least give yourself the chance of making it happen. To that extent, I hope he takes some inspiration from what I did.

Nathan did cause me some mild embarrassment on one occasion during my career. I was due to referee Bolton versus Watford in the Premier League in September 2006. We were playing football in the street the day before, taking penalties at each other. He asked me what the score would be in my match that weekend.

'It'll be 1–0 to Bolton, last-minute penalty,' I said, and mimicked taking the winning kick.

I picked him up a couple of days later from his mam's house in Chester-le-Street. Nathan had mentioned my prediction to one of the neighbours, who I knew. They started joking with me.

'I hear you knew the result yesterday before it even kicked off?'

Eh? I had forgotten all about what I'd said to Nathan. It then clicked – Bolton won 1–0 and Gary Speed scored a ninetieth minute penalty. Shit, that doesn't look good, does it? It just shows, you have to be careful what you say around kids!

I was always concerned for Nathan at school, worried that his classmates or older children might target him when I was in the news. It was not as if our surname was Smith, everyone knew he was my son. As he got older he was not even bothered about me being a referee and never really talked about it. But his indifference would not stop some kids trying to wind him up. That makes you feel helpless as a parent, you just want to be there to protect your children.

He used to get embarrassed when I picked him up from school. I lost the plot in my late thirties and bought an Audi R8 sports car – an early mid-life crisis. I thought I was so cool. Nathan didn't. He thought I looked like a dick and he was probably right. My dad had an old Ford Cortina when I was a kid. Like Nathan, I made him park around the corner from school – only that was because I didn't want anyone to know we had a Cortina!

My daughter, Mia, is a bit different in that she loves me being on the TV. She does think it's cool. She even lets me drop her off at school and always gives me a kiss before going through the gates. It might be first thing in the morning but your day does not get any better than that.

Mia was born a year after Claire and I were married. We were panicking, or at least I was, because the baby was late. I was due to go to Colombia for the Under-20 World Cup and it was a big deal for my career progression. I was buying us Indian takeaways every night, trying all the old wives' tales to hurry up the birth.

Thankfully, Mia arrived in the nick of time and has been good as gold ever since. I wind her up and say, 'Mia, your school report is bad.' She knows it's not true. Her reports reflect the girl we see at home – loving, caring and clever. I can count on one hand the number of times I've had to raise my voice with her. But I have always been the good cop between me and Claire, and that made a nice change from the day job.

Because I was not there for Nathan as much as I would have liked, I want that to be different with Mia. I want to pass on my life experiences and use them to influence and guide her. I have been through a lot – not all good – and I hope positives can come from that.

She has started to take more of an interest in who I am, beyond 'Dad'. We discovered she had been reading about me on her iPad. But it's not the refereeing she is bothered about, she loves the stuff like the Amazon Alexa advert I did with Peter

Crouch. It was great fun, to be fair. In it, I am Alexa's 'football mentor' and she is my 'voice assistant referee'. Mia thought it was hilarious when I tried speaking to Alexa at home and she came back with, 'Sorry, I did not understand that.' So much for our special relationship, Alexa needs to learn Geordie!

Mia can relate to the TV commercials and celebrity Soccer Aid matches I have refereed, they are things she and her friends talk about at school. She was even convinced I was going to be revealed as one of the contestants on *The Masked Singer* – but Alexa wouldn't be the only one offended by my northern tones were that to happen.

Mia is a friend and a daughter. I just love being around her. She is a source of happiness every day.

★   ★   ★

One point of sadness is that Mia has never met my mam. I have not spoken to her since 2012. I will detail this period later, but during that year I was accused, and later cleared, of racially abusing two Chelsea players in a match against Manchester United.

My world fell apart. I told my family not to speak to the media, and my mam did. She claimed it was a misunder-standing, but I could not escape the fact that they were her words to a journalist. I felt let down. It was all about her. She did not protect me when I needed it most, and it was not the first time.

I was flying to London a couple of years earlier to referee

a game when I read the bankruptcy notices in *The Journal*, a local newspaper in the North-East. There she was, my mam. I froze. I was in the departure lounge at Newcastle Airport and I can recall the moment vividly, such was my shock and anger. I called her immediately. She should have told me. I was upset on two fronts. Firstly, I could have tried to help her. Instead, she had declared herself bankrupt because it suited her situation. She did not think about what impact that had on me.

Secondly, as a Premier League referee, you need to know things like that. You need to inform your bosses, especially after everything I had been through a year or so earlier, when I was warned about not declaring my business debts to the PGMOL. I now had to be doubly careful.

My mam should have been looking out for me. We could have managed the issues and found a solution. Instead, it left me open to accusations of not looking after her, and that was far from the truth.

We eventually sorted things out and she came to our wedding in 2010. But the interview with the newspaper two years later felt like a betrayal at a time when I needed my family most.

It was a shame that, as I got older, more conversations with my mam involved issues around money. For me, you could be broke in life, but a loving relationship is worth far more than any material goods or cash in the bank.

The tension with my mam, I believe, caused a breakdown between the rest of our family. I do not see or talk to three of my four siblings now. As we got older, and after my dad passed away, we went in different directions. The issues with my mam came between some of us.

It upsets me that Mia will grow up wondering why she never knew her grandma. But I hope I have learned lessons on the back of what has happened. It is why I hold Mia so close, why I want to build a bond that is unbreakable.

Nathan is older, I have missed those years. But he does not need money from me to make up for that, I cannot buy back time. He needs someone to talk to, a dad to love him and guide him. I have only realised that with the fullness of time. In a way, I have used the scars of my own broken relationships to make me a better dad.

There are times when I have felt alone, detached from the family I grew up with. I have not shared the highs and lows of my career with my siblings. As kids, we were inseparable. I would play football with my younger brother for hours, jumpers for goalposts. I was very close to my older sister and we all looked after each other. Now, it is only my younger sister that Claire and I still see.

I sometimes think my mam could have done more to keep us together. It was not easy for her, with a sick husband and then being made a widow at a young age. But after that we all drifted apart. I see pictures of them now and again, but it's like I do not know who they are.

I wonder if it would have been different with my dad still around. I think my life would have been, he would have foreseen some of the problems I ran into. He would have helped me avoid them. I was in my early twenties when I lost him. I thought I knew it all. Without him to keep me in check, maybe I did run away with myself at times. As I got older and I became more high profile, I did not see myself as a role model – and because of that I did not act like one. That is where a father tells you to rein it in. Things like the private number plate that attracted so much negative publicity. Just don't do it, don't be a prick.

It was not until I met Pierluigi Collina, thirteen years after my dad died, that I felt I had that older man in my life to help me. I will talk more about Collina's influence later.

Claire is the person I turn to now. At the time of writing, I am the head of refereeing in Greece. She does not understand half of the problems I come across but she will listen and give an opinion – even if she does not know Olympiakos from Panathinaikos.

I have a group of close friends who have always looked out for me, but they will bring me back down to earth if they think I need it. Some of us first met when learning our electrical trade at Gateshead College, so to them I am not a referee. I am just Mark from college. That is what I like. They used to take the piss if I had made a bad mistake and I was often the brunt of the jokes, but a lot of the time my career was never really talked about. It only became an issue if someone outside of our circle decided to have a go at me, and my mates always had my back.

We were at the horse racing in Dubai one night and a Chelsea fan was abusing me. I had been next to him at the urinals and he was fine, chatting away. Outside, in front of his mates, he started getting in my face and the mood changed. I tried to stay calm.

'Sorry mate, I'm not here to talk about football,' I said.

He would not stop. I could see one of my friends, who was a doorman, was getting more and more irate. We gave this lad a chance to piss off, but he kept on at me. My pal snapped. Bang. It served him right. People think they are clever with a drink inside them.

I often find the best way to disarm these idiots is just to admit a mistake, regardless of whether you believe that to be the case. By saying, 'Yeah, I was crap that game, wasn't I?', it tends to put these arseholes on the back foot. I've even had some say, 'Ah right, can I buy you a drink?'

There was another incident at Cheltenham races when I was in a corporate lounge with my friends. A group of guys were on another table behind us. Again, Chelsea supporters. The day started friendly enough but then, the more drink they had, the cockier one or two of them got, showing off by hurling insults in my direction. That wasn't the only thing they threw – next thing I know a scone has bounced off the back of my head. I couldn't react, not in such a public place, not ever. My friends stepped in to sort it out without me getting involved. They were like plain-clothed security when they had to be, and I always felt safe with them around.

That is not to say I am not approachable, far from it. I have annoyed Claire on countless occasions when we have been out and a group of lads strike up a conversation about football – rather than decisions I have made – and I have left her sitting alone for half an hour.

I do wonder if people sometimes expect me to wave them away, like I would players on the pitch. But that's not the real me. Forget the idiots, if a genuine person wants to talk, then I will always engage. I wish I had a pound for every time someone has met me and said, 'You're not what I expected.'

Everyone has an opinion about me before I am introduced to them. Claire has laughed when her friends have said to her, 'He's actually alright.' What a cheek! But I just laugh with her, and I take 'alright' as a compliment.

I do sometimes long for the days of anonymity in my early twenties when I played cricket over the summer for New Hartley in Northumberland. I was refereeing in the Northern League but my cricket was a world away from football. We had a couple of Australians in the team, and as you would expect they were our Ricky Ponting and Shane Warne. We would always bowl first, skittle out the opposition and knock off the runs as quickly as possible so we could go out for a drink in Whitley Bay. I have kept in touch with the Aussies and they always say it was the best time of their lives. I can't argue with that.

The older I got, the more I found myself wanting to switch off from football, be it watching cricket or playing golf. The technical skill of the top golfers is something I have always admired but failed to emulate. I had one friend who was incredibly talented in that regard. Tragically, he died in 2013, and his loss will always haunt me.

I met Peter Jackson through Claire. He was the golf professional at Castle Eden Golf Club. Claire and Peter's wife thought we would not get on when they introduced us. They feared we would clash. What developed, to the surprise of our partners and amusement of ourselves, was a brilliant and close friendship. We would go out, the four of us, on a Sunday in Seaham for a few drinks, or me and Peter would meet up, just the two of us.

We had arranged to go out on the night of Sunday 10 November 2013. Peter had been to watch Sunderland beat Manchester City earlier that day with his son. I had just got back from a month in Abu Dhabi, where I was refereeing the Under-17 World Cup. I texted him to say I was knackered, could we leave it until next week. 'No problem,' he said.

Peter went missing the following day. It was awful. He had a wife and two children. Two weeks later his body was found in woodland in Northumberland. He was only thirty-eight years old. All of that time I was trying his phone, telling him to come home, desperately hoping he would pick up my message. He never did reply.

I saw the impact Peter's loss had on his family. It left a mark on me that will never go away. I wish I could have helped him. I often wonder, 'If only I had met him that night.'

Peter was a great guy. While I will forever mourn him not being here, I am glad to have met him and had the years of friendship we did.

Losing Peter has changed me in some ways, the sadness of

not being able to help a good person. On some level, maybe that is the reason why, in recent years, I have reached out to offer help to strangers. I do not want to disclose too many details, because that is not the motivation for doing so. But there was one story I read in the newspaper about the death of a young British person in Spain, who had fallen off a balcony. Their family could not afford to repatriate the body. I offered a sum of money to help them and later received an email saying how appreciative they were.

Money is not the only way of helping people. I did some Zoom calls during the COVID-19 lockdown, including one with a junior football club in Wales. The kids were made up and we all loved it. For me, it was nice to see some new faces and talk football after being in the house with my wife and daughter for so long!

The game has given me a wonderful life, in terms of the personal and financial rewards. It has been a wild ride and a blur of emotions at times, but it feels like I have finally stepped off the rollercoaster. With a little more freedom of thought, I want to give something back. I am very fortunate to have had a career that puts me in a position to do so.

7

THE PLAYERS

'Messi changed the way I refereed'

TOO many referees miss a trick by not engaging with players – be that before, during or after a game. I found that interaction imperative in being able to control them and, in turn, the match.

Just like with managers, by establishing a level of trust you were buying a little goodwill and understanding from those on the pitch.

Forget about punishment and enforcing the *Laws of the Game*. Talking to a player was the most powerful tool I had. Of course, you had to know when the time was right and being overly familiar would just piss them off, but I took every opportunity I could to develop a relationship.

As a referee, you are there to manage twenty-two individuals, who are highly-strung and ultra-competitive. If they all think you're a dick, how much harder is that going to be?

I always tried to understand what a player wanted from the referee. For example, I found that playing an advantage won you a lot of respect. It might sound simple, but players could not tolerate a referee who was too quick to whistle. A bad referee is one who is a slave to the laws.

But while I wanted the game to flow, I also had to adapt as my career went on. I realised that players were now multi-million-pound assets to their football clubs and I had to protect them. You never wanted to be the referee whose leniency was the cause of a bad injury. It was about striking a delicate balance between allowing a contest to breathe and at the same time establishing clear boundaries.

In some ways, that relationship with players is like earning the trust of a dog. A happy dog is one who feels safe and knows its behavioural limits.

When I was refereeing well, I felt that players did not concern themselves with every little decision of mine and instead focused on playing the game. That was always the aim – forget about me, it's about you, go and impact the match.

Whereas players were determined to leave the pitch having made their mark, I wanted to walk off having made no impression. As this chapter will reveal, that was not always possible.

With that in mind, I will instead kick off with two players who were an absolute pleasure.

* * *

Cristiano Ronaldo and Lionel Messi were the two greatest players I ever refereed. That should be a given for any official lucky enough to share a pitch with them.

The first time with Messi, I was in shock. It was 2015, Paris

Saint-Germain versus Barcelona in the Champions League quarter-final. I was like, 'This is unbelievable.' I had seen him do things on TV that I knew were special, but up close it takes your breath away.

You genuinely looked forward to refereeing games involving Messi and Ronaldo. The more the years pass, the more I realise how privileged I was. They were genius.

But they were also a challenge to referee. Not because they were difficult personalities. On the contrary, I found them easy to manage in that regard. They were a challenge because they were so bloody good.

Messi changed the way I refereed. When a player has possession you tend to watch the ball. With him you could easily lose track of it, so imagine how defenders used to feel. They would try all sorts to stop him. That is why I had to think about how I analysed situations when he had the ball. Opponents would attempt to use their upper body to knock him off balance, not that they ever could. I had to be aware of that rather than trying to follow ball and feet all of the time. He always wanted to stay on his feet, too. He would prefer to ride a challenge and score a brilliant goal than accept the foul and go down. I admired him for that.

Messi was very quiet on the pitch. I never had any interaction with him at all, really. I booked him in that game versus PSG for standing on an opponent's foot. He didn't say a word, he never did. It was as if he didn't have to, like he was above all of the verbals that others got involved with. His feet did the talking for him.

Ronaldo and Real Madrid were a challenge because they were so quick on the counter-attack. You would find yourself in a foot race with the other team trying to get on terms as they broke upfield. I should have just waited on halfway for the inevitable restart!

I will write later about Ronaldo and my respect for him. He edges Messi as the best I refereed, in part because I was in charge of the finals when he won the UEFA Super Cup, Champions League and European Championship.

I was also referee the night he scored a hat-trick in a 6–1 win at Galatasaray in 2013, during the first round of Champions League group matches. I knew then Real would win the competition that season. Ronaldo poached a couple from close range but his third was sensational. It was the last minute and it was as if he thought, 'I'm not leaving here without a hat-trick.' He went by two of their players and produced this unstoppable finish. It was mesmerising stuff.

But I remember that night as much for getting to and from the stadium. The traffic in Istanbul was a nightmare at the best of times, let alone when Real Madrid were in town. We had a police escort on the way to the ground and we were flying up the wrong side of the motorway. I was in the back of the people-carrier cowering with my hands in front of my face. I was a wreck before we even kicked off. It was a different story after the game. The home fans weren't hanging around to see their team get stuffed and the stadium cleared pretty quickly. We left, expecting more traffic hell, but we were back at the hotel within ten minutes, just in time for last orders. There wasn't a soul on the roads. So I have Ronaldo to thank for clearing our passage to the bar that night!

To be in the middle of the action with him, knowing that this one player could get 80,000 people out of their seats in an instant, it was an awesome feeling. You have to maintain a sober judgement, of course, and I always felt I had a good handle on him. But he could inspire a crowd and his team-mates through sheer force of personality. Being so close you can feel that energy, like electricity pulsing through the stadium.

Messi had that, too. You were in the presence of greatness with those two and I was fortunate enough to have the best ticket in the house. They were once-in-a-generation players who, incredibly, came along at the same time.

It was my dream to referee Barcelona versus Real Madrid with both Messi and Ronaldo playing. When I quit the Premier League in 2017, and with it went my Champions League matches, it played on my mind a little that I had never refereed El Classico. If they had been drawn together in the Champions League over the next couple of seasons – they weren't, as it happened – I would have definitely thought, 'What if?'

But at least I was not left wondering what it was like to be on the pitch with them. For that, I will always be grateful.

★   ★   ★

Gary Speed was the kindest player I ever had the good fortune to referee. It is not by chance that I have followed on from

Ronaldo and Messi with memories of Gary. That is the regard in which I held him. Sadly, they will forever be memories. Gary died aged forty-two in November 2011.

I had refereed the East Anglia derby between Norwich and Ipswich the previous day when news broke of his death on the Sunday morning. I was sitting on the sofa watching TV when I flicked to *Goals on Sunday* on Sky Sports. A text message from a viewer rolled across the bottom of the screen, 'RIP Gary Speed.' I went cold. I turned to Claire.

'What's happened? Why is it saying that? That can't be right,' I said.

I had recently been on a flight with Gary to Barbados for a Premier League exhibition event. I did not want to believe it was true. Sadly, I realised very quickly that it was. I was shivering with shock. I felt numb for days.

My relationship with Gary went back to 2004 and my first season in the Premier League. There was a lot of pressure on me given I was the youngest ever Premier League referee at twenty-nine. Gary recognised that and helped me, as I am sure he did with other referees. He did not have to, but that is the type of man he was. He found time in the heat of the battle to talk to me, to encourage me to move on if I had made a mistake, and I made enough of them during those early days. He would praise you, too. It was not to gain favour, he was just a genuine person. A gentleman.

Gary was playing for Bolton at the time, a team with a reputation for being aggressive, which they were. But that did not mean you could not be a nice person, and Gary proved that. I hope any young players reading this take note and realise – here was a Wales international, a brilliant player, who still had the heart to look out for others and be a good human being. There was a decency and an honesty about everything Gary did, on and off the pitch.

But what an awesome player. I was right there in the middle of the park with him and I saw him boss games. He could pass it, he was powerful in the air and he scored goals. He flew into tackles, yet I never booked him. He was the complete midfield player. I was also lucky that he played for my team, Newcastle, and he will always be revered in our part of the world.

Even if Gary was still with us, I would be writing exactly the same. He was a role model to all of us. I will never forget what he did for me.

Manchester City captain Vincent Kompany was very similar to Gary in that regard. He was as good a man as he was a footballer. Like Gary, he supported you as the referee and had a very respectful and calm manner.

There was one City match where I made a mistake in the first half. Everyone knew it, including me. As we came out after half-time, Kompany started talking to me.

'Mark, players make mistakes, you've made a mistake, forget about it, let's move on.'

He was a classy individual.

But unlike Gary, I did have reason to book Kompany and

even send him off. He did not let that be an issue whenever we next met and his respect for the officials never changed, even if decisions went against him.

In 2015, I gave him a red card playing for Belgium against Israel, a second booking when he deliberately stopped an attack. He accepted it.

A week or so later, I had the Manchester derby at Old Trafford. There was an incident in the first half where Kompany slipped going into a challenge with Daley Blind. It looked bad and could have been a red card. I could not be sure so went with my assistant, who advised yellow. City lost 4–2 and Kompany thanked me afterwards. He joked that one red card was enough for that month. But he was lucky we did not have VAR, because having seen it back later, I would have definitely sent him off.

United supporters certainly thought I got that decision wrong. I was flying to Belfast straight after the game to do a talk on refereeing the following day. I thought nothing of it, until I realised the Belfast branch of the Manchester United supporters club were on the same flight. They soon let me know that Kompany should have been shown red.

But thank God that decision had not impacted the result. The fans were in good spirits and were chanting from the back of the plane, 'Clattenburg, Clattenburg, give us a wave!' I was keeping my head down.

The fella next to me had been to his first-ever game at Old Trafford. They passed the season-ticket around his local pub in

Belfast and it was a lovely story to hear. He asked if I wanted a drink, but I thought better of it. I could see the headlines, 'Clattenburg toasts United derby win!'

Less than five minutes later, the air hostess tapped me on the shoulder. She had five cans of beer for me.

'Everyone at the back wants to buy you a drink. Who are you?' she said.

'Me? I'm the fella they would normally throw beer at, so this is a first!'

★   ★   ★

There are some players you would assume referees just do not like. Luis Suarez perhaps being one of them. Not for me. I respected him so much, simply because of his talent.

If you knew how to handle him, he was fine. Managing players such as Suarez helped the game. It is better for the spectacle if he knows the referee will not tolerate any of his dirty tricks, and so he concentrates on impacting the match with his skill. And boy did he have some skill.

My first game with him was Ajax versus Slovan Bratislava in August 2009, a Europa League qualifier. He scored four goals in a 5–0 win and was unplayable. He was only twenty-two at the time. I came home and told my friends all about him.

'I would love to see him in the Premier League,' I said. 'He's unbelievable. Let's hope Newcastle go and sign him.'

Fat chance. He joined Liverpool in 2011 and I knew what a special player they were getting.

My first Barcelona match, as I mentioned earlier, was their 3–1 victory at PSG in 2015, and Suarez scored twice that night in Paris. He was at his peak around this time and, having refereed most of the world's top players during that period, I believe only Messi and Ronaldo were ahead of him.

But he had that street-fighter edge to him, like Diego Costa. He would try to play the referee, if you let him. I didn't.

The first time he gave me a load of Spanish swear words, I went back at him with one or two of my own. I had them up my sleeve from refereeing in Europe. He must have taken note, because I rarely had a problem with him after that.

I also had to protect him, from both the opposition and himself. He was a player who was fouled a lot and was liable to clip – or bite – someone if he got too frustrated. I would always try to give him one or two free-kicks early on, just to calm him down. It usually worked.

I laugh when I hear some people talk about how easy refereeing should be, that it is just about knowing the laws. That is rubbish. The biggest challenge is managing volatile characters such as Suarez and Costa.

If Suarez knew exactly where he stood with you, it avoided issues down the line. He is one of the best examples of where a referee needs to apply common sense and not be a stickler for the laws.

I enjoyed the challenge of getting inside his head, I wanted to be a deterrent for his misbehaviour rather than a catalyst. Because like Ronaldo and Messi, he was a player who could take ownership of a game. And if the top players are doing that, no one is talking about the referee.

*   *   *

My time in the Premier League coincided with that of England's 'Golden Generation', and rarely did I have a problem with any of them. They were world-class players and I thought they were all decent individuals, even if some of the Manchester United boys would get in your face on what I believed to be Sir Alex Ferguson's instruction.

My biggest frustration with them was as an England fan, because they never won anything. It helped English referees when our country kept getting knocked out of major tournaments, as both Howard Webb and I benefited by taking charge of finals. But their talent was wasted in that regard.

I did have one other gripe with Wayne Rooney, but that was only because he chose to sign for Manchester United instead of Newcastle in the summer of 2004, just as I was joining the Premier League. Having later shared a pitch with him and realised how good he really was, I would have loved to see him at Newcastle. For me, he was the best of that generation for sheer ability.

Some people may think Rooney was difficult to referee because he was always chirping on, which he was. But most of it was not dissent, he was more frustrated with how the game was going. He was a different level to almost everyone on the pitch and I could see that irritation coming to the boil if things were not going his way. I had to handle that.

My method was by ignoring him, letting him play his way out of his mood, which he invariably did. There was one famous example against Newcastle at Old Trafford in 2005. He was arguing with referee Neale Barry before he ran onto a dropping ball and volleyed it into the top corner from twenty-five yards. That was him.

Rooney did cause me a lot of aggravation following an incident at Wigan in 2011, although I do not necessarily blame him for the fallout from it. He elbowed James McCarthy in an off-the-ball clash early in the game. I had seen them coming together but only in my peripheral vision. I gave a free-kick to Wigan because I thought Rooney had just knocked him over.

After the game – United won 4–0 and Rooney scored – I was accused of seeing Rooney's elbow but turning a blind eye because it was him and Manchester United. That was bollocks, and it annoyed me. I would have sent him off if I had seen it properly, it was a red-card offence.

There were calls for Rooney to be banned retrospectively, but I could not re-referee the incident and recommend that he be punished, because I had already dealt with it on the pitch by way of the free-kick. Those were the FA's rules. I was honest, I told the FA that I thought I had seen the coming-together but, evidently, had not realised the action of Rooney's elbow.

But for it to be suggested that I was doing Rooney a favour was insulting. He got off without a suspension because of the FA's stupid rules, not because I was looking after him. Once

I gave the free-kick, I could have no influence over anything else after the game.

Again, though, referees cannot speak to defend themselves. You just think, 'What's the point in all of this?' I wondered if I really wanted to continue. Your reputation is being brought into question because of something that is, in reality, beyond your control.

I cannot be aware of what twenty-two players are doing at all times. Yes, sometimes you make a mistake and call an incorrect decision. But in this instance, I felt totally wronged on two fronts. Firstly, the idea that I ignored the elbow on the pitch. Then, the ludicrous claims that I helped him avoid a ban. It was absolute garbage.

I have never spoken with Rooney about it since and all of my dealings with him have been very pleasant. In the main, I thought he was respectful to referees. Unfortunately, he had a red mist that could lead to red cards. But you have to see them to give them, as I found to my cost that day at Wigan.

*   *   *

I have no time for Chelsea Football Club after what they put me through when they wrongly accused me of racially abusing two of their players in 2012. But John Terry and Frank Lampard – two players synonymous with Chelsea – I never had any issues with.

I found Terry very helpful in that, if you had a problem with a Chelsea player, he could step in and solve it for you. I liked that. He communicated with you and it helped the game. Not all captains would do so, but I encouraged it. I found having a working relationship with captains was to the benefit of everyone.

Terry would still come after me if he thought a decision had gone against his team. He also knew I would have no hesitation in sending him off, like I did when he took out West Brom striker Salomon Rondon at The Hawthorns in 2015. But there was always a respect whereby we would listen to each other.

Lampard was less vocal and rarely engaged, but I respected him for what he said to me following the racism claims. Ahead of my next Chelsea match later in the same season, he made a point of saying there were no hard feelings from his perspective. I appreciated his understanding. He was man enough to do that and I took comfort from the fact he was prepared to acknowledge what I had been through.

Lampard was a great player, too. He had this knack of arriving in the penalty area at the same time as the ball – and I should know, because I was trying to make the same run ten yards behind him! It was a shame no England manager could find a way of getting the best from him and Steven Gerrard in the same team.

Like Terry, Gerrard was a player you could speak to. He never caused me any problems despite being so physical. He was ferocious but always tried to be fair with it.

When Liverpool were going for the title in 2014, I refereed their 3–2 victory over Manchester City at Anfield in mid-April.

It was the 25th anniversary of Hillsborough and it was an emotional day.

It had been a breathless match and Liverpool were clinging on come the end. I sent off Jordan Henderson in the ninetieth minute for a reckless challenge on Samir Nasri. Gerrard was begging me to blow the whistle. I looked in his eyes and I could see they were full of tears. As a football fan, I respected him for that.

Liverpool knew that victory over one of their nearest rivals was a huge step towards the title. Given the emotion of the Hillsborough anniversary, I saw in Gerrard's face how much it meant to him. Seeing him like that is an image that will stay with me.

When Liverpool then lost to Chelsea two weeks later and Gerrard slipped to allow Demba Ba to score, I felt for him. I thought back to that moment at the end of the City game and realised just how much he would have been hurting.

Liverpool went to Crystal Palace in their penultimate match level on points with City, who were nine better off in terms of goal difference. It was a Monday night under the lights at Selhurst Park and I sensed when I arrived that something special might unfold. What an incredible evening it proved to be, one of the most memorable of my career.

It was 3–0 to Liverpool after an hour and they had been devastating. The movement, the pace, they were dynamite. Luis Suarez, Raheem Sterling and Daniel Sturridge were unplayable.

Palace just wanted to keep the score down and their

goalkeeper, Julian Speroni, was taking his time with goal-kicks. Gerrard was screaming at me.

'Hurry him up, hurry him up!'

Liverpool were 3–0 up and I was still getting dog's abuse! But I understood why, they wanted to narrow the goal difference. They probably thought they could score nine that night alone. They were pushing so hard, and that proved their downfall.

Damian Delaney scored for Palace with eleven minutes to go. Liverpool took off Sterling and Sturridge and it seemed to affect them. I could see it happening right in front of me, they were falling to pieces. Dwight Gayle made it 3–2 and then, two minutes from time, 3–3. Palace should have even won it in stoppage-time. Liverpool had mentally disintegrated. That was the title as good as gone.

It just shows what pressure can do. I refereed them six times that season and they were the best team in the division. They should have won the league.

After the game, Liverpool manager Brendan Rodgers came into my dressing-room. I thought he was going to blame me for one of Palace's goals, that is your instinct when a team implodes like they did. He gave me a hug.

'Thank you for your efforts this season,' he said.

It was such a classy reaction after what had just happened and I saw a different side to Rodgers that night. I had great respect for what he did because he must have been hurting beyond belief. Liverpool had put everything into that season, I saw that first-hand.

They lost the title to City but did finally win it in 2020, by which time Gerrard had retired and Henderson was captain. Jordan was still establishing himself in 2014 and missed the 3–3 draw at Palace because he was suspended from the red card I had shown him versus City a few weeks earlier. I knew his mam and dad from the North-East as we lived in the same area. I spoke to him about the sending-off and he said there were no hard feelings, he accepted it was a red. He even told me that when he got back to the dressing-room, he opened his phone and his mam was having a pop at him for the challenge. At least we could laugh about that.

Jordan used to get frustrated on the pitch. He once gave me a mouthful of bad language over a decision and I turned around, calmly as you like.

'I'm going to tell your mam what you've just said to me.'

He went white, he did not know what to say. The referees' observer asked me after the game how I had calmed him down. I told him that was my secret.

I had left the Premier League by the time Jordan lifted the title in 2020, but I was happy for him. I wonder what Gerrard thought of it all; that should have been him in 2014.

Liverpool defender Jamie Carragher, another of that England generation, had retired in 2013. He was not afraid to give you a few verbals and I tried not to get involved with him. He was an unpredictable player, doing strange things at strange times. During the Merseyside derby of 2007 and with Liverpool winning 2–1, he pulled down Everton's Joleon Lescott in the penalty area in the last minute, but I missed it. He was difficult to referee because of being unpredictable.

Carragher went on to become an excellent pundit, just like Manchester United's Gary Neville. I always found Neville an on-the-pitch embodiment of Sir Alex Ferguson. He was prepped to apply pressure on you at just the right time. I thought it was funny how they all worked off the same blueprint as Fergie.

Rio Ferdinand was the same. He would get into your ribs more for Fergie's benefit than anything. But what a player. A Rolls Royce, he never broke sweat. There are certain players you appreciate more for being at such close proximity, and Ferdinand was one of them.

Michael Owen was someone I only came across in his later years at Manchester United and Stoke. He signed for Newcastle in 2005 from Real Madrid and I thought he would be my new hero after Alan Shearer retired. It did not work out and Newcastle fans, myself included, questioned his desire when we were relegated in 2009. But spending time with Owen after he retired, I appreciated what a nice guy he actually is.

Likewise with Gary Neville. I worked with him as part of the ITV punditry team at the 2018 World Cup in Russia. He is a great fella, he is smart and passionate. He even asked me to join him and Ryan Giggs in the gym one day. I assume he cleared it with Fergie first!

★　★　★

I was only ever handed a script for one match – Alan Shearer's testimonial at St James' Park in 2006.

We were into injury-time when Les Ferdinand went down in the penalty area. It was a dive, a yellow card. Not this time. I pointed to the spot. Alan was injured but on he came as a substitute to score at the Gallowgate End to make it Newcastle 3 Celtic 2. Fair play to Celtic for going along with it.

But what a night. For atmosphere it was the best I ever experienced, and that includes the three big finals of 2016. There was this incredible moment when 52,000 supporters were waving black-and-white scarves above their heads. The noise was deafening and the sight was simply awesome. Some of the players stopped following the game and were gazing around the stadium, open mouthed. We were all looking at each other just saying, 'Wow.'

I was so lucky to be part of that. Not only to be asked in the first place, but also fortunate because I had just recovered from injury. I had not refereed since January after a patellar tendon operation and had missed the remainder of the season. Alan's match, in May, was a goal for me to work towards. I was not missing this one.

Because I could not referee competitive Newcastle matches, I never had much to do with Alan as a player. But as a Newcastle fan, he was God. He was my idol. I was starstruck when he came into our dressing-room to thank us for refereeing his testimonial.

It is funny, because when I was injured that year I took the chance to go to a lot more Newcastle games, and I was there for what would prove to be Alan's last match as a professional footballer. It was a Wear–Tyne derby against Sunderland at the Stadium of Light in April. Newcastle won 4–1 and Shearer scored a penalty with his last-ever kick. He injured his knee in a challenge with Julio Arca a few minutes later and did not play again.

I could also have been injured that day. I was in the main stand and thought I would be surrounded by corporate guests. But there were Sunderland fans everywhere and they knew about my Newcastle allegiance. The banter was friendly enough when Sunderland were winning 1–0. The atmosphere changed when Newcastle scored four times in the last half hour. Even Albert Luque got a goal, and that's saying something.

The home fans were starting to target me, 'Fuck off Clattenburg, scum.' I was not hanging around. I headed to my friend's box and, thankfully, there was security on every door. I took sanctuary in there for an hour or so and then made my escape. That was the first time I had been to the derby at the Stadium of Light, and it will certainly be the last. It was a silly risk to take, as much as I enjoyed watching Newcastle stuff Sunderland.

So Alan did not play in his testimonial, which was a shame. He took part in a ceremonial kick-off but had to wait until the ninetieth minute before coming on to take his penalty.

Here is something people will not realise. It was agreed beforehand that Alan should score a penalty to make it a draw. But Celtic scored an own goal to make it 2–2 in the last minute.

We were walking back to the halfway line to kick off and John Hartson, the Celtic striker, turned to me.

'What do we do now?' he said.

We had no choice, Alan's penalty would be to win the match, which made it even better. It was a privilege to be part of that night. My family got a box and we had a few beers afterwards.

I have seen Alan a lot more since he retired. Often, it is on a flight to or from London and we always chat about our common interest – as long-suffering fans of Newcastle United!

★　★　★

I wish Craig Bellamy had never left Newcastle. Yes, in part because he was a fantastic player. But more so because it would have meant I never had to referee him.

He was the worst of the worst. Every referee felt the same. He was rude and could be abusive. His biggest problem was that he could not see it himself. He thought it was perfectly acceptable to behave the way he did. He had zero respect for you as a referee, and he certainly did not like me.

Manchester City were playing at Bolton in December 2009 and he was up to his usual tricks with the verbals. I booked him for dissent. At half-time I spoke to one of City's coaching staff.

'How do you put up with him every week?' I said.

In the second half, I gave Bellamy a second yellow card for a dive and sent him off. I got it wrong. He was fouled and it should have been a penalty. Of all the players to make such a mistake with! Of course, he forever held it against me.

The game ended 3–3 and City manager Mark Hughes accused me in the press of being biased against Bellamy. He also revealed the comment I had made about Bellamy at half-time. I felt let down by that, because what is said during a game should stay there. If I reported managers and players for everything they said to me, they would be a few quid worse off from the FA fines they would incur. They can't have it both ways.

But my relationship with Bellamy was over, not that we ever had one. He was always a problem player and made your life difficult. You were like a teacher having to deal with one unruly child, and you risked losing focus elsewhere.

Later, I was refereeing a City match at the Etihad Stadium and, for a split-second in the tunnel, I thought he was about to offer his hand in peace. Don't be daft. He grabbed my balls, and I don't mean my match-balls. I took it as a joke. Although given the pressure he applied, I am not so sure!

Whereas Bellamy caused offence, some players just irritated you. Arsenal goalkeeper Jens Lehmann was one of those. I always felt like saying to him, 'Give it a rest man, will you?' He would moan about the colour of the grass if he could. He was irritable and was constantly on at you. It detracted from what was a very good goalkeeper. I noticed that opposition teams played on that weakness and wound him up. They would niggle him before corners or stand on his toes and he would react.

Lehmann was not enjoyable to referee, but that was in part because he did not seem to be enjoying himself. I understand some players are like that, they need conflict to get the best out of themselves. But with some, such as Lehmann, it was detrimental and disruptive to himself, his team and the referee.

Spurs striker Robbie Keane was another annoying player. He always had to have the last word. He would argue the ball was orange if you said it was white. Players like that make life unnecessarily awkward for you. I sometimes wish they would stop and think, 'Why am I being such a dick?'

Then there are those you have to watch like a hawk, such as Roy Keane at Manchester United. He wanted nothing to do with referees on a personal level. He was not one for a quick chat in the tunnel before the game. That was all part of his hard-man exterior, he wanted to intimidate everyone.

On the pitch, you never knew what he was going to do next, and that unnerves you. If you missed a nasty challenge and he had hurt someone, you would get the blame, not him. He was not enjoyable to referee.

But then I spent quite a bit of time with him during the 2018 World Cup in Russia – he was also working for ITV – and I loved his company over dinner or in the bar, not that he ever had a drink. It was fascinating to listen to the stories from his playing career and his time as manager of Sunderland. I was just a football fan lapping it all up. It was proof that these characters can be very different away from a competitive environment, where they are so driven to win, and Roy is perhaps the best example of that.

Saying that, I can't see me and Craig Bellamy sitting down for dinner any time soon.

★　★　★

'Adam, you've changed since you played for England, you never used to be like this.'

Those words caused me so much aggro, and they shouldn't have done. It was a farce what happened.

To explain, Southampton were playing at Everton in December 2013. They were getting beat 2–1 when their midfielder, Adam Lallana, appealed for a penalty late on. I waved it away. From nowhere he gave me this volley of abuse. I'd never had a problem with him before, he was a nice lad. I thought, 'Fuck you.' That is when I told him he had changed since being capped by England, and I meant it.

I could have sent him off for what he said to me. I chose to manage it in a different way by telling him a home truth. I never liked to resort to a red card for dissent, it was not my style. Lallana had said something in the heat of the moment and had gone too far. I went back at him and, for me, that was the matter closed.

Only the following day Southampton complained to the PGMOL. They released a statement saying I had 'abused and insulted' one of their players. Mike Riley, my PGMOL boss, called me.

'Did you say what they're alleging?' he asked.

'Yes, of course I did. I've got nothing to hide. I would say it again.'

I thought it was such a petulant reaction from Lallana and Southampton. How dare he use that foul language towards me and then go crying to his club when I had a go back. The

PGMOL supported me from the start on this, which was re-assuring if unusual for them.

When it was revealed what I had said, everyone laughed. I think people thought, 'Where is this abusive language?' It was an absolute nonsense and was dismissed as such by the PGMOL.

Lallana signed for Liverpool that summer and we spoke about the incident the next time we met. He was sheepish. He tried to protest that it was not him who made the complaint. Okay, maybe it was driven by those above him, but he was still silly enough to mention it to someone at the club in the first place, sparking the chain of events that brought needless grief to my doorstep.

'If that's how you want to play it, then the next time you swear at me I'll just send you off,' I said to him. 'You can't have it both ways. Either I give you a red card or you respect how I manage you.'

I had not sworn at him or overstepped the mark. But again, I was in the headlines for the wrong reasons. People were starting to think, 'Oh no, not Clattenburg, it's always him.' That was frustrating, especially when this was an example of sensible refereeing.

Another player who swore at me once was Arsenal's Andrey Arshavin. He was Russian and barely spoke any English, so I was a bit shocked. I then noticed some of his team-mates laughing their heads off. Arshavin clearly did not have a clue what he was saying to me. Mischievously, the Arsenal boys had taught him the odd swear word. It was funny, I let him off. I did then arm myself with one or two Russian equivalents just in case I ever needed to fire back at him, but Arshavin was a gent.

That was not true of all players, of course, but on the whole I would like to think I had a good relationship with the majority.

Kasper Schmeichel, the Leicester goalkeeper, once said in an interview he liked me because I would tell players to 'fuck off'. If I did do that then it was a very rare occasion, because I always tried to keep my language clean when I was being forceful.

In the main, I felt players responded to my style in a positive way. Like with managers, I allowed them a degree of tolerance. I wanted them to feel as if I understood what they were going through. And I did have empathy – we were all out there together, trying to do our best under intense scrutiny. All I asked for was a little bit of understanding in return. Some did, some didn't, that's life.

But I will say this – the number of players I liked and respected certainly dwarfed the number I did not.

8

THE ACCUSED (PART TWO)

'Fucking hell, he's swinging for me'

AS I boarded the British Airways flight from Newcastle to London Heathrow on Saturday 27 October 2012, little did I realise the storm to which I would return.

Twenty-four hours later and I would be plotting an escape route with airport staff to smuggle me from the terminal, desperately trying to avoid a pack of journalists, photographers and cameramen.

By then, news would have broken that Chelsea Football Club were accusing me of using inappropriate language towards two of their players, the Nigerian midfielder John Obi Mikel and Spanish playmaker Juan Mata. They were calling me a racist.

The story was leading every news bulletin across every channel, and they all wanted the first footage and pictures of the man at the centre of it – me.

But as I flew to London on that Saturday afternoon with my assistant referee, Mick McDonough, my only thoughts were on the game in front of us, Chelsea versus Manchester United. Chelsea were the European champions and top of the

Premier League, Sir Alex Ferguson's United were four points behind. It was Super Sunday, a match that was sure to dominate Monday's headlines.

It certainly did that.

★　　★　　★

United were 2–0 up inside twelve minutes. David Luiz scored an own goal when Robin van Persie's shot came back off the post and rebounded into him and over the line. Van Persie then smashed one of his own and it looked like being an easy afternoon, for United and me. How wrong was I?

Mata bent in a free-kick to pull one back on forty-four minutes. It had been a breathless half, not that it was done yet. Just as I was preparing to blow for half-time, Chelsea striker Fernando Torres caught Tom Cleverley with a high boot.

Jesus, that doesn't look good. It looks high, but how high? Where did Torres catch him? I can't tell from my angle, Cleverley has his back to me. In fairness, I think Torres has gone for the ball, it looked as if it was there to be won. But he was definitely late, and he didn't get the ball. Cleverley looks winded. Is it a red card? It could be. It happened at such high speed, I can't be sure. I can't give a red if I'm not 100 per cent. My assistant isn't certain, either. This is on me. It's a big match. Emotions are running high. Use your common sense, use a yellow to calm things down.

When I watch the incident now, it is a red card every time. With VAR, Torres would have been sent off in an instant, his studs landed on Cleverley's chest.

As we came off at half-time, United's players were asking why I had only given a yellow. I told them it was a borderline decision. I did not infuriate them further by insisting it was a booking, I tried to calm them by accepting it could have been a red. I always considered the pressure players were under during occasions like this, and that played a part in me giving Torres a second chance.

Chelsea started the second half how United began the first and they equalised when Ramires headed past David de Gea. It felt as if Chelsea were now the likely winners.

But then, on sixty-three minutes, Ashley Young ran through on goal and Chelsea defender Branislav Ivanovic clipped the back of him. Young went down. I glanced over to Mick McDonough for confirmation but I knew it was a red card, Ivanovic had denied a clear goalscoring opportunity. It was an easy call and off he went.

If only it was that easy sending off a Chelsea player at Stamford Bridge. Some of their fans could be vile, even when the decision was justified. Despite knowing they would now have it in for me, I did myself no favours five minutes later.

That's a dive, Torres has dived. He's nicked the ball past Jonny Evans and thrown himself to the ground. Why is he holding his knee? Evans was nowhere near his knee. That's a second yellow, I'm sure of it. He's got to go.

I should have been smarter. There was an option of play-on and I should have taken it. I should have protected myself rather than send off a second Chelsea player. There was a chance Evans had made slight contact – probably not enough for Torres to go down – but I should have used that to allow play to continue. Knowing what I do now, I wish I hadn't sent off Torres. It proved the catalyst for everything that would follow.

Technically, when I watch it back, I think I was justified in showing a second yellow. Evans brushed Torres on the lower leg and he went down clutching his knee. That told you he was trying to deceive me. But I had to be cuter. Instead, I left myself exposed to the poison of Chelsea and their supporters. If United won, it was going to come back on me.

On seventy-five minutes, the inevitable happened when Javier Hernandez made it 3–2 to United, and it just had to be controversial.

Hernandez was only a few yards out when he hooked the ball in from Rafael's cross. It looked tight for offside but there was no flag from Mick, so I gave the goal. Only later did we realise Hernandez was marginally off. It was one of those awful decisions for an assistant to make, because the player was jumping back from offside to onside. He was among a crowd of bodies and it happened in a flash. At the point of Hernandez making the touch to score, he was in an onside position. It is a mistake you can understand.

I was powerless in that situation, not that Chelsea saw it that way. Their players, including Mikel, were protesting about the goal. I booked him for dissent. There was a seat ripped out by a supporter and thrown towards the pitch, and a steward was injured. It had descended into anarchy. I blew for full-time – United had won – and I just wanted to make it back to the referee's room in one piece.

The tunnel at Stamford Bridge is narrow and can be intimi-dating even on a good day. There was a real nastiness in the air as I entered it here. United's players and staff were celebrating, some of Chelsea's were waiting to hurl obscenities, they weren't even bothered about debating my decisions. It was a recipe for trouble and I just needed to get to the other end unscathed.

My assistants and I were eventually bundled into our dressing-room, a small room down a corridor away from the teams. Given how volatile it had been coming off the pitch, I expected the Premier League match delegate, Nick Cusack, to be there before us. His role would be to hold a debrief with me and my team. He should also have been there to witness anything that might unfold away from the cameras. There was no sign of him.

But the dressing-room felt like a sanctuary. I sat down, still in my kit, and tried to sift my way through the chaos. I reasoned that my decisions, in isolation, I had got right. We also did not know at this stage that the Hernandez goal was offside.

I knew to expect a tirade of abuse from Chelsea supporters on social media, and their players and manager Roberto Di Matteo were sure to criticise me in their post-match interviews. But I was not beating myself up over my performance. It was then that I heard a commotion outside the dressing-room door.

What the hell's going on out there? I walk towards the door to take a look. Before I get there it swings open, and with some force. I jump back, instinctively. What the fuck? John Obi Mikel bursts in. I can see the rage in his eyes. Di Matteo and coach Eddie Newton are holding him back. Mikel is out of control, he's trying to get at me. 'I'm gonna break your legs!' he shouts. Fucking hell, he's swinging for me. There are arms everywhere. I'm ducking to avoid them. A security guy is grappling with Mikel, pulling him away. That's not easy, Mikel is strong. I can't go back at him, you can never retaliate, I'd get nowhere near anyway. I've got my boots on, I'm slipping all over the place. I'm knocked backwards into some seats. I just try to defend myself. He's still hellbent on hurting me. Get him out of here! Mikel is eventually dragged back into the corridor. I'm shaking. What the fuck has just happened?

Never in my career, be that the Northern League or Premier League, had a player tried to get at me like that. They know the consequences are severe for an attack on an official. It was incomprehensible what Mikel had done, he was putting his career in jeopardy.

I was struggling to deal with what had happened. I couldn't get my breath and my legs had turned to jelly. There was another knock at the door. Oh God, here we go again. The security guy came in and asked for his flip-flop back, it had come off during the scuffle! I can laugh about that now.

Di Matteo eventually returned to my dressing-room. Like me, he was shaking, he was in shock. We spoke about United's winning goal, which we now knew was offside, and also about what had happened with Mikel just moments earlier. I got the impression Chelsea were concerned about what I was going to include in my report.

I have to be clear here – and this is extremely important – at this point there had been no mention of racism to me, either from Mikel or Di Matteo. No one had made any accusation of that nature.

Was I going to report Mikel for what he had done in the dressing-room? Absolutely. My team of officials were witness to it. To the FA it would be a cut and dried case, there was no disputing what he did. Mikel would be facing a lengthy ban.

Cusack, the match delegate, made a belated appearance and I relayed to him what had happened and the details I would include in my report. He went off and explained to Chelsea the process that would follow, during which I believe he spoke to their chief executive Ron Gourlay.

In all of my discussions to this point, I got the feeling Chelsea were panicking about the consequences of what Mikel had done. By the time I left the stadium, I was not aware of the allegations against me.

Di Matteo used his post-match press conference to criticise my performance, but there was no mention of racism.

'We are massively disappointed that these key decisions were wrong,' he said. 'It always seems to be in favour of the opposition. It was a good game of football with two good teams, and the officials ruined it.'

I left Stamford Bridge in the people-carrier and, as we made our way out of West London towards Heathrow, I had just one thought in my head. 'Get me out of here.'

My phone is buzzing in my pocket. I shouldn't get it out, I'm going through airport security. I take a quick look, there's a social-media notification on the screen ... 'BREAKING NEWS: CHELSEA ACCUSE REFEREE MARK CLATTENBURG OF RACIST COMMENTS.' What the fuck? Is this a joke? A fake account? Mike Riley, my PGMOL boss, calls immediately. I answer. It has been leaked to the media that Chelsea are saying I racially abused Mikel and Juan Mata. My conversation with Riley is short and we don't have any details beyond what is being reported. It seems the press have more information than we do. This is bullshit. Claire calls, she is panicking, like me.

'What the hell is going on?' she asks.

I haven't got a clue. I haven't got any answers – for her, for Riley, for anyone.

The flight back to Newcastle was the most tormented fifty minutes of my life. I must have looked in a daze to anyone else. I was locked in my own head, oblivious to my surroundings. It was mental torture knowing what was being said about me on the ground, and knowing there was nothing I could do about it.

Before boarding I spoke to David Laws, a former referee who was the chief executive at Newcastle Airport.

'Davey, I've got a problem,' I said.

'I know you've got a problem!' he replied.

'The press will be waiting for me at the airport, I don't want to go through the main terminal doors. My car is in the car park.'

'No problem, leave it with us.'

We took off from Heathrow and my phone lost signal. That should have been a relief. Instead, it meant I was alone with my thoughts.

What am I supposed to have said? Has something been misheard? Have they misunderstood my Geordie accent? A lot is said on a football pitch, but I would never say anything racial, this is absurd. What are Chelsea playing at? I've sent off two of their players and we've missed the offside goal, but would they really go this low to get back at me? Or is this a diversion tactic? Are they trying to find a cover for what Mikel has done in the dressing-room? That makes sense. They will know he could be facing a long ban. Or is this about Chelsea captain John Terry? He missed this game because he is serving a four-match ban having been found guilty by the FA of racially abusing QPR's Anton Ferdinand. Is this Chelsea getting back at the FA and I'm caught in the crossfire? I know the club are furious about the way the FA handled that case.

That might be it. But would any of this have happened if Chelsea had won the game? Are they lashing out just because they lost? All I have is questions. I hope by the time we land it's all been cleared up, that whatever this is about was a mistake. I just want this to be over.

Sadly, this was just the beginning. There was a lighter moment on the flight when another passenger recognised me. I did not want to speak to anyone but this guy was trying to be friendly.

'I've just read the match report,' he said. 'They've made it sound like you had a nightmare!'

He was not aware of the racism claims and I did not bother to update him. I thought, 'You don't know the half of it, pal.'

I switched my phone back on as soon as we landed. Claire called, she was crying. Some journalists had knocked at our front door. She was scared. My daughter, Mia, was sixteen months old. I just had to get home to them as quickly as possible.

I've been told I have to come through the domestic arrivals gate, just to keep things legal. The press are waiting outside the terminal, lenses trained on the revolving doors. But there is a side exit and I am guided to it. A member of airport security staff is waiting in a car. I jump in and he whisks me to the spot where I have left my car, avoiding the front of the terminal. I was here yesterday, parking up without a care in the world. That seems a long time ago now. I drive through the security barrier

*and leave the press pack behind. If only I was leaving all
of my troubles there.*

Word must have been passed between the photographers at
the airport and those outside my house that I had not got off
the flight, and by the time I got home to County Durham there
was no one waiting. The stakeout soon resumed the following
morning.

*I am trapped. A prisoner in my own home. A prisoner in
my own head. I am not allowed to speak. Not allowed to
tell the world I am innocent. I can't sleep. No chance. I'm
upstairs, downstairs, cups of tea at 3 a.m. I'm reading
the newspapers online. I'm watching the TV news. I'm
checking social media. It's not healthy but I need to know
what is being said, I need to try to make sense of this. The
bolt is on the door but my head is being invaded by the
outside world. If I dare to look out from the window the
photographers and journalists are there, waiting. Then
they hide, like snipers, all around, all wanting the first
picture. I do not dare take the bins out. There have been
lots of tears. This could ruin my career. It could ruin my
life. The fear is worse than going to prison. I am being
called a racist. That is a real life-sentence, you don't
come back from that. Guilty until proven innocent, that
is the English way. Chelsea say I did it and I'm scared
that people are believing them. What is happening to me?*

During those early hours overnight on the Sunday and into Monday, I realised the power of football clubs, the hold they have over the media and their influence on public opinion, driven by the blind loyalty of their fanbase. It was terrifying. It was the European champions against a referee – who would you believe?

I was already a villain, the guy who shows red cards and disallows goals. The man on the street does not have much sympathy for a referee. It is not as if I had a band of supporters ready to jump to my defence. I was alone. I knew I was innocent, but I would have to prove it.

I'd ask Claire every so often to take a look from the window to check if the press were still outside. As much as I despised what was being spun in the newspapers, I so wanted to walk to the front door, invite them all in and tell my side of the story. Chelsea were feeding their friends in the media every lurid and libellous detail, why couldn't I come out and give my response to their bullshit? I was being thrown to the wolves and it was a daily feeding frenzy.

The only time I left the house during those first couple of days was to attend our fortnightly referees meeting at St George's Park. The PGMOL said I could stay at home but I wanted to go, I needed some support from my colleagues. I was desperate for a friend.

Michael Oliver picked me up and I was pictured leaving the house. It did not stop the photographers following us down the A19. We enjoyed trying to escape them, ducking in and out of traffic, and we eventually lost them at Wetherby Services. It was a fleeting moment of fun, not to mention freedom. I returned home that night, back to confinement.

I have to say, the backing I got from my fellow referees that afternoon meant everything to me. Referees can be bitter and they often want others to fail to further their own career, but on this they were right behind me. It united us as a group. One of their own was being attacked and they were not going to lie down and accept it. They thought it was a witch-hunt. They could not understand why Mikel had not yet been charged by the FA over the attempted attack in the dressing-room. There was even talk of boycotting Chelsea matches.

Part of me realises that they had to wait for the facts to be established, but I could have done with more support than I got from the PGMOL during the first few days. It was all too obvious that they could not publicly back me, just in case I was guilty. I was in dialogue with them and explained my version of events, but my word was not enough. They were using lip-readers to review the footage and at no point did Mike Riley say, 'Mark, we believe you.' With them I always held the fear they wanted rid of me, and this might just be their chance. It was only later that I felt they truly sided with me.

Within twenty-four hours of the game, my team of officials at Stamford Bridge told the PGMOL they had heard no racial language down the headsets. The sound quality is crystal clear, it was inconceivable that my two assistant referees and fourth official would not have picked up on something of that nature being said.

Chelsea were leaking information to the press every day, trying to control the narrative. They let it be known that the Mata allegation involved me calling him a 'Spanish twat', which simply was not true. That claim had appeared as early as Monday's newspapers.

It was suggested that Chelsea defender Gary Cahill would be used to confirm what I had said to Mata. Gary spoke to a mutual friend and it was communicated to me that he was not getting involved. I was also told that some of Chelsea's senior players were not comfortable with the allegations.

Two days after the game, Chelsea midfielder Oriol Romeu revealed that Mata had, in fact, not heard the words 'Spanish twat'. The club withdrew the allegation and Mata later gave an interview in Spain in which he confirmed he had heard nothing.

It was also reported on the Tuesday that Mikel himself had not heard any racial language, although I still did not know what it was they were alleging. Chelsea were now briefing the press that Brazilian players Ramires and David Luiz would back up the club's claims.

Surely this undermines the entire thing? How can we trust anything coming out of Chelsea? They're making it up as they go along. This is all bollocks. For God's sake, the newspapers were saying yesterday that Mata was 'shocked' when he heard my 'insult'. Now he didn't hear a thing? And neither did Mikel? The other officials have also confirmed they heard nothing. This has to be over, right?

Wrong. Chelsea had consulted external lawyers for advice and made a formal complaint to the FA on Wednesday 31 October, three days after the game. They were saying I had racially abused Mikel and, for the first time, I was made aware of the specifics of their accusation, which was also leaked to the press later that day.

According to Chelsea, I had said to Mikel, 'Shut up, you monkey.' The language disgusted me, it was damaging and fictitious.

I'm crying. I feel sick. Why? Fucking why? Where has that come from? My friends and family have never seen me like this, I'm beaten. Chelsea are out to get me and they're going for it, and it seems like people believe them.

I was told that a formal process would now begin and the FA opened an investigation. I was stood down from that weekend's fixtures, but at no point was I suspended.

It was reported that the Society of Black Lawyers were calling for Chelsea to take the matter to the Metropolitan Police, saying that what was being alleged against me was a 'hate crime' which should be dealt with properly, not just by the FA. The police did not pursue the matter because no alleged victims came forward and I was never interviewed. But it felt like every day I was being hit with something new, as if a queue was forming to take shots at me.

Chelsea also confirmed that Ramires was the only player who had heard the word 'monkey', and not Mikel. To add further incredulity to their case, it was now said that Luiz's part in the matter was to translate for Ramires what his team-mate thought he had heard me say.

Once I had composed myself and considered all of the new information, in a strange way it reassured me, because I knew I had not said what they were alleging. I also knew Ramires spoke hardly any English. It strengthened my belief that this was a smear campaign, manufactured for reasons known only to Chelsea.

But then, it also frightened me. If Chelsea made a compelling and emotive case, the FA might just believe them. It felt like the club were throwing as much mud as possible, hoping some of it would stick. If you read the newspapers and the reaction on social media, they were doing a good job in that regard.

Back at home, locked away and struggling to sleep, obsessively going over the events of Sunday, I began to slip into a dark place. Friends were concerned for my welfare, and with good reason. It was then that I found an unlikely friend.

'Mark, it's Sir Alex Ferguson,' came the unmistakable Glaswegian accent down the phone.

I was such a wreck, I did not even say much back to him.

'I have spoken to my players and they did not hear you say what Chelsea are alleging. We don't believe you said it. I believe in fairness, so we will support you.'

Sir Alex did not have to make that call and he did not have to defend me in public, which he later did. But he did so because he believed what Chelsea were doing was wrong. He put his neck on the block, not for me, but in the name of truth and justice.

On the Friday of that first week, Sir Alex used his pre-match press conference to reiterate what he told me on the phone.

'I don't believe Mark Clattenburg would make any comments like that,' he said. 'I refuse to believe it. I think it is unthinkable in the modern climate. I just don't believe it – simple as that. There is no way a referee would stoop to that, I am convinced of that.'

I was later told Chelsea threatened to sue him for insinuating they were lying. But Sir Alex stuck to his guns, he thought it was nonsense. Not for the first time he would be proven right.

Battle lines were being drawn in the media and I could tell which reporters and newspapers Chelsea had onside. But managers were now coming out in support of me. Leeds boss Neil Warnock joined Ferguson in casting doubt over Chelsea's motives.

'I have got to say I am disgusted with what's gone on. I'm on Mark Clattenburg's side,' he said.

'We ask referees to man-manage and that's what he does. I'm sure he might have said a few things, but are you telling me if Chelsea had won that game that there would have been one iota of a complaint?

'I hope if it is proved wrong that the players, whatever they alleged Mark to have said, get done as well. I think he made a mistake [with the Torres red card], but they are trying to kill him and I don't agree with that at all.'

The Premier League media team were calling every day to ask if I was okay. No, I wasn't okay. They also revealed something that disturbed me. They asked if I'd spoken with Sir Alex. Yes, I told them. They said a journalist had called them claiming he was aware of the conversation.

How has it come to this? I'm having my house swept for bugs and my phone checked for a tap. We can't find anything. But the front room in which I spoke to Sir Alex, I'm scared to step foot in there now. Is anything I do or say private? Who or what can I really trust? This is insane.

To this day I do not know how the fact I had spoken to Sir Alex became known by a journalist. Was the reporter taking a punt by asking the Premier League? Was it a chain of information passed on by word of mouth? Or maybe it was something more sinister involving my mobile phone?

Whatever the truth, it intensified my paranoia. The fact it never appeared in the press also made me think that perhaps the information had been acquired by improper means. I will never know.

By fate, Chelsea played Manchester United in the League Cup on Wednesday 31 October back at Stamford Bridge. United's fans unfurled a banner, 'Clattenburg: Referee, Leader,

Legend', mocking a similar banner about Chelsea's John Terry. I appreciated the support from United and it was a rare chance to smile, but it provoked more vitriol from Chelsea's supporters towards me.

Chelsea won 5–4 after extra-time and apparently it was a cracking game, not that I could bring myself to watch it. I could not face any football. In fact, trying to do anything to distract myself was impossible. This was consuming me, my every waking minute. When you're not sleeping, they are long and lonely days.

I was losing weight despite not leaving the house. That was a combination of stress and not eating properly. Claire was also in pieces. We tried to support each other, but that is hard when you both feel so drained. She could not go to work, in part because of the photographers camped outside. But I needed her at home with me, I did not want to be left alone.

I was bombarding Claire with questions and she listened to it all, even though we had no answers. We had to get away. I told Mike Riley we were going to Spain for a few days and he was fine with that. The PGMOL said I could have carried on refereeing if I wanted to, but come on? I was in no fit state.

Are the photographers there yet? I ask Claire to check out of the front window. It's 7 a.m., the coast is clear. We pack our bags into the car and head for Newcastle Airport. Five days ago I was being smuggled out of here, now I'm trying my best to get back in undetected. I'm wearing a baseball cap and keeping my eyes on the floor as I push Mia in her pram through the airport. We get on the plane without any issues. There is a couple sitting behind us and one of them is reading a newspaper as we taxi across the runway.

'Do you think he's guilty?' the wife asks her husband.

'Nah, a referee would never say that,' he says.

'You never know,' she says back to him.

I'm grabbing Claire by the leg, both of us are desperate to turn around and put her right. We think better of it. We'd best get used to this.

The following day we are in my friend's bar in La Cala De Mijas. It's quiet and there is an elderly couple sitting in the corner. Sky Sports News is on the TV but the sound is down. We have a drink and head back to the apartment. My mate who owns the bar calls an hour or so later.

'You know that old couple who were here?' he says.

'Yeah?'

'They've just asked if I think the referee is guilty, your picture came on the TV.'

'What did you say?'

'I told them, "You should have asked him yourselves, he was sitting right here an hour ago!" The wife said, "Was that him? God, he's lost loads of weight, he looks fat on the TV!"'

At least Claire and I can laugh about that. But I can

feel people staring at me in the street, even here. County Durham or the Costa del Sol, I'm still a prisoner. When will this ever end?

There was one question to which I needed an answer, a thought that had been troubling me from the start – when exactly was I meant to have said what Chelsea were accusing me of? If we had a specific time in the match then we could review the footage, that was my best hope of getting at the truth. But Chelsea would not reveal that moment, meaning it remained a case of my word against theirs.

On the flip side it gave me confidence. Others in the media were starting to ask the same question – when did this happen? Surely, there would be a reaction from the players? I knew there was no reaction because I had not said it.

I was being sent messages via third parties from journalists who were expressing doubt over Chelsea's story. Of course, they were casting themselves as a sympathetic ear and wanted me to speak to them, which I could never do. But it was comforting to know not everyone was falling for Chelsea's spin.

After returning from Spain, I was called to the first FA hearing in Manchester on 8 November, where I was interviewed by a two-person panel led by Jenni Kennedy, the FA's head of off-field regulation. So, too, were my assistant referees Mick McDonough and Simon Long and fourth official Mike Jones.

My mental state was already fragile, and when the panel started asking their questions I got the impression they thought

I was guilty. Even though all of the match officials told them they had heard no racial language down the headsets, I felt unsettled by the tone of their approach. Our microphones were not recorded during the game and that was a real problem. How could I prove my innocence without a recording?

But we should have been dealing in facts, not hearsay, why could the FA not see that? There was no consistent evidence against me because, quite frankly, there was no evidence against me, it did not happen. I spoke to my lawyer, who had been appointed by the PGMOL.

'I'm adamant, I want to know the moment Chelsea say that this happened, then we can disprove it from the footage,' I said to him.

The FA panel said they could not tell us because they did not know. Instead, they showed me a series of clips from the TV coverage of the game which 'may' have been the moment. They asked what I had said at each point.

'I don't know,' I told them. 'I'm not going to make something up just for the purpose of this. I cannot remember everything I said, but I know what I did not say. Look at the screen, there is no reaction from any players at any stage. Do you not think Mikel or Ramires would have said something to me?'

The panel listened and made notes. There was no sign of any emotion, no hint of understanding. I wanted to scream.

What the hell are we doing here? This is crazy. We're going around in circles. I'm stuck in the middle of an investigation based entirely on the evidence of someone who doesn't even speak English. At no point in the footage we have does Ramires react to anything I have said. It's a stitch-up. When will this ever end? I can't referee. I'm on the back pages of the newspapers every day. I just want to prove my innocence and quit. If this is football then forget it, I do not want to be part of it. I'd rather be back working as an electrician.

In reality, I knew that I could not leave refereeing, I was too far gone to start again in a different world. I had to fight to save my career, to protect my income and my family.

Before leaving the interview, my lawyer made the point that there must be more footage available and requested that the FA ask Chelsea to provide it. The panel agreed and the request was made. I was told Chelsea were awkward at first and it took a few days – and an FA reminder – before they handed over the feed from an overhead static camera.

I was called to a second interview in Manchester on Monday 19 November. A few days earlier the panel had re-interviewed Ramires.

For the first time, Chelsea revealed the exact moment of their allegation. They said it happened in the sixty-ninth minute and not the seventy-sixth when I had booked Mikel, as the press had previously speculated.

I believe Chelsea thought they were being clever, because there was a break in the TV footage as a replay was shown of a

Van Persie shot. When the live pictures returned, I was on the screen with Mikel in the background. My lawyer said it looked like Chelsea were trying to make their allegation fit.

But now, because of the footage from the static camera, it proved beyond any doubt that I was nowhere near close enough to Ramires when he claimed to have heard me use those words. The images showed that I was around ten metres away and, not only that, but Ramires had his back to me. The panel also took into consideration his lack of English.

There were two more players in closer proximity to me than Ramires – Chelsea defender Ashley Cole and United striker Wayne Rooney – and both of them told the panel they had heard no racial language, and neither had Mikel.

On Thursday 22 November, twenty-five days after the game, I took a phone call while waiting to collect my son, Nathan, from school.

It is the FA, I answer in a flash. 'Mark, you have been completely exonerated, there is no case to answer.' I was expecting the news, but I feel the relief run through my body. But then, I feel empty. I have not won. I simply haven't lost. I call Claire. She arranges for us to meet some friends and we go for a Chinese meal later in the evening. I'm not here to celebrate. It's not a party. It's just something to mark the end of the agony. We share a toast to the future, not that I feel particularly enthused about mine.

The FA had dismissed the case. They had presented all of the evidence to an independent QC, who said there was no case to answer. I was not guilty, something I had known all along.

But I will always wonder what might have happened had the new footage not come to light, bringing a swift end to the investigation. Would it have run on for months? What verdict would the FA have reached? Even if it was 'not guilty', there could still have been an element of doubt hanging over me to this day. Some might have always wondered, 'Did he say it?' The thought of that being the case is scary.

My instinct from the start was right, I did have to prove my innocence. Only the emergence of the static camera enabled me to do so beyond any doubt.

I released a statement following the FA verdict.

'To know you were innocent of something but that there was the opportunity for it to wreck your career was truly frightening.

'Racism has no place in football and this experience should not discourage those to speak out if they genuinely believe they are a victim of abuse.

'However, there are processes that should be adhered to in order that any investigation can be carried out in a manner that is fair for all parties involved.

'I know first-hand the ramifications of allegations of this nature being placed into the public domain ahead of a formal process and investigation.

'I hope no referee has to go through this in the future.'

THE ACCUSED (PART TWO)

It was also confirmed on the same day that Mikel had been charged by the FA over the incident in the referee's room.

He was later given a three-match ban and the FA explained to me they had to be careful not to be too harsh, because they did not want to deter other players from coming forward to report allegations of racism.

I make no apology for how I felt in that moment.

Three matches? Are the FA taking the piss? He should be banned for the rest of the season, if not more. Go for a referee like that at grassroots level and you're lucky if you ever play again. So how on earth is a professional footballer allowed to get away with three games? That's the same as you'd get for a bad tackle. Was this the real reason for Chelsea's accusations against me? As I suspected on the flight home after the game, was it all an attempt to mitigate against what Mikel had done? If so, Chelsea have won, Mikel has dodged the ban he deserved and I'm still the biggest loser in this, the one who has just been through the worst twenty-five days of my life. Hell, I have missed more matches than Mikel will. That's not right. I'm furious.

I still think about that now, the true motivation for Chelsea's allegations. The FA said Ramires had acted in 'good faith' and that the club were right to report the matter.

I do not know what their intentions were, but I do know

they made my existence unbearable by the manner in which they went about it. They fed the media and left me exposed to the hate and suspicion, and all for something I had not done. They did not give a damn about me. They did not care about the effect on my wife and baby daughter or my son at school, they only cared about themselves.

If they believed their player's allegations to be genuine, they should have made a formal complaint to the PGMOL and FA, instead of leaking it to the media. All parties could have been interviewed in private, without the investigation being played out in public. We would have arrived at the same outcome, but the hurt and humiliation suffered by myself and my family would have been avoided.

How could a Premier League club not realise the consequence of their actions? I found their conduct appalling at the time, and I always will.

The impact on me aside, why was Chelsea's first thought to make public what were very sensitive allegations? Surely, they should have shown more respect for their own players, if they believed their claims to be true? There will always be so many unanswered questions.

Sir Alex Ferguson called it right all along, and he welcomed the verdict.

'I did not believe it anyway,' he said. 'The unfortunate thing for Mark is that he has had to carry that stain for the last few weeks. Everyone in the game is pleased for him now – apart from Chelsea.'

I had been cleared but we still had the press outside the front door. The Premier League sent a media officer to help manage the situation and we arranged for the photographers to get some pictures as I went for a jog. It worked. Once I had satisfied them with those shots, they left. But it did not end there.

My first game back was as fourth official for Spurs versus West Ham on Sunday 25 November, three days after the verdict. Because of the media interest, I had to travel to the game by myself and did not stay in the hotel with the other officials.

I walked out of the tunnel at White Hart Lane before kick-off and you would have thought I was being unveiled as Spurs' new manager. Every camera lens was pointed towards me, all I could hear was the clatter of shutters.

I don't want to be here, stood on this touchline. I am because I have a mortgage to pay. And I'll carry on, I have little choice. It might feel better one day. But not now. How I feel about Chelsea and Mikel – resentment, anger, disgust – those feelings aren't going anywhere in a hurry. Everyone here is being very nice – the players, staff, managers, and I appreciate that. It feels like there is genuine sympathy. But none of that can heal the wounds of the past four weeks. Right now, I feel like I have fallen out of love with this game.

Chelsea and Mikel never did apologise. Am I surprised? Not at all, it fits entirely with their original disregard for me.

Richard Scudamore, the Premier League chief executive, did bring Chelsea chairman Bruce Buck to a meeting with all of the referees a few weeks after the verdict. The group were threatening to go on strike and Scudamore was trying to avoid such action.

The strike was not my idea, but I supported it. My colleagues wanted answers from Chelsea as to why this had been allowed to happen. It could, they said, be any one of them going through this in the future.

Buck showed up at St George's Park and went around the room shaking everyone's hand. He gestured to shake mine. Don't you fucking dare. He moved on.

He did not make a good start when he opened by saying he did not understand what our issues were. We all looked at each other in disbelief – was this clown taking the piss?

My fellow referees spoke passionately in response. They explained that the club had, very publicly, accused one of our senior referees of being a racist, causing undue suffering and reputational damage. They stressed that the allegations were unfounded. Considering all of that, they asked if Chelsea would be issuing an apology.

'No, we were duty bound to report it,' Buck said.

He was reminded that it took them three days to make a formal complaint but less than three hours to leak their allegations to the media. Still no apology? No.

We left the meeting angrier than we had entered it. Buck was so out of touch with the real world. He thought referees were like players, that we lived in a gated community and were protected by security. He had no understanding of the living nightmare his club had put me through. It was a farce that reinforced our opinion of Chelsea as a club looking out only for themselves.

Scudamore spoke to me privately and made reassurances about my career and the treatment of referees going forward. I spoke with some of my colleagues and we decided that a strike was not the best way to make our point. But they were ready to walk out, I have no doubt about that.

As for Mikel, I have no time for him whatsoever. I cannot forgive someone who has refused to apologise to me. I made tons of mistakes as a referee, but I would always say sorry if I thought it was the right thing to do.

Mikel says he took Ramires for his word. Okay, if the circumstances were different then I can understand why you would continue to believe your team-mate. I appreciate the need to report all alleged racism, that is not the issue here.

But Mikel must know that I did not say those words. He was stood far closer to me than Ramires at the exact point of the allegation and admitted he heard nothing. Further still, he knew Ramires did not speak English.

From the start he should have been brave enough to say to Chelsea, 'This did not happen.' Were he and Ramires encouraged by the club to do otherwise? Only they and Chelsea can answer that.

The next time I refereed a match in which Mikel started

was a Nigeria friendly against the United States in Florida ahead of the 2014 World Cup. We did not shake hands before the game.

There was a 50–50 challenge in the first half where the opponent probably went in with too much force on Mikel. I could have blown for a free-kick, it was a tight call, but I chose not to. Why should I protect him when he did not protect me?

People will say I should be impartial as a referee and ignore what has gone before. This went beyond that, this was about someone who had accused me of being a racist and tried to physically assault me, yet he had refused to apologise or even acknowledge the pain I had endured.

He later chose to antagonise me when speaking about the matter to the media, making a point of stating he would not say sorry. When he does that it attracts widespread coverage and brings back a lot of the anguish.

There were death threats against me in the weeks after the United match, although I was all too used to them by that point. I never believed anything would come of them, as unpleasant as they were. Even today there is online abuse and that will never end. So forgive me when I say, I have absolutely zero respect for Chelsea Football Club.

I refereed them on plenty of occasions after 2012 and I always did a professional job. I even gave them a penalty in my next match when they beat Swansea in April of that same season. Juan Mata, of all people, was the player fouled. There had been a lot of talk about the abuse Chelsea's supporters were

Sport was in my genes. The Clattenburg family name only came to the UK when my granddad, Larry Clattenburg, arrived from Canada. He was a professional ice-hockey player, a netminder, and came over to play for Durham Wasps. Larry is in the back row, far left.

(Courtesy of the author)

Butter wouldn't melt.
The classic school photo.

(Courtesy of the author)

October 1998. I got a call from the Northumberland FA to say I would be fourth official for Newcastle United versus West Ham at St James' Park. I played it cool on the phone, but when I hung up I started dancing around the room.

(Courtesy of the author)

Showing Dinamo Zagreb's Jerko Leko a red card during a barely believable Champions League match against Lyon in December 2011.

(Igor Kralj/Pixsell/PA Images/Alamy)

John Obi Mikel waves a finger at me during the infamous game between Chelsea and Manchester United at Stamford Bridge in October 2012. Chelsea and Mikel never did apologise for events that day.

(Back Page Images/Shutterstock)

They called it the 'Battle of the Bridge': Chelsea versus Spurs in May 2016. I felt more like a policeman that night than I did a referee.

(Will Oliver/EPA/ Shutterstock)

Gary Speed was a gentleman, one of the best and kindest players I ever had the good fortune to referee.

(Action Images/John Sibley)

After one game, I was shocked when Cristiano Ronaldo came into my dressing-room with a signed shirt. I hadn't asked for the jersey, it was just a kind gesture because, over the years, our relationship had grown.

(Nick Potts/PA Archive/PA Images/Alamy)

Kasper Schmeichel once said in an interview he liked me because I would tell players to 'fuck off'. If I did do that then it was a very rare occasion, because I always tried to keep my language clean when I was being forceful.

(David Davies/PA Wire/Alamy)

Over the years, I had plenty of opportunities to see Sir Alex Ferguson up close, especially when I was the fourth official.
(Joe Giddens/EMPICS Sport/ Alamy)

Sam Allardyce was a manager for whom I had a lot of time. He would be kicking your arse one week but having a laugh and a joke the next. He never held a grudge.
(Ppauk/Shutterstock)

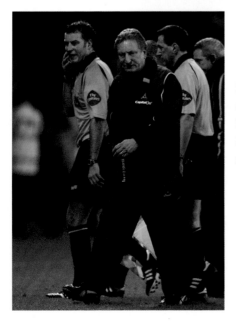

Neil Warnock was a real character. I wish there were more like him in the Premier League. But he could also give you hell.
(Mike Egerton/EMPICS Sport/Alamy)

The 2016 FA Cup Final

Sir Alex Ferguson greets me in the tunnel ahead of the big match between Manchester United and Crystal Palace. This picture caused a bit of a stir.

(Michael Regan/The FA/ Getty Images)

Sending off Chris Smalling after he had fouled Yannick Bolasie. It was an easy second yellow and Smalling knew it.

(Ian Kington/Getty Images)

Getting my message across to Palace's Pape N'Diaye Souare.

(Mike Hewitt/Getty Images)

The 2016 Champions League Final

It's the Champions League Final. Real Madrid versus Atletico Madrid at the San Siro. And I'm the referee. Picking up the match ball.

(Stuart Franklin/UEFA/Getty Images)

A Madrid derby was always going to be a lively affair. Showing a yellow card to Atletico's Gabi.

(Shaun Botterill/Getty Images)

Real's Cristiano Ronaldo protests to me about something or other. In the end, he scored the winning penalty in the shootout.

(Matthew Ashton/AMA/Getty Images)

The 2016 European Championship

A flare on the pitch heightens the tension still further as Croatia and the Czech Republic play out a 2-2 draw in their group match in Saint-Etienne. Mario Mandzukic tries to go across to plead with the Croatian ultras to calm down.

(Jeff Pachoud/AFP/ Getty Images)

Receiving the support of my boss Pierluigi Collina ahead of the European Championship Final between Portugal and France in July 2016.

(Kieran Mcmanus/BPI/ Shutterstock)

Leading out my fellow match officials and the two teams. A very proud moment.

(Bob Thomas/Popperfoto/Getty Images).

Heading out for my very last Premier League game: West Brom versus Leicester City at The Hawthorns on 29 April 2017.

(Matt Bunn/BPI/Shutterstock)

That's it. I've just blown the final whistle. Just like that, my days of officiating in the Premier League are over.

(Shaun Botterill/Getty Images)

Taking charge of a Chinese Football Association Cup quarter-final between Guangzhou Evergrande and Shanghai SIPG in Guangzhou, July 2019.

(Visual China Group via Getty Images)

going to give me that day. There was not one word, it was as if even they were embarrassed by the club's behaviour.

On the day after the verdict, the back page of the *Daily Mail* read, 'Chelsea almost ruined Mark Clattenburg's life – and they don't even have the decency to say sorry.' The article also speculated that I would pursue legal action against the club. They were right, I fully intended to. I met a lawyer in London in the January of 2013 and he outlined to me the strength of my case. I began to make enquiries as to how I would go about bringing a claim for defamation. I was then told by Mike Riley that, to do so, I would first have to end my employment as a Premier League referee, if I wanted to sue a Premier League club. It quickly became apparent there would be opposition to me engaging lawyers against Chelsea. I stepped away from it and, in the end, it became something I put to the back of my mind. That frustrates me when I look back now.

I still believe Chelsea's motive could have been a retaliation to John Terry's suspension. The FA had found Terry guilty of racially abusing Anton Ferdinand on the 'balance of probability'. Chelsea believed, like the criminal investigation, it should have to be proven to the standard of 'beyond a reasonable doubt'. Terry was found not guilty in a court of law.

That is why, I believe, they may have pursued the allegation against me, to test the FA's 'balance of probability' standard. Chelsea must have known I did not say those words after speaking to all of their players, yet they still made the formal complaint. Why? Maybe because they wanted to expose what they felt was a flaw in the FA's disciplinary process.

Not all of the hurt that still exists is directed towards Chelsea. The actions of the Society of Black Lawyers amounted to irresponsible opportunism. I could not speak out at the time and I had to allow them to have their moment, but it felt like they were using the case as a vehicle for publicity, even though they were not in possession of the facts.

Will I ever be able to bury all of these feelings for good? I wish my answer to this question was different, but I think it would be impossible to ever make my peace with what happened in 2012. Reflecting now, retracing events step by step, has reminded me of the malicious and political world in which I found myself caught up.

But I moved on in my career, I had to. So when I walked out for the finals of the Champions League and European Championship in 2016, it felt like a 'fuck you' to all of those who tried to destroy me. They had failed.

If I can take one positive, it is that the experience made me stronger.

9

THE REFEREES

'He was a snake'

IT is a strange game, refereeing. We are largely unpopular to the outside world and plagued by in-fighting and bitching on the inside.

You would think there would be a siege mentality, us against everyone else. Other than the support I received in 2012 following Chelsea's unfounded racism allegations, that was rarely the case.

There is more camaraderie at grassroots level than there is among the elite, but experiences throughout my career taught me that only a handful of my fellow officials could be trusted to have my back.

Maybe it was the type of personality the profession attracts, those who are drawn to it by a want for authority and status. It is no surprise a lot of referees have a background in the police or teaching. They are climbers, out for themselves and happy to see others kicked down the ladder along the way.

I would like to think I was never like that. I had ambition, yes, but that was driven by a desire for personal improvement. I did not need my colleagues to fail for me to be successful.

Was I disliked within our group? I certainly felt like an outsider as opposed to one of the ringleaders. That was fine, it suited me. I would argue I was close to the good guys, the normal ones.

As for the rest of them? They were a bunch of weirdos half the time, as you will discover.

★   ★   ★

One official I came across was a snake. The smiling assassin. Nice to your face but happy to stab you in the back.

This is the first time I have spoken about this, but in 2015 he reported me to the PGMOL – he suspected me of match-fixing. Why did he think that? Because I had just bought an Audi R8 sports car. He was, I am told, concerned about how I had the money to afford it. Angry does not come close to describing how I felt. He knew an allegation like that would risk destroying my career, and all because he had a hunch, apparently.

I had bought a nice car with the money I had worked hard to earn. My wife had a decent job and I had done eleven European and international matches that season. That was an extra £60,000 straight away. Who gave a damn what I did with my money? One official clearly did.

He went to Mike Riley, the PGMOL boss, with his suspicions. Riley told him to go away and get some evidence and

Howard Webb was later instructed to investigate. Howard was retired by now and was PGMOL technical director.

I was told they were looking into several matches where I had not performed to my usual level. Christ, even my poor games were better than half of the other Premier League referees at their best. They did not tell me which matches but Howard looked into it and found nothing. He told them if they suspended me and made this public, it would ruin my career. For that, he said, they needed evidence, and they did not have any.

I was still called into a few meetings and asked to explain why I had met a certain individual in Dubai. This fella was a 'fixer', but not a bloody match-fixer! He could get you discounts on water parks and restaurants. It was ridiculous what they were insinuating. He was a friend of Mark Halsey, the former referee. Mark, who is one of my good friends, called and arranged for me and this guy, Mohammed, to meet for a coffee. I was in Dubai with Claire on holiday. I met him, but we did not need him in the end.

But here I was, having to prove to the PGMOL that he had not paid for my flight to Dubai. What were they trying to imply? It was absurd. He was the type of bloke who knew everyone. He'd had his photo taken with loads of players and managers over the years. I was just another one of those.

I can honestly say, I have never been approached about match-fixing. English officials are regarded as clean the world over. I found it sad that Riley even entertained the idea. It was as if they would always take any opportunity like this, always hoping I had slipped up. My colleagues were not subjected to the suspicion which I felt under – or if they were, no one ever heard about it – and it always seemed to be me caught up in these episodes.

It did not go any further and the matter was dropped, but I was sick. I had let it go in 2008 when I was suspended and sacked before being reinstated. I would not have done this time. I would have sued them had it got out and damage been done to my reputation. It felt like I was always on guard, always waiting for their next attack.

I once got a phone call from someone inside the Premier League who was looking out for me.

'The PGMOL want to suspend you,' he said.

'What for?'

'You have filled your expenses in wrong. You have claimed for travel back from London after a European match, but you flew straight home.'

I checked the dates.

'Sorry, that's right. I apologise,' I said.

'Change it immediately and send them an email,' he said.

So I did. But it had come to this, people tipping me off that the PGMOL were trying to suspend me over the most innocuous thing. That is what the PGMOL were like. I detested them.

★   ★   ★

I actually liked my colleague Chris Foy for a while during my early years in the Premier League, but I was naive to think he was trying to help me. He showed his true colours come the end.

I was driving back from a game at Norwich in 2014 when I got a phone call saying Foy had reported me for the behaviour of my guests at a Newcastle match that same day. I was irritated anyway. Driving home from Norwich, it takes two hours to get back to mainland England! So this phone call really pissed me off.

One of my friends, a barrister, had asked if I could get him tickets for the Newcastle game. I sorted them through Darren Cann, the assistant referee at Newcastle, who gave me his two guest tickets. It was Darren who called and explained what had happened, that Michael Oliver was also there watching Newcastle and had told Foy about some of the guests misbehaving. Rather than investigate himself, Foy reported me straight to the PGMOL.

I started making some calls, trying to find out what the hell was going on. I discovered pretty quickly that two of the tickets allocated for the officials had been given to a guy who drove us to and from stadiums, and he had passed them on to two Newcastle fans, who were the rowdy pair.

It had nothing to do with my guests. My friend was not even a Newcastle fan, he was just in the city for the weekend, so I thought the accusation was odd. I phoned Foy and went off it with him. I lost respect for him after that, it opened my eyes.

Looking back now, I cannot believe I put up with the likes of Foy and the backstabbers within the PGMOL for as long as I did.

★   ★   ★

Howard Webb was an outstanding referee, he had real presence and personality.

We started together in the Football League in 2000. He was this big policeman from Sheffield and I was a daft electrician from Newcastle, but we got on well. He was promoted to the Premier League in 2003, a year before me. We were blessed with some top referees at the time – Graham Poll, Graham Barber, Paul Durkin, Alan Wiley, Dermot Gallagher – but Howard took it to another level.

In 2010, he was the best in the business. He refereed the Champions League and World Cup finals. I was like, 'Wow.'

We had built a good relationship over the years. We were similar characters and always enjoyed a beer if we were together on a European trip. We would sit in one of our rooms after the game and just have a laugh and a few drinks. He raided my mini-bar one day and I had to pay for it. He was from Yorkshire, don't forget.

I respected him massively as a referee and really liked him as a guy. But then my opinion of him changed during Euro 2012. He was England's referee at the tournament and I was one of his additional assistants, who patrolled the by-line next to the goal. Martin Atkinson was also part of our team, and we had never got on.

We had a last-16 tie in Warsaw. Portugal beat Czech Republic 1–0 and, as ever, Cristiano Ronaldo scored. Afterwards, we had two cars taking us back to the hotel, and I had the beer left for us at the stadium by the sponsors in my bag. I thought the team were all having a drink in one of our rooms.

I arrived at the hotel a little bit later than the car carrying Howard and Atkinson. I got changed and knocked on Howard's door. No answer. That was strange. I tried again ten minutes later, still no answer. His phone was also ringing out, so I just had a beer and went to bed.

The following day I realised they had gone to a party that the BBC had organised, and it seems I was not invited. I was hurt. Don't do that to me. My relationship with Howard changed after that. As soon as our tournament was over I got the next flight home, I was not hanging around with our 'team'. Fuck them.

It felt like I had lost someone who could have been a close friend in Howard. He did later help me escape the Premier League when I replaced him as director of refereeing in Saudi Arabia in 2017, and for that I will always be thankful. But I never fully trusted him after the incident in Poland. For all of the good decisions he made during his career on the pitch, I thought he made a poor one that night. It perhaps betrayed what type of person he really was.

★　★　★

Martin Atkinson represented a lot of what I do not like about refereeing.

He formed cliques. I found it pathetic how many other officials wanted to be part of his little gang. You would be on a European trip and one of Atkinson's minions would be with you as fourth official, and you knew he was reporting back to his master.

I clouted him once in training and he had a go back. Rather than move on, he was bitter, and that feeling intensified the more I became a threat to his career.

Atkinson was a good referee. He got the Europa League Final in 2015 and did well. He should have been proud of that and focused on himself, but he was always distracted by me and how I was doing.

There was a period when Atkinson and Howard and I were part of UEFA's Elite group of referees. I believe Atkinson thought he would become top dog when Howard retired, and it bothered him that it was me who took over as our best referee when I was awarded the finals of the Champions League and European Championship in 2016.

I did not care about his performances, I looked after myself. Maybe if he had done the same he could have achieved more.

I found Atkinson boring company, like I did most referees. The Christmas parties were dull. They were tight with money as well. You would go to the bar and a queue of referees had formed behind you, all waiting for someone to buy them a drink.

Michael Oliver, a fellow Geordie, got caught under Atkinson's spell. Michael and I used to travel together because of where we lived in the North-East, and we got on well. But as Michael got older and more established, I felt he started to play petty games like Atkinson's lot, and it came between us.

There were a few great lads among our group and I will come onto them. But, on the whole, I never fitted in. I was different to most of them, thankfully.

Graham Poll was a referee who I wanted to emulate during my early years, but he was a strange fella. He once reported me for taking a man-bag on a European trip. It was only a little shoulder bag, to carry my laptop. He said it was not appropriate for referees. But what was appropriate? Were you supposed to wear your pants around your nipples? Did you have to dress like a fucking square? After that I could not trust him.

But, as a referee, I looked up to Graham and modeled a lot of what I did on him. He managed players so well and they respected him. He could be quite cutting and below the belt with what he said to them – I heard that down the headset if I was fourth official – but it was a style that meant he had control. He was very sure of himself.

It was a shame for Graham that he lost a lot of credibility after showing three yellow cards to one player before sending him off at the 2006 World Cup. He came back to the Premier League that summer with his tail between his legs. That lasted about a month before he was back to his old ways.

I liked him for that brashness, but the incident with the shoulder bag meant I could no longer respect him the way I once did. That is what some of these older referees were like, always trying to bring you down a peg or two, especially if you were threatening their position.

I had no time for Rob Styles. He reported me to the PGMOL

following an Everton versus Manchester United FA Cup tie in 2005, for which he was referee and I was fourth official. There was a hostile atmosphere because Wayne Rooney was back at Everton. All sorts were being thrown on the pitch and one fan launched a mobile phone towards United goalkeeper Roy Carroll. Styles picked it up and brought it to me. Sir Alex Ferguson shouted over.

'Mark, I hope that's Vodafone. If it's not then get rid of it!'

Vodafone were United's kit sponsor at the time. I made a joke of it and put the phone to my ear, as if I couldn't hear Ferguson, who laughed.

Styles did not see the funny side and reported me for not being professional. I got an arse-kicking off my PGMOL boss Keith Hackett, who said it was not appropriate. Referees, it seemed, were not allowed to have a bit of fun.

As time went on and I was promoted to UEFA's Elite group, I became the senior referee responsible for my team of officials when we travelled abroad. I never reported any of them for their choice of bag, that is for certain.

I always tried to make sure we had a good time. Why not have a few beers after the game and see the world? We were fortunate to be working in some places you might never get the chance to visit ordinarily, so my attitude was always, 'Let's enjoy ourselves.'

Lee Mason was always good craic on these trips, I enjoyed his company. He was part of my team when Malaga played Zenit St Petersburg in the Champions League in 2012. I had an apartment near Malaga and my friends out there were asking to meet up after the match. I wanted to wait and see how the game went first, you could not be going out if you'd had a shocker. Malaga won 3–0 and there was nothing controversial – book the taxis!

We dumped our bags at the hotel and went for a drink in Torremolinos. One of my friends, an ex-pat, brought his mate with him, Joe. This Joe was a bit of a hard lad, a big Everton fan. He started talking to Mason, who was good fun but could sometimes speak first and think later. Mason started telling this fella how Liverpool were the best team on Merseyside, and I could see it was winding him up.

Joe pulled me to one side.

'What am I going to do with him?' he said.

'Please don't clip him, it'll just end up in the newspapers,' I pleaded.

'Okay, but I'm gonna get him.'

Joe then went to the bar and I was watching him. Next thing, he has laced Mason's drink with spirits. Should I say something? Nah, it'll teach Mason a lesson when he tastes that!

It was all good-natured, but that was a little reminder – as a referee, you have to play the political game when meeting new people. Just tell the lad that Everton are the greatest team you've ever refereed. You never know how some folk are going to react to you, what preconceived ideas they may have, so just play it safe. It is a funny job we do, and people can be funny with it.

★   ★   ★

Mike Dean is proof that you can be a really good guy and a top referee.

He was a former ballroom dancer and used to work in a chicken factory, and that explains a lot. He was mad and he liked a drink, he was just great value to be around. He was the joker of the group but everyone respected him.

Some people on the outside criticised Mike for his eccentric behaviour, like celebrating goals after he had played an advantage and his theatrical hand gestures. I did not mind any of that. He was a guy enjoying his job and having a bit of fun with it.

Mark Halsey was another great bloke. He cared about everyone. He sacrificed a lot of things for other people and was genuine. That is probably why he did not get on well with the PGMOL, for he was not scared to speak his mind.

He had a terribly difficult time when both he and his wife were diagnosed with cancer. He fought so hard to come back and it was inspirational to witness, I was so happy for him. He is one of the few referees with whom I have kept in touch. He loves football and understands the game, and that is what made him one of our best referees.

When I first joined the Premier League in 2004, Phil Dowd took me under his wing. I was twenty-nine, the youngest referee in Premier League history. Phil was the master mickey-taker in the group and, like Mike Dean, you wanted to be in his company.

I once landed in Moscow ahead of a European game and Phil was just leaving. He had been part of another refereeing team the previous night and the people-carrier that had dropped them at the airport was waiting to pick us up. He texted me and said, 'Look in the back seat.' I leaned back and found a little bit of folded paper. It was a note of all the best nightclubs in Moscow! That was typical of him.

Phil and I had a bit of a problem with our weight and supporters hammered him for years about being fat. But he could always laugh it off, if not run it off.

It was around 2005 that PGMOL boss Keith Hackett brought in a rule where referees had to be weighed at the end of the season. If you came back heavier the following season, you were fined. Me and Phil were in trouble. He started thinking of ways to beat the system. On the morning of the end-of-season weigh-in, he sat me down to explain his masterplan.

'Right, before we get weighed, let's go to the canteen and stuff our faces,' he said.

'Why? We'll look overweight if we do that,' I protested.

'Exactly,' he said. 'That way our target will be easier to beat ahead of next season!'

So we did just that – chips, bread, pasta, as much as we could get down our throats over lunch. We were so distracted by the attempt to expand our waistline, we were late for the weigh-in. Phil was running up the stairs when he stopped, turned around and looked at me.

'Why the fuck am I running?' he said. 'I don't want to go losing any weight, do I?'

Phil was old school, like a lot of the guys were when I first started. When we had our referee get-togethers at Staverton Park in Northamptonshire, the lads would play golf during the day and turn up for dinner steaming drunk. There was a real drinking culture. I used to sit back and laugh at it all, and Phil was at the heart of it, the best character I ever came across in refereeing.

Over time, his type were slowly replaced by a new breed. Now, when I look at the Premier League group, there are very few personalities. That shows in how they referee – there are no leaders, those who command respect by strength of character. That is reflected by PGMOL boss Mike Riley. They need better leadership at the top of the organisation if they are to succeed on the pitch.

Riley never liked me and that dates back to an incident in Milan in 2007. He was referee for a Champions League group game between AC Milan and Benfica, and I was the fourth official.

We were heading out for some lunch on the day of the game and, because the cleaner was in my room, I asked Mike if I could quickly use his bathroom. We then went into the square for some food and came back to the hotel for a sleep in the afternoon, which was our usual routine. Except for Riley, he went for a massage. I was lying on my bed, just dozing off, when someone started banging on my door.

I answered and it was Riley. He was effing and jeffing, and he hardly ever swore.

'You've nicked my fucking speakers,' he said.

'What the fuck are you on about?' I went back at him.

'You took them and hid them, when you used my bathroom earlier.'

'Mike, I haven't got them. Go away.'

I went back to bed.

We later met for sandwiches, coffee and biscuits in the hotel before leaving for the game. He was still banging on about these bloody speakers.

'Mike, I haven't got your speakers. If I had them I would have told you by now. The joke would be over.'

We arrived at the San Siro and Riley was one of these referees who made the fourth official go and check the players' boots before the game. It was a pointless exercise, they used to have about six pairs each.

'Which ones are you wearing?' I would ask.

'Er, I don't know yet,' they would say.

Great. I'll just check six pairs of boots of every player then, shall I? It was a waste of time.

I got back to our dressing-room and could not believe what I saw. All of the stuff from my bag had been tipped out on the floor. What the fuck? Who has done that? Riley said it was him.

'I'm looking for my speakers,' he said.

Those speakers . . . I was ready to throttle him.

'Put that stuff back in my bag now, or I'll fucking clip you,' I said, and I was not joking.

He had stepped way out of line. He put the things back in

my bag and we got ready for the game in an awkward silence. If only we'd had some speakers for a bit of music!

A week or so later I asked if he had found them. He had. When he got home he realised he had left them behind on his bed. Did he apologise? Of course he didn't. We barely spoke after that while he was still refereeing.

He retired in 2009 but, sadly, that was not the last I would be seeing of him. Far from it. He was appointed manager of the PGMOL, replacing Hackett. Mike Riley was now my boss. My problems with him were only just beginning.

10

THE MATCHES

'Clattenburg, I'm going to kill you'

THE bigger the game, the bigger the fallout.

It is a high-wire act when you are refereeing Sky Sports' *Super Sunday* fixture most weekends. Take a wrong step and you are going to get a kicking all the way down.

But that is the price on the ticket if you want to operate at the top of our trade. If I made a mistake, it was blown up into headline news. If any other referee made a mistake, it would blow over within twenty-four hours.

Do a good job, however, and that feeling of satisfaction was my equivalent of scoring a goal, even if no one made mention of it. That was always the aim – get in, get it right, get out, get lucky. Refereeing those marquee matches was all about survival.

But on more than one occasion I was left clinging to my reputation for dear life, and that is why I will start with a chastening afternoon on Merseyside.

Saturday 20 October 2007.
Everton 1 Liverpool 2. Premier League.

If referees are better remembered for their bad games instead of good, then this has to rank as my worst. Most football fans will recall this match, and sadly that is more so because of my performance than it is the football.

I had recently refereed the Manchester and North London derbies and did okay in both, well enough not to make headlines anyway. The PGMOL thought I was the right man for this Merseyside derby. I thought I was the right man. That was part of the problem, I got complacent. It was only my fourth season in the Premier League.

We walked out at Goodison Park and I realised straight away the noise and intensity was at a different level to those other derbies. Some derby matches can feel corporate, as if they have lost what they once were. This was raw. It was like the Tyne–Wear derbies I had been to as a Newcastle fan – the atmosphere is feverish, you can feel the anxiety and desperation to win coming down from the stands and every decision is contested. It caught me by surprise.

I was lucky in that the first half was relatively straightforward for me and Everton were winning 1–0 after a Sami Hyypia own goal. There were no controversies and, at half-time, I thought I had nailed it. How wrong was I? It was me the home fans were ready to nail forty-five minutes later.

The second half was an absolute disaster. The game stepped

up and I did not go with it. On fifty-four minutes, Steven Gerrard went through on goal and Everton defender Tony Hibbert pulled him down. The foul was committed entering the area and I thought it was just inside. I awarded a penalty and TV replays showed I was right.

What upset Everton supporters, and I understand why, is that I pulled out my yellow card only to swap it for a red and send off Hibbert. The TV footage looked as if Gerrard had influenced me because, at the point I am changing the cards, he walks towards me and appears to say something.

But Gerrard was going to get the ball. If he did speak, I wasn't listening. I had simply taken the yellow from my pocket by mistake. Martin Atkinson, the fourth official, was talking to me down my headset.

'Mark, do you know you've got the yellow card in your hand?'

I quickly changed it for the red. What I should have done was keep hold of the yellow. It had tape on the back where I made a note of the cards I had issued. I should have shown Hibbert the red and then written it down on the back of the yellow. Instead, what I did looked terribly messy, as if I had changed my mind, and I get that.

But to be clear, I was always going to send off Hibbert. It was an obvious red card because Gerrard was through on goal with only the goalkeeper to beat. The decision was correct. The timing of Gerrard then walking past me – and the angle it was shown on TV – was unfortunate. Everton fans pounced on that but for them to suggest Gerrard had overturned my decision was bollocks, it just was not true.

Dirk Kuyt then scored the penalty to make it 1–1, and there is nothing like a red card and seemingly controversial goal to dial up the temperature of a derby. This was already at boiling point when another of my decisions threatened to blow the roof off Goodison Park.

The ball was running towards Everton's Phil Neville on the touchline when Kuyt flew in to challenge him. I call it a challenge, it was more like a kung-fu kick, not that I realised at the time. I had a bad angle where my view was obstructed, and that was my fault. I thought it was a genuine attempt to stop the ball being played down the line, although I knew Kuyt was clearly late. Having later seen the replay, it was outrageous.

Darren Cann was my assistant referee, one of the best in the world, and he told me there was no contact. He advised that it was a yellow card and I agreed. I was wrong, I should have been in a better position to make the call.

There was no contact but that was not the point. Kuyt was out of control, off the ground and endangering Neville's safety. It was a blatant red card. In fact, it was worth two red cards! With VAR there is no doubt he would have been sent off.

Everyone in blue was gunning for me now, whether they were in the stands, on the touchline or on the pitch. Two big decisions had gone against Everton and, even though one of them was correct, that did not matter to them. They were hurting and felt cheated. It soon got worse.

Everton were holding on for a point when, in the last minute, Neville saved a Lucas Leiva shot on the goal-line with his hand. I sent him off and awarded a penalty. It was the right call and no one can dispute that. What intensified Everton's sense of injustice was the sight of Kuyt stepping up to score from the spot. The Liverpool forward should not have been on the pitch, and that was down to me.

Then came the moment that makes me angry to this day, and my annoyance is with no one but myself. We were deep into injury-time when Everton launched the ball into the goal-mouth. There was a crowd of bodies and lots of jostling. All of a sudden Everton's players were appealing for a penalty. I did not know why. I thought it was desperation. I was wrong, again.

I had a bad view and was obstructed by a player running across me – again, that's on me – and I had missed Jamie Carragher dragging down Everton defender Joleon Lescott. He manhandled him. It should have been the easiest decision in the world. To give Everton a penalty would have put some balance back in the game from a refereeing perspective; it was a gift.

I honestly believe that, if I had awarded the penalty and Everton scored to draw the game, I would have escaped with far less criticism. Everton would have been elated with taking an injury-time point while down to nine men. That would have made the headlines, not me. Rafa Benitez had also substituted Gerrard with twenty minutes to go, which seemed bizarre, and I am sure that would have been the story as much as anything else, had Liverpool failed to win.

Everton manager David Moyes came into my dressing-room after the game, and he was spitting feathers. I have always said we should avoid those situations. Emotions are raw. I tried to explain myself and that made it worse. Given more time and a chance to analyse the decisions, I would have said sorry to Moyes. In the heat of the moment, immediately after full-time, it does no one any favours to be thrust into such a scenario where conflict is always going to arise. It's stupid, really.

Moyes was not the only angry person connected to Everton. I could see the fury in the eyes of everyone in the area outside my dressing-room, it was a very uncomfortable walk back down the tunnel. Even though a couple of the big decisions were right, they all went against Everton. There was no balance, it had all gone Liverpool's way.

It was only as I got older that I began to think more about that word – balance – and how important it is, not only in helping to control players during the game, but also in protecting yourself from criticism afterwards.

First and foremost you have to get decisions right, of course. If you get five big calls correct and they are all for one team, then so be it. But you also have to realise when there is injustice and you have made mistakes at the expense of one side, like I did in this game.

I made an error in not sending off Kuyt but I had the chance to restore some balance by awarding Everton a penalty in injury-time, and I missed it. I left myself exposed to the subsequent fallout.

What I am trying to explain is that, as a referee, you have to protect yourself, because no one else will. I failed to do that in this match and paid a heavy price. I wish I could go back and award Everton that penalty, for I would not have received the condemnation and death threats that followed.

I left Goodison Park and tried my best to look composed as I walked towards the people-carrier. The hate being screamed by Everton fans in that moment is the worst I can remember. Once we were in the car I got a text message from my friend, Neil Saxton. He is the son of Bobby Saxton, who was Peter Reid's assistant manager at Sunderland. He said, 'Reidy wants to kill you.' It was a joke and I took it as such. Reid is a good guy, an Everton legend, and he was understandably upset like the rest of the club's supporters. They even started a petition to get me banned for life. I would not be surprised if one or two inside the PGMOL added their signature!

But some of the other abuse was vile. Because of press reports available on the internet, the area in which I lived in Newcastle was in the public domain. The postman used to think he was doing me a favour when he delivered letters addressed to 'Mark Clattenburg. Gosforth. Newcastle.' It would often be an Everton fan threatening to kill me. They were always typed, never hand-written. The first time it happens, it scares you. But over time you become immune to death threats. I never did believe any of them were a genuine threat to my life, as unpleasant as they are to receive. If someone wanted to kill me, they wouldn't put it in writing first! I reported every letter to the police and PGMOL, but there is not a lot anyone can do.

There was one idiot, an Everton fan, who somehow got my home telephone number. He would call late on a Saturday night. I think he was pissed and trying to impress his friends. He used to shout, 'Clattenburg, I'm gonna fucking kill you!' He stopped when I blew my whistle down the phone one night. I hope it burst his fucking eardrum.

I was taken off Premier League duty the weekend after the Merseyside derby. It was the right decision given the scrutiny I was under. My head was in a spin. I went to Spain to get away from it all and spent the entire time thinking, 'God, how bad was I?' I thought my career at the top could be over. Paranoia consumes you in such moments and I started wondering whether I might be demoted to the Football League. To think I had gone into the match believing, 'I've made it here.'

But in some ways the whole experience, as horrible as it was, helped make me the referee I became. It served as an unfortunate but valuable lesson. Some might laugh given the perception of me as arrogant, but it taught me humility. It reminded me – don't ever think you've cracked it.

I paid for my mistakes as I never got to referee another Merseyside derby, and that is a special fixture to miss out on. I regret that. I even had to wait more than four years to referee Everton again, when they drew 1–1 at Aston Villa. Sadly, their fans used it to target me and it brought back a lot of the hostility. At least Everton's players had moved on. The likes of

Leon Osman and Phil Jagielka were good pros and nice people and nothing more was said of it.

I eventually returned to Goodison Park six years after the derby and, in time, things settled down. It was a shame, because I have a lot of respect for Everton as a football club. The passion of their supporters is similar to Newcastle in the love of their team and knowledge of the game. But I got on the wrong side of them and I understand why. I was dreadful that day. I cannot apologise enough.

Monday 2 May 2016.
Chelsea 2 Tottenham Hotspur 2. Premier League.

The Battle of the Bridge . . . I felt more like a policeman this night than I did a referee. It is one of the most infamous matches in Premier League history. I showed a record twelve yellow cards and the fallout saw both clubs given record fines totalling £600,000 for failing to control their players.

Could I have controlled them better? I certainly could have refereed it differently. I could have shown more yellow cards earlier in the game, which may have then led to red cards. Instead, I chose to step back from it and let the players slug it out.

It is like a policeman going into a riot. Do you charge in with a baton and start fighting straight away? That is the worst thing you can do. I let this battle play out in the belief it would settle as the game went on. Ultimately, my approach did not deter the fouls and fighting, the players were hell bent on destruction no matter what any referee did. But I still believe I made the right call, and I will try to explain why.

I have called it an 'infamous' match, but I do not think that should have a negative connotation. It was a throwback to the sort of game about which many fans romanticise, two teams going at each other hammer and tongs. If this match had been from a bygone era – like the brutal clash between Leeds and Chelsea in the 1970 FA Cup Final – it would be remembered fondly.

It was rare to see a game like this in the Premier League. I often think the modern-day interpretation of such matches is one of outrage that players should behave like that. Okay, I take that point. It was not a particularly good look and it was certainly not a good example to any young players. But I bet supporters and neutrals enjoyed it. A Premier League executive later told me it was a 'guilty pleasure' watching it all unfold. It was arguably the most talked-about game of the season and, you know what, I even enjoyed it myself.

One misconception is that I deliberately chose not to send players off. That is not true. It was not as if I kept my cards in my pocket, I booked more players in one match than any referee had done in twenty-four years of the Premier League.

Yes, I accept there should have been red cards, but without VAR some of those I simply could not see. Those players would have been sent off had I witnessed the relevant incidents, either in real time or with the help of technology. There was one red-card offence that I did see and should have acted on, and I will come to that.

Before I go into more detail, it is important to revisit the background to the fixture. Spurs were trailing league leaders Leicester by eight points with three games to play. They had to win every one of them to stand any chance of taking the title. The world was watching because anything other than a Spurs victory meant Leicester were champions, and everyone wanted to see the underdogs win the Premier League. Chelsea were tenth in the table. They'd had a shocking season. All they cared about was stopping Spurs from winning the league. I expected it to be lively, and boy was it that.

Chelsea midfielder John Obi Mikel and Mousa Dembele squared up to each other early on and were flinging their arms about. It was enough for me to stop play and I had a word with both players.

'Just calm it down,' I told them.

No chance. There was then a late Danny Rose challenge on Chelsea striker Diego Costa. Again, I chose to talk to him rather than show a yellow card. It was a final warning for Rose, and we had only played thirteen minutes. My resolve to keep my cards in my pocket was certainly being tested.

Spurs defender Kyle Walker seemed in the mood for trouble from the start. He was the first player I booked on twenty-seven minutes for a foul on Pedro. The TV cameras also captured Walker flicking his boot at Pedro after another coming -together. I did not see it.

There were three more bookings before half-time – Jan Vertonghen for a shirt pull on Costa and Rose and Willian for their part in sparking a mass scuffle, which would prove the first of several. They tangled right in front of the dugouts and were shoving each other. Spurs boss Mauricio Pochettino ran onto the pitch and jumped between them. All hell broke loose. Pochettino was a smart guy but even he was caught up in it. It sent the wrong message to his players.

It was during this moment that we missed Dembele's eye gouge on Costa. There were bodies everywhere and so much to take in. My mind was racing trying to process it all. It might not look like it from the footage because I step back and seem pretty relaxed, but trust me, your heart is pumping. I was trying to get a view of as much as possible without getting physically involved.

My assistant referee, Simon Beck, was closer to Dembele and Costa than I was, and I wish he had seen it. It was a horrible thing for Dembele to do and, if I had been made aware of it at the time, I would have sent him off. But we missed it and Dembele stayed on the pitch. He was later banned for six matches. What I cannot believe is Costa did not turn around and punch him. It was one of the few occasions when he did show restraint. Part of me thinks he was enjoying it too much to risk getting sent off and missing out on more conflict.

Spurs were 2–0 up at half-time after goals from Harry Kane and Son Heung-Min. They should have come out in the second half and taken the sting out of the game. They had the scoreline they needed. Instead, they lost their heads. It was stupid what they did.

Spurs winger Erik Lamela went through Cesc Fabregas on the touchline with a wild challenge. Yellow card. Christian Eriksen also went into the book for a cynical foul on Eden Hazard. What were they trying to achieve?

On fifty-eight minutes, Chelsea pulled a goal back through Gary Cahill. From that point, Spurs hit the self-destruct button. They were not clever enough to see the game out. Hazard equalised seven minutes from time and that was it, Spurs did not care about trying to win the match now. It was as if they decided the title was beyond them. They just wanted to fight. They were like a raging bull.

No matter what I did, it would have had no effect. I know that, I was right there in the heat of the battle with them. I could smell it. They did not give a shit about the consequences in terms of cards or suspensions, or even the result. They were young players who had not been in this situation before. They could not handle failure. That is why they behaved the way they did.

Chelsea were more than happy to go along with it, by the way. I do not want to paint them as the victims. They were giving as good as they got, but Spurs were the instigators.

There was an incident where Fabregas accused Lamela of stamping on his hand. He was in my face showing me the apparent stud marks. I had not seen it happen and I could not take action based solely on his word. I dismissed his claims. But with VAR, Lamela would have been sent off.

I then booked Spurs midfielder Eric Dier for a lunge on Hazard and almost every player raced to the scene. I was getting knocked about in the middle of it and I booked Obi Mikel, who had rushed in and was barging into me and others.

Come injury-time, it was like nothing I had ever refereed before. I booked three Spurs players – Dembele, Kane and Ryan Mason – and after every one there was a shoving match. It was carnage.

The one player I should have sent off was Dier. It was a blatant second yellow when he flew in late on Fabregas. I put the whistle to my mouth and would have shown the red card had I blown, only Chelsea had possession and were breaking upfield. I played the advantage. It was the last minute, I wanted to give them the chance to score, that was always my style. But I was wrong. For a second yellow like that, you should kill the game and deal with it.

The attack was finally stopped when Mason brought down Hazard at the other end of the pitch and I booked the Spurs midfielder. There was another angry melee. It was right on full-time and I overlooked going back to show Dier his red card. That was a mistake.

We weren't done there. Coming off the pitch, it all kicked off again entering the tunnel. Chelsea boss Guus Hiddink was knocked over, he could have been seriously hurt. I was being verbally abused by a member of Chelsea's technical staff. I got back to my dressing-room and tried to make sense of all that had happened. I knew my merit mark from the assessor would be low, but I did not care about that. It would have been impossible to score highly.

But had I been right to referee the game the way I did? I took a risk, I knew that much. I allowed a level of tolerance. I tried to find the balance between applying the *Laws of the Game* and understanding the occasion and the emotion of it.

Some will argue a referee is there to simply administer the laws. I never wanted to be a slave to that. Yes, they are your first thought. But for me, it was as much about managing people. I also wanted the game to be played and not stopped for every foul, and that is why I believe those in football liked my style.

Former Premier League referee Dermot Gallagher said it was a 'gamble too far' and called me a 'maverick' when he analysed this game. Maybe he was right. But it was an approach that got results and took me to the top of my profession. Did it backfire here? Well, that depends on your interpretation and enjoyment of the game.

I have spoken to several of the players involved since and they say they loved playing in that match. I also think the executives inside the Premier League did not mind it. It was being talked about all over the world. Do not forget, these guys think more about the value of TV contracts than they do the value of fair play. And this was box office.

I will be criticised for saying this, but I allowed Spurs to beat themselves that night. Could I have sent off one of their players in the first half for a couple of yellows, even if some of them were borderline? Yes, I probably could have done. But who gets the blame for Spurs losing the title if there is a contentious red card? The coverage would have been about a picky referee, who failed to understand the pressure of the occasion and panicked by flashing his cards too early. The referee could not win here.

But I repeat – I did not wilfully ignore or turn a blind eye to any obvious red card in front of me. I got it wrong on Dier and I missed Dembele's eye gouge, I regret those two instances. Lamela and Walker probably would have been sent off with VAR, but I did not see those incidents.

There has been a lot written and said about my performance in the years since. I would challenge anyone to do a better job in those circumstances. I had a plan and I gambled on the players responding to that. They didn't. Chelsea were determined to ruin it for Spurs, and Spurs were determined to ruin it for themselves. It was madness. There was not a lot I could do to change that.

But I am glad I handled it the way I did. The alternative, I believe, would have been worse, like pouring petrol on a fire. I made a choice and I stand by it.

Leicester, of course, won the Premier League that night. I had refereed them two weeks earlier when they beat Swansea 4–0 at the King Power Stadium. I was only on that match because Jon Moss had had a nightmare the previous weekend when Leicester drew 2–2 at home to West Ham. He sent off Leicester striker Jamie Vardy and gave penalties for both sides that were controversial. So the PGMOL sent me for their next game. They won well in the end, but I could feel their nerves.

They were so close to this monumental achievement and only Spurs could stop them.

But Spurs lost their own nerve. They lost their discipline. They lost everything that night at Chelsea. For that, they only have themselves to blame.

Sunday 16 March 2014.
Manchester United 0 Liverpool 3. Premier League.

Manchester United versus Liverpool is unique, by far the best Premier League fixture for rivalry and a sense of occasion. I relished being part of it.

Earlier in the season, I refereed their League Cup tie at Old Trafford, which United won 1–0. It was Luis Suarez's first game back for Liverpool after a ten-match ban for biting Chelsea's Branislav Ivanovic. The atmosphere was red hot, there was real spite in the air. To think the importance of the League Cup is often downplayed – not when United play Liverpool it isn't.

Wayne Rooney and Steven Gerrard were the captains that night. They were England team-mates. Two Scousers and good friends. Not that you would have known any of that in my dressing-room an hour before kick-off. They came in to exchange the team-sheets and did not even acknowledge each other. Often, you see hugs and handshakes. There was none of that here. It felt like two generals about to declare war. That is what makes this match so special.

It was David Moyes' first season as United manager. Come this Premier League game in March, Moyes was under huge pressure. United, who were defending champions, were seventh in the table. The club had lost its aura overnight when Sir Alex Ferguson retired. It was not the same under Moyes, nor any of the managers who followed him.

You could tell that visiting teams were turning up at Old Trafford expecting to get a result. I knew they could smell blood by the way they approached matches. There was belief, whereas before there had been fear.

It was the same for referees. Old Trafford became just another ground like all the others. The intimidation was no longer there. It was remarkable to experience the difference, all because of the removal of one man.

I gave Liverpool three penalties on this day, and it should have been four. Suarez won the first on thirty-four minutes, when he knocked the ball past Rafael and the defender handled. It was a penalty, there were no complaints and Gerrard scored.

I gave the next one within a minute of the start of the second half when Phil Jones clattered into Joe Allen. It was clumsy. Again, a clear penalty and Gerrard scored for 2–0.

The third penalty, on seventy-eight minutes, I got wrong. Daniel Sturridge went down when Nemanja Vidic slid across him. It looked like a foul and I pointed to the spot. I sent off Vidic for a second booking but I had this nagging doubt that Sturridge had dived. My assistant referee said penalty, so I stuck with the decision. Vidic did not get the ball and, later, I heard

Gary Neville say in commentary that the defender deserved everything he got for being so reckless. But Sturridge did dive. I wish I had gone with my gut feeling. Gerrard missed the penalty for his hat-trick when he hit the post.

A minute or so later and Sturridge went down in the area after Michael Carrick clipped his ankle. I'm thinking, 'Jesus, not again, this is never-ending'. It was a tight call. Gerrard and Jordan Henderson were screaming for it.

'I've given you three already, and one of them was dodgy!' I told them, as I waved away the appeal.

But the result was never in doubt. Liverpool were far superior on the day and Suarez made it 3–0 late on. Moyes was sacked within a month.

Louis van Gaal was appointed that summer but, come January 2016, he was clinging to his job when they went to Anfield in the Premier League. United had won two from their previous eleven matches. I was in charge and I could tell the home crowd were desperate to see off another United manager.

This fixture is different at Anfield, the rivalry goes up a level. The fans are closer to the pitch. It feels claustrophobic but makes for a more intense atmosphere. You can feel the energy from the crowd transmit to the players.

After five minutes I was saying to them, 'Whoa, calm down.' In the end, it wasn't a great game and Rooney scored the only goal late on to win it for United. Van Gaal survived, at least until the end of the season.

But even the scrappier matches between these two were a

pleasure to be involved with. Because their hate was directed towards each other, it also meant the referee often slipped under the radar – even when you had given three penalties to Liverpool at Old Trafford.

Wednesday 7 December 2011.
Dinamo Zagreb 1 Lyon 7. Champions League Group Stage.

This game did not sit right with me, and it never will. It was the final round of group matches and Lyon were in third position. They could still qualify for the knockout stages but they needed to win in Zagreb and hope that Ajax lost at home to Real Madrid in the other game. The goal difference also had to swing by seven in favour of Lyon.

I booked the Dinamo captain, Jerko Leko, for a foul midway through the first half. Then, a few minutes later, he tripped a Lyon player. It was an obvious second yellow and I sent him off. He shook my hand before running off the pitch. It was odd – most players are pissed off, even when they know they're in the wrong.

Dinamo went 1–0 up on forty minutes and Lyon equalised right on half-time. Within the first three minutes of the second half, Lyon had scored twice more. I knew that Ajax were losing 2–0 at half-time. I wanted that information, as I had an uneasy feeling about what was happening in my game.

By the seventy-fifth minute, Lyon were winning 7–1. Their

striker, Bafetimbi Gomis, had scored four, including the quickest ever Champions League hat-trick inside just seven minutes. Ajax were losing 3–0 and Lyon were heading through to the last 16.

But a few of the goals did not feel good. I do not want to accuse anyone of anything. All I will say is that some of Dinamo's goalkeeping and defending was not of Champions League standard. Watch it back and you will know exactly what I mean.

The final quarter of an hour was like nothing I had seen before. Dinamo barely went into Lyon's half. The ball stayed in play and Lyon just kept it. It was not football. Dinamo had no fight, no pride. I blew for full-time and everyone seemed happy. But I wasn't.

I landed back at Newcastle Airport the following day and I got a phone call from Chris Wild, UEFA's head of refereeing services. He asked if I thought there was anything suspicious in the game. I had felt uncomfortable, yes. But had I seen or heard anything that would form a concrete allegation? No, I hadn't. This was a matter for UEFA to investigate. They had to look into betting patterns around the fixture. Footage had also emerged of a Dinamo defender appearing to wink at Gomis after one of the goals. It was not a good look for the game. Ajax were angry and wanted answers.

But, ultimately, nothing was proven. There were no suspicious betting patterns. One of the goals had been marginally offside and some people were asking questions of us. But hold on, the one thing accepted around the world is that English officials are clean. We were just as concerned as anyone at what had played out in front of us.

It was not my place to say whether this game was correct or otherwise. I did not know. UEFA said there was no evidence of wrongdoing and that was that. You have to accept it and move on.

Saturday 11 August 2012.
Mexico 2 Brazil 1. Wembley Stadium.
London Olympics gold medal match.

This is right up there as one of the most enjoyable fortnights of my career, refereeing at the London Olympics of 2012. We were staying in the Mayfair Hotel, right in the heart of the city. Every football confederation in the world had officials there and I was so proud to be Great Britain's representative. It was a magical time for the whole country.

We went to the opening ceremony at the Olympic Stadium in Stratford, but it was impossible to get tickets for the bigger events. I watched some of the road cycling around London and had to blag my way into the beach volleyball. I confess, I used my Wikipedia page on my phone to convince the guy on the door to let me in, but it was worth it. I was living the dream.

It was also a stepping stone for me to a major tournament, so I wanted to be at my best. As a FIFA-organised competition, I knew the refereeing chiefs would be watching closely.

I refereed a 1–1 draw between Egypt and New Zealand in front of 50,000 at Old Trafford before taking charge of the Mexico versus Senegal quarter-final at Wembley. Mexico won 4–2 and there were 82,000 spectators. It was just incredible, this wave of happiness and goodwill that you could feel everywhere you went.

It was then announced that I would be refereeing the gold medal match between Brazil and Mexico. What an honour that was, at our home Olympics.

Brazil's team was immense – Neymar, Oscar, Thiago Silva – yet Mexico won 2–1. I was happy with my performance, although it was a strange match to referee. The crowd was mainly made up of families and it felt a bit like a pantomime – every time a foul was committed they all went 'Ooohhh . . .'. I could have closed my eyes and I would have known when to whistle for a free-kick. We had a party afterwards and Sepp Blatter, then FIFA president, turned up. Unfortunately, we did not get a gold medal.

Instead, I later got my first tattoo. The design, on my wrist, commemorated the Olympics and the gold medal match. No one knew about it until four years later when I got the Champions League and Euro 2016 logos tattooed on my arm. I had worn long sleeves during that entire time because I was worried it did not look professional. That was silly. I should have worn it with pride. It is a memory of a special time.

WHISTLE BLOWER

Sunday 11 August 2013.
Manchester United 2 Wigan Athletic 0.
Wembley Stadium. Community Shield.

The Community Shield was my fourth Wembley appearance in eighteen months, and it was the only one that left a bad taste. It was exactly one year on from the Olympics and, before that, I had refereed the 2012 League Cup Final between Liverpool and Cardiff.

Finals can be cagey, but that one wasn't. It was 1–1 at full-time and 2–2 after extra-time. Both teams played with freedom and bravery and I just stood back and enjoyed it.

Liverpool won on penalties but I felt for Cardiff. They were the underdogs and made it a cracking match. Anthony Gerrard, Steven's cousin, missed the deciding penalty. You could not have scripted that. The final had been pure drama and I was proud to be part of it, my first match at Wembley.

The only problem was, what with extra-time and penalties, it meant the meal for the officials did not finish until 11 p.m. By the time we got out for a celebratory drink in London, everywhere was closing. It had been such a good day that we did not want it to end.

The Community Shield, though, I would rather forget. It was not a difficult match. Manchester United won 2–0 and it was easy to referee. But it was spoilt for me by a senior football official.

He was sitting behind our families in the stand and they could hear him calling me 'arrogant', saying I was having a poor game.

'Clattenburg's shit,' he said. 'He's just like Howard Webb.'

Claire turned around.

'That's my husband,' she said.

He did not seem to care. I reported it to Mike Riley at the PGMOL. He told me to let it go. That was typical of him. Instead of standing by one of his referees, he was happy to allow the official to upset my family. That was also the type of bloke this guy at Wembley was, I never liked him. He should have had more respect, for me and my wife.

Like a lot of those I came across in such elevated positions of authority, they had disappeared so far up their own backsides that they had forgotten how to behave like decent human beings.

Tuesday 12 August 2014.
Real Madrid 2 Sevilla 0. Cardiff City Stadium. UEFA Super Cup.

I was travelling back from Spain with Claire when I got a message saying Pierluigi Collina, my boss at UEFA, had been trying to get in touch with me. My phone had been switched off on the flight. Your first thought is always, 'God, what have I done?' You never expect good news. I called him immediately. Claire was standing next to me at Newcastle Airport.

'What did he want?' she said.

'I'm going to referee the Super Cup,' I told her.

'Great. Where is it?'

'It's usually in Monaco.'

'Ah, I would love to go there.'

'Me too. I can't wait.'

I then got a phone call from Chris Wild at UEFA to confirm the appointment.

'Congratulations,' he said. 'But do you want the bad news?'

'What's that?' I said.

'The game is in Cardiff.'

'I thought it was in Monaco. Are you taking the piss?'

I have nothing against Cardiff, but come on. Claire did not even come in the end, and she was not the only thing I left behind. I have never told this to Collina, but I forgot to take my communication headsets. It was the night before the game when I suddenly realised. It was a real 'Oh fuck' moment.

I rang Claire. I had a plan. I would get her to send them down to Cardiff with a courier company. I did not care about the cost. It was my mistake, I had to rectify it. I made some calls as a backup, just in case my courier idea went wrong. The Welsh FA insisted straight away that they had some headsets we could use. They said we would get them before the game. I told Claire not to worry about sorting the courier, it was all in hand. I went to bed a relieved man.

The next day I received the communication sets from the Welsh FA. My God. They belonged in a museum. The technology was older than me. There were also only four of them – and there were six of us!

This was a nightmare, and it was all my fault. We had no

choice but to use them. I took two for myself and the fourth official and gave the other two to the additional assistants on the by-line. They needed them as it was their only method of communication. The assistant referees had their flags. We all had the wires in our ears, just to look the part, but only four of the six were hooked up and able to hear each other. We were going to have to wing it.

It was the first game in a UEFA club competition to use vanishing spray to mark out the distance of the defensive wall at free-kicks. There is a joke in there somewhere about vanishing spray and my communication kits, but I was not in the mood for laughing at the time.

The match was going well but then, in the second half, there was an offside flag that I was hopelessly late to react to. There was no great consequence but it did not look good. The game finished 2–0 to Real and Cristiano Ronaldo had scored both goals. Had I got away with it? Collina pulled me up after the game.

'What was the problem with that offside?' he said.

I did not have the nerve to tell him the assistant referees weren't wired up. I just fudged it. But how bad was that? I had got lucky in that my cock-up had not been exposed.

I was quite emotional afterwards. It felt like a big step towards my dream of refereeing the Champions League Final. I went for a drink with some friends and I was a bit of a wreck, but not in a bad way. I was relieved that I had done okay and Collina seemed happy, one offside apart.

It felt like things were heading in the right direction for me. You have plenty of bad days as referee, this was one of the good ones. And I never forgot my headsets ever again.

Thursday 1 May 2014.
Juventus 0 Benfica 0. Europa League semi-final, second leg (Benfica win 2–1 on aggregate).

This was the only match in my career in which I showed three red cards, even though two of them were to players not on the field at the time.

I sent off Benfica's Enzo Perez for two bookable offences midway through the second half and his team-mates were clinging to a 2–1 aggregate lead approaching the final ten minutes.

The final was going to be played at the Juventus Stadium in Turin, so Juventus were desperate to turn the tie around. I could feel the tension rising, a sixth sense as a referee when you just know something is going to boil over.

Juventus had a goal disallowed for offside with about five minutes remaining and it was the right call. Not that the referee being right does much to soothe a feeling of injustice. To Juventus' irritation, Benfica were wasting time at every opportunity and I did not manage it well. I should have come down harder on the Portuguese side. It made me appreciate just how cynical some European teams can be in such a scenario.

All of a sudden, it exploded in front of the dugouts. There was pushing and shoving and fists being thrown. There was management, coaches, players, physios – the only person not involved in the brawl was me.

I picked out who I thought were the two worst offenders – I could have chosen twenty-two – and I showed red cards to Juventus forward Mirko Vucinic, who was an unused substitute, and Benfica's Lazar Markovic, who had not long been taken off.

Benfica held on to go through and that meant Markovic was suspended for the final. There was an appeal by the club and UEFA arranged a telephone conference where I had to explain my decision. I said that I recognised Markovic as a guilty party because he had long hair and had just been substituted, he was fresh in my memory. That was enough for them to reject the appeal and he missed the final, which Sevilla won on penalties.

That summer, Markovic signed for Liverpool for £20 million and I refereed them early in the season. He was waiting for me in the tunnel. 'Oh God,' I thought, 'I remember Turin, he's a hot head, he is going to have a pop at me here.'

'Hello, Mr Clattenburg,' he said, before shaking my hand and walking off.

What a polite young man. If that had been an English player he would have killed me!

Sunday 24 October 2010.
Manchester City 0 Arsenal 3. Premier League.

This was the quickest red card I showed in my entire career. City surprised everyone by bringing in 19-year-old Dedryck Boyata to start at centre-back. We had only played five minutes when he mistimed his challenge on Arsenal forward Marouane Chamakh, who was running through on goal just outside the penalty area.

I did not need any clues as to what had happened – my mind was made up straight away – but young Boyata put his hand on his head before he had even looked at me. He knew.

It took me thirty seconds to get the usual suspects like Arsenal's Cesc Fabregas out of my face, waving imaginary cards. But there was no doubt, it was a red. Boyata was the last man and he had denied a clear goalscoring opportunity.

Try telling that to City manager Roberto Mancini and their supporters. Mancini later said it was not a sending-off. Was he taking the piss? He tried to say City would have won with 11 v 11. Maybe they would have done, but that was irrelevant. Whether this was the fifth minute or the ninety-fifth, it was a red card.

I also gave Arsenal a penalty when Vincent Kompany needlessly fouled Fabregas, who then missed the spot-kick. Again, it was an obvious decision.

But the abuse I got from City's fans was something else, and they had eighty-five minutes after the red card to let me know exactly what they thought. Sometimes you cannot win. Even in the face of such blatant decisions, supporters' tribalism still comes to the fore. There aren't many jobs in the world where you get attacked for getting things right.

Saturday 29 November 2014.
Middlesbrough 1 Blackburn 1. Championship.

I include this game because I did not get the chance to referee Middlesbrough too often, given my North-East connection. And this proved to be my last match at the Riverside Stadium, not that Boro's supporters were complaining.

It was the ninety-fifth minute and Boro were winning 1–0. Blackburn swung a corner into the box and the ball dropped for Rudy Gestede to equalise. I gave the goal. What I had missed, somehow, was a blatant barge by Chris Brown in the back of Boro keeper Dimi Konstantopoulos. There was probably another foul on Boro defender Ben Gibson. My position was poor, very poor.

Boro boss Aitor Karanka was screaming at me, finding whatever words he could in English and Spanish. I sent him off, but I shouldn't have done that. My decision had influenced the result. That is the worst feeling as a referee. I should have realised Karanka would not have reacted like that without a genuine grievance.

Because it was an error against a team on my doorstep, I

have probably taken more flak in person for this decision than any other in my career. If ever I am driving down the A19, I will not stop for petrol near Middlesbrough, for the chances are someone will recognise me and mention it. I made the mistake of doing so once and this guy shouted at me across the forecourt.

'Clattenburg, you had a fucking nightmare!'

I am sorry, Boro fans, I got it wrong. Please let me fill up in peace from now on.

11

FA CUP FINAL

'I felt anger, embarrassment, injustice'

Saturday 21 May 2016. FA Cup Final. Wembley Stadium.

*I really don't want to walk up those steps. How many are
there? A hundred and odd? This is going to be torture.
I don't even want my medal. I would prefer to disappear down the tunnel. What enjoyment will there be in
this? Being booed by Crystal Palace fans with the world
watching on TV. I know there will be certain people
taking great satisfaction. They will be loving this. But I
can't escape it now. Here goes. Just get it done and get
the hell out of there.*

BY 2016 I was regarded as the best referee in the country.
I felt at the top of my trade. Is that arrogant? I would say it
was more the confident exterior you need when dealing with
competitive athletes and their egos, and I had worked hard to
get to that level.

Yet, I had still never refereed the FA Cup Final. Why? That
would be David Elleray, the former Premier League referee who

was now chairman of the FA Referees Committee. I always felt he resented my success. He chose who refereed the final and, I believe, never wanted me to get it. He even picked Lee Probert ahead of me for Arsenal versus Hull in 2014. I was refereeing the biggest clubs in Europe, and Elleray chose a middle-of-the-road domestic referee? It felt like bullying.

Elleray had tried to put me down so much over the years that I no longer cared if I was given the Cup Final. I seriously was not bothered, and that is sad given what the occasion had meant to me as a boy. As an elite referee, I was more focused on the Champions League and making it to a major international tournament. Ultimately, Elleray could not control either of those, even if he wanted to.

My problems with him dated back to Blackburn versus Sunderland in August 2002, a Premier League match for which he was referee and I was fourth official. I was still a Football League referee at the time but was being talked about for promotion to the Premier League. At twenty-seven, that was unprecedented.

I turned up at Ewood Park with a bit of stubble on my face. Elleray started laying into me about not being professional. I should have known he was not joking, because he did not have a sense of humour. He was a teacher at Harrow School – one of the most expensive boarding schools in the country – and he was talking to me like a child. I hated that. He thought he could talk down to people and I saw him do that with others, not just me. He was pompous and we did not speak the same language. I would never dream of socialising with someone like him. He drank Earl Grey with his pinkie finger in the air. He once asked me to make him a cup and I felt like saying, 'Where do you want it? Over your fucking head?'

He reported me to PGMOL boss Keith Hackett for the facial hair. How did me not having a shave affect my ability to perform? It felt like an attempt to intimidate a young referee who was trying to make his way in the game. It was as if he felt threatened by me. It was pathetic. We never got on from that moment forward. He was, in my mind, deliberately out to hinder my progress.

Ten years later and I was in Lisbon during the 2012/13 season on a UEFA course. Elleray was also there. By now he had retired from refereeing and was in his FA role. He asked to see me. He said I would not be part of his thinking ahead of Euro 2016. He was going to push Martin Atkinson and Michael Oliver as the FA's preferred representatives. Fuck you. I walked off.

I had just refereed the gold medal match at the 2012 Olympics at Wembley, and he was casting me aside like that? It was ridiculous. It was proof, for me, that this was about more than refereeing ability. I got the impression he wanted me to fail. But, you know what, it spurred me on. I just could not tolerate the man.

Come April 2016, he could no longer ignore me. It was circulating in refereeing channels that I was going to get the Champions League Final. It would have been embarrassing for

Elleray if I took charge of the European showcase having never done my own domestic final. The media would have picked up on it and asked questions. It would have been obvious that ulterior motives were at play.

I believe he panicked and made a snap decision. It was announced that I would referee the FA Cup Final between Manchester United and Crystal Palace. A statement was released and I talked about it being an honour. And it was, I would never disrespect the FA Cup Final, but it was not the same prestigious event that it once was.

As a fan in the Eighties, I would watch the TV coverage from first thing in the morning all the way through to the trophy being lifted. The Cup Final we know now does not have that magic, it is just another game amid a seven-day schedule. Sadly, my own Cup Final experience did nothing to change that feeling.

As a referee, it is downright idiotic what the FA make you do the night before the game. It is their precious Eve of Final Rally at a hotel in central London, a formal event 'steeped in tradition', they say, with the match officials as the guests of honour. It is full of geeks, former referees and old public schoolboys. It was not my scene at all.

So here I was, with Claire, in the back of an FA car, crawling through London traffic. The sun is burning through the glass and all we can see in front of us are red brake lights. I should be in the hotel preparing for the game, not getting wound up by this nonsense. I was hot and bothered, in every sense.

The event itself is just not enjoyable. I had to stand up in front of the room and introduce my team. You then sign hundreds of Cup Final programmes. The entire time I was thinking, 'What on earth am I doing here?'

There was no meal so we went to an Italian restaurant afterwards. It was near enough midnight by the time we got back to the Hendon Hall Hotel in north London. I was tired and pissed off. The whole thing is needless and outdated, a stuffy tradition for the suits. Scrap it. Let the officials relax and get the best preparation. The FA should be prioritising the referee's performance ahead of keeping up appearances with their old boys' network.

I went down for breakfast and Claire was not allowed to come. It is like some secret society full of toffs. You do all the schmoozing with the FA lot, but it is awkward. Lunch as well, it is all so formal and stiff. We then met for photographs on the lawn and travelled to Wembley, although it was far too early. You are sitting around for ages, signing more programmes and shaking hands.

I do not want to come across as ungrateful. I desperately wanted to embrace the day. But it is like going to work for a bad boss who has treated you like a piece of dirt for years and years. I had no respect for Elleray and he had no respect for me, despite what I was doing for English refereeing on a European and international stage. In the moment I was trying my best to enjoy it, but it was forced, I did not feel comfortable the entire day. I will not try to hide that now.

Truth be told, I was the wrong appointment anyway. Palace supporters had it in for me because they had not won any of their previous ten Premier League matches with me as referee. That was a quirk of fate. It wasn't my fault they could not win games. There was even one against Aston Villa, who were hopeless at the time, where Palace goalkeeper Wayne Hennessey chucked the ball into his own net for a 1–0 defeat. There was no bias, it was just one of those things. But fans do not see that. I was on a loser with them before a ball had been kicked. They seized on my appointment and attacked me in the weeks leading up to the final. Elleray should have seen that coming.

There was a lighter moment before the game. Sadly, it was blown up into something it was not. I was coming back into the tunnel after my warm-up. Palace manager Alan Pardew and Steve Coppell, the former Palace boss, were chatting to Sir Alex Ferguson, the former United manager. They all wished me good luck and Sir Alex mimicked pulling an envelope from inside his jacket pocket, making a joke about offering me a bribe.

'God, Sir Alex, you've been doing that for years,' Pardew said.

Everyone laughed, it was funny. But it was also caught on camera and twisted into something else, something quite serious.

The following day, one newspaper wrote, 'Had Pardew seen Clattenburg laughing and joking with Sir Alex Ferguson before kick-off, he may have thought something untoward was going on. Indeed, the official mimicked taking cash from the former United manager.'

Pardew was standing with us, for God's sake!

But I could not speak out to set the record straight. That was always a frustration. So much rubbish was spun or deliberately misinterpreted, yet you were not allowed to say anything about it. What was I meant to do in that situation with Sir Alex and Pardew? Just ignore them? No, it was harmless fun. Given how tedious most of the day can be, it was actually one of the more enjoyable moments.

The game itself, I have to say, was not enjoyable. I made a decision in the seventeenth minute that Palace fans will forever hold against me. Their striker, Connor Wickham, was away down the left. United defender Chris Smalling was tugging at him and both players went down. I blew immediately for a free-kick to Palace but I snatched at the decision. It was not like me, I always allowed the advantage. I should have let play run for a couple of seconds and given Wickham the chance to jump back up, which he did. He then ran into the penalty area and scored.

Maybe the occasion got to me. It certainly affected the singer, Karen Harding, who missed her cue for the National Anthem before the game. I was the opposite. I was too anxious to blow my whistle, like a player who wants an early touch.

Wickham put the ball in the net and Palace's players were in my face, as good as accusing me of disallowing a goal. But let me be clear – should I have played an advantage? Yes, absolutely. I regret not doing so. But was it an obvious goalscoring opportunity? No. Wickham was out wide, there was still an awful lot to do before he scored. Yes, he can argue he did score, but the United defenders had stopped, they were half-hearted.

I booked Smalling for the foul and this is what Palace fans forget, because that yellow card led to him being sent off later in the game, giving them an advantage. But I knew right away that this 'disallowed goal' would be a major talking point. I also knew Elleray and his mates upstairs would be loving it.

Palace took the lead in the seventy-eighth minute. It was a superb goal from substitute Jason Puncheon. The ball was dropped in behind and he ran onto it, one touch to steady himself and a volley to finish across David de Gea. My assistant, John Brooks, made a brave call, because he looked offside. He kept his flag down and replays showed Puncheon was just on. It was a brilliant decision on such a big stage. I had no idea from my position, so it was all on him and he got it spot on.

Puncheon had been dropped by Pardew and I could tell by his celebration that a lot of frustration was coming out. I spoke to him and just reminded him to keep a check on his emotions. I understood how he was feeling and we all want to see that passion, he had just scored a goal he had dreamt about his entire life. But, as a referee, I also want to keep players on the pitch. It was my job to manage those emotions. You are doing the player a favour by working with him, not against him.

I did not see Pardew's infamous dance at the time. He did a little jig after the goal. But that is the type of bloke he was. I found him a strange individual and could not engage with him at all. It was as if he was looking down on you. That dance captures him really – a bit aloof, a bit of a wally.

United equalised three minutes later when Palace allowed

Wayne Rooney to run through them and he crossed for Juan Mata to score. It was another sweet volley but there were mistakes all over the place in the build-up. Puncheon was not smart enough to foul Rooney as he ran through the middle. He should have taken a yellow card for the team, stopped the attack and preserved their lead. Then, they did not prevent the cross. And, when the ball did land in the box, the defending was slack and Mata was unmarked. You can't blame the referee for all of that, can you? Palace had the chance to win the match when they led 1–0 with ten minutes to play but they blew it. That's on them.

We went to extra-time. Right on half-time, still at 1–1, Smalling fouled Yannick Bolasie. It was an easy second yellow and Smalling knew it. So now Palace had an extra man with fifteen minutes to get back in front. Again, what an opportunity.

They failed to take it and Jesse Lingard won it for United with a volley worthy of settling any cup final, it was an awesome strike.

I blew for full-time and, rather than be gracious in defeat, Palace were griping on about a decision I had made two hours earlier. That was all they cared about. I thought that was unjust given how the game played out. They were looking for an excuse when, really, they only had themselves to blame.

I went up to get my medal and was booed, by both sets of supporters. That is not a nice feeling. It was a long and lonely walk. I knew it would happen, at least from the Palace fans, and I did not want to go up those steps. I felt anger, embarrassment, injustice. I had put everything into that match during

120 minutes. Now, I was wishing I had never been awarded the final in the first place.

Palace were always looking for a reason to hammer me and I gave them that chance with the Wickham decision. I regret not allowing play to run on, of course, but I will always maintain that it did not influence the result. If I felt that it had, I would admit as much.

Annoyingly, the controversy also gave Elleray the chance to smile. Claire was upstairs in the lounge with him and Neale Barry, the FA's head of refereeing. She overheard them saying things like, 'I bet that's knocked him down a peg or two.' It made her feel uncomfortable. They looked happy that I had made a mistake, which was no surprise. But could they not keep their glee to themselves in front of my family?

We went for dinner with all of our wives that evening to a French restaurant near Harrow School. Elleray had arranged it. He was sorting the tables and deciding where everyone sat. He tried to move me and Claire apart. Who are you? You're not the schoolmaster now. We just sat where we wanted to in the end, but people were frightened to order a drink. There was a bad atmosphere.

I did not want to be there anyway. I was flat because of the fallout from my decision. I was frustrated because I thought more was being made of it than was fair. I had refereed the match perfectly fine on the whole, that incident apart. I just could not rid myself of that irritation. An awkward meal with Elleray was the last thing I needed.

We got back to the hotel and I went straight to bed. Claire and I went out in London the next day and had a few drinks around Covent Garden, but it was still eating away at me. I was not great company.

Was I being too sensitive? If I made a mistake then I accepted what followed, as unpleasant as that could be. That goes with the territory. But, in the case of the Cup Final, it was the fact I was being vilified for one error that had been blown into this huge, game-changing moment. It was not as significant as some were making out, and that pissed me off. As did the mischievous reports about Ferguson's 'bribe' – it felt like there was an agenda against me.

We got the train home and I had twenty-four hours to snap out of it. The Champions League Final was the following weekend, and I was not going to let anything spoil that. From there I was heading to the European Championship in France.

I look back now and do not have any love for my memory of the FA Cup Final. I try to blank it out. I am proud of the achievement, but that is different to having affection for it. My medal is there with all the others. I never look at it. I have never even watched the game back. What would I achieve by reliving it? I would just get a negative vibe, and that has as much to do with the whole weekend as it does the game itself. If that is how the FA want to make people feel, people who had worked hard for them over many years, then I want nothing to do with them.

One moment did provide me with some perspective on the

day, and I will always remember this. United manager Louis van Gaal knocked at my dressing-room door after the game and had a signed shirt for me. I liked him a lot as a man, he had a bit of fire about him.

'Mark, thank you for everything. It's been a pleasure knowing you,' he said.

'Eh? What's up?' I asked.

'I've just been sacked!'

So while I felt bad about myself, it was nothing compared to what he was feeling. And I still had plenty to look forward to that summer.

12

CHAMPIONS LEAGUE FINAL

**'72,000 fans and 400 million more watching on TV . . .
I was terrified'**

Early hours of Saturday 28 May 2016. Milan, Italy.

I can't sleep. Even the few minutes I do manage are invaded with nightmares. In one of them, my alarm doesn't go off and I miss the match. But that's stupid, it's an 8.45 p.m. kick-off. I finally nod off and it starts again – I forget my cards, my shorts split and they fall down during the game. This is torture. Thankfully, by 3 a.m., I am too tired to even dream. I fall into a deep sleep. I am going to need it. Tomorrow is the real dream. It is the Champions League Final. Real Madrid versus Atletico Madrid at the San Siro. And I'm the referee.

I WILL never forget the phone call. I was driving down the M1 to St George's Park for our fortnightly referees' meeting when my mobile rang. It was Pierluigi Collina, the head of referees at UEFA. Oh no, I usually got a bollocking when the boss called out of the blue. I pulled over, I wanted to take the call properly. You don't shout down the car phone to Collina.

What followed took me completely by surprise. It had been reported that week in the Spanish media that Jonas Eriksson, from Sweden, would referee the Champions League Final. I was close to Jonas, one of my best friends in refereeing, so I was happy for him. Part of me was hoping to be fourth official. That would have been another step towards a major European final of my own. I had refereed the Atletico Madrid versus Bayern Munich semi-final, and no one had ever done that and the final in the same season, so it was never in my thoughts. I was still half expecting a ticking-off.

Collina started by congratulating me on getting the FA Cup Final, which had been announced a few days earlier. This was all very positive. Where is he going with it?

'How would you like to go to Milan?' he said.

'Wow, great,' I said. 'It would be a pleasure to be fourth official to Jonas.'

'No, you're going to be referee.'

'Who? Me?'

'You don't want to?'

'No, no, no, of course I do!'

'Okay, then. I think you deserve it.'

I rejoined the motorway in a blur and tucked into the inside lane, trying to process it all. Well, at least I did once I'd stopped screaming!

My goal at the start of the season had been to get a

Champions League semi-final, and I had done that. But this was surreal. During the call I was still thinking, 'Why me? I'm just a daft Geordie who used to be an electrician!'

I'd had so much shit thrown at me over the years. I thought about all those barriers, especially the opposition from Mike Riley and David Elleray. This was two fingers to all of that. I thought, 'You know what, Collina believes in me, he always has.'

The first person I called was Claire.

'What? You're refereeing the Champions League Final?' she said.

I had gone from Collina to my wife, she didn't have any belief in me! The conversation quickly turned to fashion and questions like, 'What shoes will I wear?' But Claire was right, a bit of practical thinking. The reality kicked in. It is all well and good calling your friends and family and getting the congratulations, but then you realise, 'I've actually got to referee this game. Oh, and it's a Madrid derby!'

I walked into St George's high as a kite but Collina had warned me not to say a word to the others. We did our usual session and Lee Mason said to me, 'Wow, you trained well.' No wonder, I was still pumped full of adrenaline, especially as I knew it was being announced at 5 p.m.

I was upstairs in my room watching *Sky Sports News*, ready for it to break on the hour. Straight away the messages started arriving. For all the abuse referees take, moments like this were what I had spent twenty-five years working towards – from a linesman in the Northern League to refereeing the Champions League Final. In that instant, it all felt so worthwhile.

I walked downstairs into the dining room and all of my colleagues stood up and applauded. That was special. Put aside the politics of refereeing, to get acknowledgement like that from my peers meant the world to me. Even though me and Martin Atkinson did not see eye to eye, he still had the decency to clap. He would have been hurting inside.

There was always a bitterness in refereeing that meant some did not want others to do well, especially in the Champions League. So yes, part of me was thinking to a few people, 'Fuck you.' Certainly to Riley, my PGMOL boss. I had made it this far without his support, but that drove me on. I needed people against me to perform, it motivated me in proving them wrong. If Riley and Elleray had actually backed me, I do not think I would have achieved what I did, I would have got bored. They did not do it deliberately with that in mind, it was not clever reverse psychology. They did it because, I believe, they preferred to see others doing better than me.

I always felt it irritated them when I was doing well in the Champions League. That was beyond their remit, they could not affect Collina's thinking. And I believe I performed better in Europe than I did domestically. Maybe that was because of the pressure. If you made glaring errors in a UEFA game, you might not get another that season. It could be quite brutal like that. The financial rewards also sharpened your focus. We got around €6,500 per game. If you did ten matches a season, you suddenly felt a lot more comfortable. It was the difference between a summer in Durham and Dubai.

I remember having a shocker when Bayern Munich played Juventus in the Champions League quarter-final of 2013. I missed an obvious red card when Bayern forward Franck Ribery stamped on Arturo Vidal. I got a low score from the observer and the media coverage was pretty scathing. I came home and told Claire that I had messed up, that I might not get another game.

'What? All season?' she said.

As a family you get used to that extra money and the nice holidays. So the pressure was huge, from all sides!

But I had made it to the Champions League Final, the absolute pinnacle of the club game. Now I had to start preparing for it. I spoke to my team one by one at St George's Park. Jake Collin and Simon Beck were my two assistant referees. Andre Marriner and Anthony Taylor were my additional assistant referees.

When Jake was first assigned to me for a Champions League game in 2014, Elleray had not nominated him as one the best eight assistants for the competition, yet he was now giving him to me. It felt like, 'Fuck you, Clattenburg.'

I rang Jake at the time and said to him, 'Welcome to my team.' He started getting emotional.

'The hard work starts now,' I told him. 'You need to lose weight, because you're a fat fucker like I was, so start grafting. If you work hard, I'll support you.'

Our first game together was a Champions League play-off in August 2014, Leverkusen versus Copenhagen. He was brilliant, top notch. I sent a message to Elleray afterwards, hoping it would wind him up. 'Jake was excellent, thanks.'

I was then down to referee on Champions League Matchday One the following month. I got a phone call from Jake. He was upset. He told me he was no longer an assistant and had been made fourth official. Elleray had changed it, stabbing me in the back.

I called UEFA and spoke to Hugh Dallas, our referees officer. I told him I was quitting and didn't hold back. I was not putting up with crap like this anymore. Hugh calmed me down.

'Mark, please, don't worry, we'll sort it.'

I only ever spoke to Elleray when I had to after that. And that was fine by me.

*   *   *

My team and I met in the Hotel Sofitel at Heathrow Airport on Thursday 26 May, two days before the Champions League Final.

I could feel the tension among the group, myself included. I had refereed the FA Cup Final the previous Saturday, and that had been a disaster. We had a beer and tried to relax but my mind was racing with all the logistical stuff, such as match tickets, flights and hotels for our guests. You want everyone to have the best possible day, not just you.

But then going through Heathrow on the Friday morning, it felt like I was floating on air. You don't often experience that as a referee, you're normally weighed down by some worry or other. But here we were, all looking dapper in our suits, people wishing us good luck, heading off to represent our country in the biggest club match on the planet. It was a rare moment of appreciation.

When we landed in Milan it was the VIP treatment, whisked off in blacked-out people-carriers with a police escort to the hotel. We had to train at the San Siro that evening, although I usually preferred to find a park for a jog, just to avoid all of the media at the stadium. We did a bit of running on the pitch just to look professional, because you never knew if Collina was watching.

It also gave us a chance to get the photos out the way. I hated it when any of my team took selfies on matchday. We're not tourists, we were here to do a job. And this was some job. I was being consulted on everything from the coin toss to the timings of the pre-match singer to where the medals would be collected. I felt like a party-planner.

We got back to the hotel and were told we could not go out into Milan. Thankfully, Collina and Dallas were heading out for dinner, so at least we could have one beer. There was never any chance of a drink with Collina around. When the big fella was there, you were even careful about what you were reading. We went to bed after 10 p.m. But not to sleep, no chance.

Finally, after a day of clock-watching, pacing my room and studying the teams and their tactics one last time, we left the hotel for the San Siro two hours before kick-off. The journey was hell. It was like the chase scene from *The Italian Job*. It was 30°C and you are in a suit. I felt sick. We were weaving in and out of traffic and it was chaos, horns and sirens blaring all around us.

I was so wound up by the time we arrived that I had to take five minutes to myself during the warm-up. I sat there on the pitch, doing a few stretches and looking all around the stadium, this iconic venue that I had first seen on TV during Italia '90. It is a truly magnificent place for football.

'This is it,' I thought, 'the biggest game of my life. Do it well and it will be the best game of your life.' Then the nerves kick in . . . 'What if I make a big mistake?' I had to force all of that from my thinking. I had to remind myself why I was here in the first place.

The tunnel at the San Siro is long enough for a thousand thoughts to race through your mind in those moments after leaving the dressing-room for the last time. Have I forgotten my cards? Where's my coin? Is my whistle loud enough? I got to the end of the tunnel about seven minutes before kick-off and waited. And waited. The singer, Alicia Keys, was taking ages. Sergio Ramos, the Real Madrid captain, was standing next to me.

'Go and tell her to quit, will you?' he said.

'What can I do? You go and tell her!' I told him.

It eased the tension, for both of us. I got the nod to start walking towards the pitch and all I'm thinking is, 'I've got to pick this matchball off the plinth without dropping it.' It is ridiculous what goes through your head when under stress. Even for the coin toss I was worried about getting the flick right, to the point where I'd been practising!

Then, as you emerge into the stadium, in front of 72,000 fans and 400 million more watching on TV all around the world, it suddenly becomes very real. I can honestly say, I was terrified.

★   ★   ★

My plan was to let the match breathe, at least within the *Laws of the Game*. After ten minutes I said to my team down the headsets, 'This isn't working.'

Both sets of players were constantly in my ear. That is what this lot were like, every decision was being challenged. I thought, 'I need a yellow card here, I need to take control.' Real defender Dani Carvajal flew into Antoine Griezmann. That was my moment – thank you. It presented itself and I thought, 'I'm having that.' The game calmed down. Well, at least it did for five minutes.

Then, from a Toni Kroos free-kick, Ramos bundled the ball over the line from a couple of yards out to make it 1–0 to Real. The stadium erupted, a feverish noise that I had to block out. I was trying to process what had happened. I had not watched Kroos take the free-kick. He was behind me and I was standing on the edge of the penalty area, observing what was going on in the box. I knew these players too well, someone would be trying to bend the rules somewhere.

As the ball came in, I saw Real forward Gareth Bale flick it on with his head. It landed in a crowd of bodies in the goal-mouth and Ramos poked it in.

Simon Beck was my assistant at that end. He'd had a bit of a rough time in Europe that season and I was slightly concerned about him going into the final. I was shouting to him down the headset.

'Simon, do you understand there was a Real touch before the ball got to Ramos? Are you sure Ramos was onside?'

There was no answer. I am panicking now. I said it about four times and there was still no response. I looked across to the line and I feared that Simon had frozen. He was staring up at the big screen, looking for help.

It was too late. We did not have VAR. It was the most critical moment of the game so far, and I was getting nothing from Simon. I was telling him there had been a flick by Bale but the information was not going in. After about ten seconds, he came back to us on the headsets.

'I'm okay, I'm okay,' he said. 'The headset went off.'

Rubbish. They did not stop working all of a sudden. I gave the goal, I had no choice, Simon was not telling me to disallow it. I was unnerved, because I suspected Ramos was offside.

As we walked off at half-time, still 1–0 to Real, I could tell by Simon's body language he was not comfortable. He was trying to look at his mobile phone in the dressing-room to see if he had made a mistake. I hated that and never allowed it. I tried to cajole him, we still had a big half in front of us and that decision had gone. Before we headed back out, it was said to me that Ramos was just offside. As a referee, if there has been a perceived error, I then have to manage that.

In the tunnel, Griezmann and the Atletico captain, Gabi, were waiting for me. They asked about the goal. I told them I thought it was marginally offside. Gabi could be spiky and I was expecting a nasty reaction, but he just touched my arm and said, 'Okay.' He accepted the mistake. If I had denied it or tried to defend the decision, you cause more aggravation, it intensifies their feeling of injustice. If you lie to players, you lose them.

Some people might be surprised at what I am about to say, but I was now waiting for a decision in Atletico's favour to get some balance back in the game. I would not give them something unwarranted, absolutely not. And if the next big call was a penalty for Real, then so be it. But you have to be conscious of what has gone before, because it helps you control players' emotions.

I only had to wait one minute into the second half when Real defender Pepe came through the back of Fernando Torres in the penalty area. It was a senseless challenge. Torres was clever, he put his body in a position where he knew Pepe would catch him if he dived in, which he did.

When you are presented with that decision after the injustice of Real's goal in the first half, you are going to take it. It restored the balance. I had not made it up, I was not giving them a soft penalty to say sorry for the offside goal. Not at all. It was a clear penalty.

What I am trying to explain is that, in terms of game

management, me awarding Atletico a penalty evened things out in the minds of their players. They would be easier to control after that. For Atletico, the aggravation of the offside goal was forgotten about.

I still had Pepe to deal with and he was a handful, a player who would challenge you from first minute to last. He came towards me, screaming that it was not a penalty. I spoke to him calmly.

'Your first goal was offside,' I said.

It defused the situation and it shut him up.

Listen, two wrongs do not make a right – and this was a penalty, I stand by that – but you have to understand the psychology of a footballer's logic. Me saying that to Pepe gave him a reason to accept the decision, and he did.

Griezmann then stepped up and smacked the penalty off the crossbar. I had to laugh in my head, 'You've had your chance to even it up, you can't blame me now.' The game was easier to manage after that moment. The players began to influence it, not me, and that is what you want.

Atletico midfielder Yannick Carrasco equalised with eleven minutes remaining, smashing in from a couple of yards out. It was pure theatre, Carrasco running to his girlfriend in the crowd. I did not mind that. Some referees might have booked him, I thought it added to the occasion, and it did not cause a delay. The contest had now grown into the spectacle we all hoped for, and I felt in control.

It was 1–1 after ninety minutes, it had been a cracking game.

Sadly, extra-time was a waste of time. Both teams had given their all and it felt like neither had the energy to go and win it.

Pepe, though, always had enough in reserve for trying to con the referee. He started rolling around on the floor, trying to get Carrasco sent off. It was nothing, he had barely brushed his face. Pepe reacted exactly how I knew he would, lashing about as if he had been punched on the nose, it was laughable. I just stood over him, shaking my head. Did he think I was stupid? He was not spoiling the biggest game of my career by tricking me into giving a red card. Get up, you soft shite. He did, eventually. It makes both sets of players realise you will not be fooled and it showed Pepe up for what he was.

But that is when I did it, that thing with my tongue which people will be asking me about for the rest of my life, licking my lips at twenty to the dozen. It became known as 'Clattenburg's Lizard Tongue' on social media. People always ask, 'Were you calling him a pussy?' Maybe subconsciously I was, not that I realised at the time. I don't know what I was thinking. The fact I was so dehydrated is perhaps the best explanation.

But what Pepe did was embarrassing. The likes of him, Ramos and Atletico defender Diego Godin, they had all been at it. They were sly, you could not trust them. I had refereed them so many times that I just ignored their deceit, whereas another referee might get sucked in. That is where Collina was clever in appointing me to this fixture. Yes, they would still try it on, but the players knew where they stood with me, I had made my position clear over several seasons.

We got to the end of extra-time with the score still at 1–1. It was a relief. Like the players, I was on my last legs and I told my team as much during those final few minutes.

'I'm not seeing things properly here, help me out!'

When you blow for penalties, it is perfect for a referee. You are leaving it to the players. There is always a hero and a villain, and it is never you. Juanfran missed Atletico's fourth, meaning Real had to score their fifth to win.

Here he came, his Lordship. Cristiano Ronaldo, shorts hiked up around his thighs. He had done jack shit all game and here he was, this was his moment and he was not going to miss. He was carrying an injury and he probably shouldn't have played. He had barely had a kick. But I knew he would make this one count, that is what the greatest players do.

All I cared about was getting the matchball. That was mine. I felt like I was in the starting blocks, ready to sprint for the back of the net. Goalkeepers often used to boot it away in frustration when they lost a shootout, and I could hardly go climbing into the stands asking for my ball back. Ronaldo stepped up and scored. Of course he did. Real were the champions of Europe.

I only caught sight of Ronaldo ripping off his shirt from the corner of my eye. My focus was locked on the ball, which had bounced out of the goal and was rolling through the six-yard area. Not for long it wasn't. It was soon in my possession, and that was where it stayed.

A word on Ronaldo. He was the best player I ever refereed. He was never a problem and I never once had cause to book him. I knew how to handle him. When he was playing well, he was easy, he was happy. When he or his team were struggling, just leave him alone. He could be moody and you risked antagonising him with needless chatter. I had that knack of measuring his temperament.

But it was a luxury to be on the pitch with him. He had this God-like power whereby he could lift an entire stadium and every one of his team-mates, just at the moment when they needed it most. I swear you could physically feel the energy he generated. It was genius. I respected his mentality so much. He was a winner who got every last ounce of potential from himself.

After one game, I was shocked when he came into my dressing-room with a signed shirt, 'To Mark, Best Wishes, Cristiano Ronaldo.' I had not asked for the jersey, it was just a kind gesture because, over the years, our relationship had grown. Every time I refereed one of his finals, his team won. So maybe that and the fact I never booked him was the reason for the surprise gift!

And here we were in the Champions League Final. He had done close to nothing for 120 minutes and it was still The Cristiano Ronaldo Show. I had to smile. Fair play to him.

But after his winning penalty I suddenly felt on edge, just like I had before kick-off. A week earlier I had been booed by both sets of fans at Wembley as I went up to collect my medal after the FA Cup Final. Would it happen again?

I began the walk towards the steps at the San Siro. I

would have settled for no reaction, for my ascent to pass by unnoticed. But as I climbed the stairs I realised people were on their feet and were applauding. What? No booing? My anxiety was gone in an instant, I relaxed and took it all in. I thought of my dad and hoped he was looking down; he would have been here.

As I received my medal, FIFA president Gianni Infantino leaned over and spoke in my ear.

'I look forward to seeing you at the World Cup in 2018,' he said.

Infantino did not know I would quit the Premier League the following year, and neither did I at this point.

When I got back to the dressing-room, Collina was waiting for me outside. He gave me a big cuddle. He thanked me for controlling the game – a big derby, a lot of hatred. I broke down, weeping in front of my boss. I had been on a long and difficult journey and Collina was the one who backed me more than anyone else. But I needed to stop crying. What I needed was a beer, and quick.

Thankfully, Heineken were one of the sponsors. During the match they had left 120 bottles in the winning dressing-room. The losers got bugger all. I walked back into the referee's room and there they were, 120 green bottles stacked on the floor.

'Heineken must think we're winners, lads, get stuck in,' I said.

And so we did. We sat there and had a few beers, exhausted but elated. It had never tasted so good. Maybe I was on a high, but I really believed this was the best I had ever refereed, certainly in terms of managing an occasion and a rivalry that had the potential for trouble. I had not influenced the result and either team could have won.

A lot of people wanted me to fail after the FA Cup Final, all because I did not play one advantage to Crystal Palace. I was going into the Champions League Final plagued by negative thoughts because of that. So to sit here, with my kit still on, enjoying a beer with my team, knowing that Collina was happy, it felt so good.

Some Atletico fans do still blame me for them losing the final. But, like Palace, they had their chance to win the match, regardless of any earlier decisions. Diego Simeone, the Atletico manager, came up to me on the pitch afterwards and pounded his chest and said, 'Well done.' He meant it, I think. That meant a lot to me. I liked Simeone. He was passionate and I respected how he managed his team, his players responded to his energy.

I finally switched my phone back on in the dressing-room. It would not stop buzzing. Here I was, on the greatest night of my career, and my WhatsApp has been taken over by clips of 'Lizard Tongue'! Even Collina mentioned it. I played it straight with him, 'Nah boss, I was just thirsty.'

From the San Siro we went straight to a restaurant for a celebration dinner for the officials. It was after midnight by now and they had kept a private room open for us. My team and I turned up with our wives. Mike Riley and Keren Barratt from the PGMOL were already there, which was not planned. I did not want them to be, I did not like them. UEFA had invited them thinking there was no problem. If they had asked me, I would have blocked it.

Barratt was the Select Group manager. He made life awkward for me. There was one example in 2012 when he knew I was landing back in Newcastle from a game in Bilbao at 10 p.m. on a Friday evening, and yet he appointed me to West Brom versus Aston Villa the following day, 200 miles away. I managed to change my flight to suit me better with the help of UEFA, but that is what he was like. If I wanted to be in London for the weekend, I would request a game up north, knowing he would appoint me to a southern match just to spite me.

But I was not letting them two spoil my night here, even though Riley was sitting next to me. He is a boring fucker. He had a few drinks and promised that, if I was awarded the Euro 2016 final in July, the PGMOL would pay for all of our guests to fly out. Of course, I later did get the final. He paid for my guests but only half for the rest of the team, which was shameful.

I did enjoy watching him eat a dessert of humble pie that night in Milan. I always felt he wanted me to fail, that he wanted Martin Atkinson, one of his neighbours, to get the Champions League Final. From giving me a one-match suspension for going to an Ed Sheeran concert to putting me on a Shrewsbury game over Christmas just to piss me off, it was like he was trying to break me. But he couldn't, and that night with my Champions League medal on the table in front of us, he knew it.

I got back to the hotel at 5 a.m. but Claire was not allowed to stay with me after the game. I rang her at 7 a.m., I was crying. It panicked her.

'What's wrong? Have you been attacked?' she asked.

It sounds soft – and maybe I'd had a few beers and was tired – but the emotion of it all just hit me. There was a feeling of great satisfaction but also emptiness. It was all over.

I also thought of my dad and how he would have loved to be in the San Siro watching me. And where was my mam? We had not spoken for four years by this stage. I wondered what pride my parents would have felt, had they been there. Everything came out in that moment, a release of emotions I had probably bottled up over years and years.

We stayed an extra day in Milan and went out shopping. Claire took me into Zara. I have just refereed the Champions League Final and I am standing on my own outside a changing room in fucking Zara. Talk about a come-down.

My friend, Ian King, and his wife had been to the game and we met them for a drink. Michael Laudrup, the former Barcelona and Real Madrid forward, came into the same restaurant and joined us for a little while. It picked me up massively, sitting among friends and sharing stories from our weekend.

But then, on the flight home, you realise that normal life starts again – the school run, the dishwasher, the gym. You feel lost. It took me a few days to recover, not that I had any longer than that. Now, I had to get my head right for Euro 2016. It was relentless, but I could not rest on what I had already achieved that year. I was chasing a hat-trick.

13

EURO 2016

'I never thought I would be so desperate for England to lose'

Monday 27 June 2016. Irish Bar, Enghien-les-Bains, nine miles outside of Paris, France.

Iceland are winning 2–1. It's injury-time, only a few seconds left. England have been poor. I am angry, because I'm an England fan, but fuck that. Hold on, Iceland, hold on. If England are going home, I'm not. There are other England fans here in the bar. They are screaming England forward. I'm sitting on my hands. Clear it! And there it is, the full-time whistle. Relief. Joy. Disappointment? Not anymore. England deserved to lose, so forget them. We are the winners tonight, me and my team. I do not say anything to them but, inside, I am ready to burst. I know what this could mean. It means I am now favourite to referee the final of Euro 2016. Lads, what you drinking?

I WAS in the people-carrier with my team travelling to referee Leicester City versus Chelsea in December 2015 – the match which turned out to be Jose Mourinho's last as Chelsea manager – when Pierluigi Collina's name came up on my phone. Why is the boss calling me on a Monday night just before Christmas?

'Congratulations,' he said.

'What for?'

'You're part of the selection process for Euro 2016. But keep that to yourself for now.'

'Okay, boss. Thank you.'

I told the team, they were sitting right next to me after all. No matter what Christmas might bring us, nothing would beat this. As a kid, I would not miss a kick of World Cups and European Championships, so the thought of going to one as a referee stirred that child-like excitement.

If selected, and at this point I thought that was a formality, it would be my first major tournament as a referee. I had been expecting to go to the 2014 World Cup in Brazil – I was on the shortlist and did all of the camps in preparation – but Howard Webb decided he wanted to stay on, even though it was thought he would step aside after refereeing the 2010 final in South Africa. I do not know why he did that. Had the PGMOL encouraged him to, just to scupper me? I never did get an answer.

But now, after all of my problems with Mike Riley, the PGMOL and the Football Association, to get this opportunity to go to Euro 2016 felt like proof that I had beaten their resistance.

It was only the following day when all of the referees met up at St George's Park that I discovered Martin Atkinson was also part of the selection process. That soured it. I did not think UEFA would send two referees from the same country – they had not done previously. It killed my good mood.

As I have written about earlier, Atkinson and I did not get on. I thought he was very jealous and was more interested in seeing me fail, when he should have been concentrating on himself. We had both been to Euro 2012 as additional assistant referees in Howard's team. Atkinson had also refereed the Europa League Final in 2015. In the opinion of some, he was probably favourite to go to the Euros ahead of me. I just kept my focus. I wanted to give Collina and UEFA a headache. I might not be the FA and PGMOL's preferred man, but I would show UEFA that I deserved to go instead of Atkinson.

Thankfully, Collina broke the usual protocol and picked both of us, and I was happy with that. I did not care if there was one of us or ten of us from England. Atkinson no doubt thought he was our number one. Maybe he was, but not for long. By the end of the 2015/16 season, I had refereed the FA Cup and Champions League finals, elevating me above him going into the Euros.

But at that point in December 2015, I was determined to push harder to get ahead, and that is exactly what I did.

I used Steve Bennett, the former Premier League referee, to help me from a mental perspective. I asked if I could call him every now and then just to sound off, especially when I felt opposition from the likes of Riley and David Elleray. Steve calmed me down and got me to use that frustration to my advantage.

Physically, I started going to the gym every day. I did not afford myself any rest. UEFA actually warned me I was doing too much. But I could not and would not stop. My weight came down to 75 kg – when I started in the Premier League it was 95 kg. I was watching my games back and I was like Billy Whizz. There was one clip, and Gary Neville made mention of it in commentary, where I kept pace with Liverpool's Daniel Sturridge during a counter-attack and I was going past defenders. My ability to run further and faster than ever before was driven by the motivation to be the best referee at Euro 2016.

We arrived in France in early June, a week before the tournament kicked off. My team was the same as from the Champions League Final just a week earlier. Simon Beck and Jake Collin as assistant referees, Andre Marriner and Anthony Taylor as additionals. Atkinson had Michael Oliver and Craig Pawson as his additionals. People often ask why I did not have Michael with me, us both being Geordies. It was an FA decision and I was happy to stick with it. I trusted my two assistants and I cared about that more than anything else. We had a good team and we protected each other. They knew that if I failed, they failed. I worked hard to keep a good spirit between us.

During the tournament, all of the referees were staying in a hotel overlooking a lake in Enghien-les-Bains, just outside of Paris. It was an amazing place. We had a week-long training camp before the tournament and, on the last night, I took my team out for a meal and a beer. A newspaper got some pictures of us and tried to make something of it. We just laughed it off.

Simon and Jake were good craic to have a beer with as well, they were just normal lads. I liked Taylor and Marriner but they were slightly different, they were a bit more geeky about refereeing. I loved being a referee, do not get me wrong, but I still enjoyed life. I wanted to be true to the lad I always was growing up, not conform to how some referees thought they should behave. Just be yourself.

One concern going into the tournament was terrorism. The Paris attacks, in which 130 people were killed, had happened the previous November. There was a bomb outside the Stade de France that night and my family were worried the tournament would be targeted. But we felt safe. You could not walk five metres without seeing a policeman with a gun and we always had security around us when on official duty.

The hardest thing, I found, was waiting between matches. The first round of appointments were announced and I was not involved. Do they not like me here? I wanted an early game, it was torture not knowing when or where I would be refereeing first.

The first big match of the group stage, between two of the fancied countries, was Belgium versus Italy, four days into the tournament. The email with the latest appointments landed at midday, every day. We were all in the dining room, everyone looking down at their phones. There it was – Belgium versus Italy, Mark Clattenburg. Get in! I was pumping my fist under the table. It felt like a marquee game, and Collina trusted me with it.

Monday 13 June.
Belgium 0 Italy 2. Parc Olympique Lyonnais, Lyon.

UEFA wanted this match to set the tone for the tournament from a refereeing perspective and I felt that I managed it well. Belgium were poor and Italy deserved to win. It was such a good feeling to get my first game at a major tournament under my belt without any controversy. I got a nice message from Collina afterwards. I texted back, 'Thank you, but I'm sure there are small improvements I can make.' It never paid to be too cocky with the boss.

We got called into a debrief the following day with Collina and his team, Hugh Dallas and Marc Bator. These debriefs could be just as important as the game, it was no time to be snoozing. Collina's style was to praise what you had done well but also to challenge you. He turned to me.

'Why did you play an advantage to Italy in the ninetieth minute when they're winning 2–0? They wanted the free-kick. Why are you being stupid?'

He was right. Italy wanted to absorb time, not push for a third. Realising little things like that made me a better referee. You should be adaptable, able to read the situation of the match. Players respect you more when they feel you understand the game.

At Euro 2012, the tournament started on a negative for the officials when Spanish referee Carlos Velasco sent off Poland goalkeeper Wojciech Szczęsny for a foul in the penalty area.

The decision was right but there was some debate about it. The media started to attack and that carried on over the next four weeks.

But Euro 2016 had started well. We were looking to protect the players but also trying to get as much playing time as possible, keep the ball alive. That suited my style. We were also very clear on what would be punished and what would not, and that strength of conviction came from Collina.

My tournament began how I finished the Champions League Final, allowing the players to get on with the game. It was a relatively new approach. In the past it was always whistle, whistle, whistle, whereas I would let a player lie on the floor if I thought he had gone down easily. Just leave them, they'll soon get the message. Players started to stay on their feet. We did not fall into their trap. Instead, they were falling into ours. The tournament was all the better for it.

Friday 17 June. Czech Republic 2 Croatia 2. Stade Geoffroy-Guichard, Saint-Etienne.

As referee, I was never called into the security briefing on the morning of a match. I was here. The game, I was told, would be stopped at some point by hooligans and there would be crowd trouble. The match was high risk because the locals in Saint-Etienne had sold tickets to Croatian ultras. It caused UEFA a serious headache. They did not know who they were or where they would be, it was a nightmare scenario we were facing. They briefed me on what to expect, although they could not be sure when it would happen.

We got to eighty-five minutes but still nothing. It was 2–1 to Croatia. Then, what on earth? Fireworks and flares were coming towards the pitch, there was fighting in the stands. Croatia striker Mario Mandzukic tried to go across to plead with them to stop. Is he daft? He could get badly hurt, this lot didn't care about him. I quickly took him out of the situation. Above all else, I had to make sure everyone was safe.

I stopped the game and led the players to the side of the pitch, far enough away from danger. But I was not taking them back to the dressing-room. Bollocks to the idiots. If we go off, they win. You just think, why? Why spoil it for your own team? But this was about politics at club level in Croatia. They were not interested in what happened in this game, they just wanted to cause disruption and make headlines.

I had a plan in my head of how to deal with it and all went well, until I realised I had forgotten to stop the clock. When we restarted I did not have a clue how long was left. Small details like that I did not like getting wrong.

Within a couple of minutes I gave a penalty to Czech Republic for handball, a fair decision. They scored and the game finished 2–2. Refereeing wise I left the pitch and felt I had done well. I got another message from Collina saying as much. 'Brilliant,' or so I thought.

We had our debrief the following day back at the hotel.

Collina said I was not at the same level as the previous game. Oh God. He said I looked tired. Maybe it was two games in five days? But if he thought that, I was listening. It did not matter how wonderful I thought I was, I took the advice. I told him I agreed.

Looking back, I think he was worried about my participation later in the tournament. He wanted me at my best. Now, I know why he said that. He was protecting me.

My additionals, Taylor and Marriner, asked me after the debrief why I had agreed with Collina, they thought it could cost me. But it does not cost you, I told them. If you are honest with people then they think better of you. Refereeing always seemed to be about hiding mistakes and trying to get away with it. Yes, you have to survive and protect yourself, but you cannot hide. Try to improve, that was always my way. Tackle things head on and deal with it. Do not be a bluffer. I knew Collina respected that.

Sunday 25 June.
Switzerland 1 Poland 1 (Poland win 5–4 on penalties).
Stade Geoffroy-Guichard, Saint-Etienne.

Collina had said to me in the previous debrief, 'You're not on holiday, Mark. Be prepared.' That was at the forefront of my mind.

I was now tasked with the first knockout game of the tournament, and that felt significant. If I did well and England went out, I knew I was one of the leading candidates for the final.

That was still a little way off, of course, but the thought was there, especially after what Collina had said. Perhaps I was distracted or even unsettled by that prospect, because there were certain elements of this game with which I was far from happy.

Five minutes in and the ball was heading towards Anthony Taylor, my additional assistant on the by-line. Switzerland's Stephan Lichtsteiner, who was on the attack, touched the ball as it went out. Was the touch before it crossed the line? Was it a goal-kick or corner? From my angle, I could not really tell. I gave the goal-kick. Lichtsteiner ran past, giving me a load of verbals.

'It's a fucking corner!' he was yelling.

I never liked Lichtsteiner, he was always a pain in the arse. At the same time, Taylor was in my headset.

'Corner, corner, corner!' he was shouting.

My assistant referee, Simon Beck, was saying the same. I stuck with a goal-kick. I then heard Taylor.

'Just forget about it Mark, move onto the next one.'

I went back down the headset.

'Give it a fucking rest, man. It's only a corner or a goal-kick. Bloody hell, it's not a big decision.'

We moved on but I was getting a bit sick of the guys, they were irritating me. An injured player was being led away from the pitch by the physio. Jake Collin, my assistant, was screaming down the headset.

'Stop the game! Stop the game! The medical bag is still on the pitch.'

Was he winding me up?

'Mate, pick the bag up and bring it off yourself, it's right next to you,' I said.

It was common sense, don't shout down my headset when I'm following play. Little things like that were annoying me.

Earlier in the game, the balls were soft. I always got Simon Beck to check them. It was the fourth official's job but I used to say to Simon, 'Don't trust anyone else outside of our team, just trust ourselves'. Simon did not check them, and they were flat.

This was Euro 2016, not a Sunday morning kickabout with your mates. Details like that make you look incompetent, and apparently Collina was going mad. It was amateurish. The last-16 of a major tournament and the balls are soft. Because of us. Because we did not check them. I went crazy with Simon at half-time. Maybe I was getting anxious. We were into the latter stages and had been away from home for three weeks. I knew the stakes were high.

The game went to extra-time and then penalties after a 1–1 draw. We did the coin toss and I walked towards the penalty box with the two goalkeepers. I explained to them about staying on their line. I did not know this at the time but me instructing the goalkeepers was being broadcast to the world. UEFA liked that. It was proactive refereeing. What we did not want was to re-spot a penalty. That is never a nice feeling. For me, if a player misses, he should miss, not get a second chance because a keeper steps a foot from his line. Switzerland's Granit Xhaka missed the only penalty here and Poland were through to the quarter-final.

Then, just when we thought we were done, a scuffle broke out among the players coming off the pitch. Bloody hell, I can do without this, a brawl on my watch. I got involved and pushed a few people away. I calmed the situation and got the teams back into the dressing-rooms, but this was a negative. Could I have managed it better? I was on edge. Collina texted me, 'Well done.' I'll take that, it had been a stressful afternoon.

We did the debrief the next day. Collina starts with the incident involving Lichtsteiner.

'Mark, we've got the audio, although we'll not repeat what you actually said.'

That was probably for the best, given my language. He asked me to explain the decision.

'The ball has definitely come off Lichtsteiner. But I'm not sure if he was on or off the pitch,' I said.

'So then why did you not follow the advice of your team?' Collina asked.

'Do you want my honesty?'

'Yes.'

'It doesn't matter if this decision is right or wrong, it's a matter of millimetres either way. But if I give a goal-kick and it's wrong, the TV companies will show the replay once. They'll say it should have been a corner and move on. But if I give a corner and it's wrong, and Switzerland score from it, it will be replayed twenty times. It will be the major talking point from the game. The headlines will be about us costing Poland a goal.'

I waited for Collina's reaction, like a kid in the classroom.

'That is clever,' he said.

He turned towards Anthony Taylor.

'Anthony, look at this referee and what he does, you should start thinking like that.'

My team were not trying to turn me over, they genuinely thought it was a corner. But they did not protect themselves. They did not think about decisions that could have a consequence. If I went with their call and I did not get lucky, my tournament could be over. Collina could see I was thinking like him. And, for the record, the footage proved that it was a goal-kick.

Collina then showed us Xherdan Shaqiri's equalising goal for Switzerland, an overhead-kick from twenty yards. When Shaqiri scored I actually said to him, 'Fucking hell, that was some strike.' Collina wanted our take on it, and I knew why.

As Shaqiri connected with the ball, there was a Switzerland team-mate in an offside position in front of Poland goalkeeper Lukasz Fabianski. By law, you could argue he was offside. He was potentially distracting the keeper.

But, for me, Fabianski had no chance and I thought he had a good enough view of the shot. The Switzerland player was fully ten yards away and had ducked ever so slightly. I was not going to give Fabianski an excuse, because no one wants this goal to be disallowed.

We watched the replay. Collina broke the silence.

'My God, if you had disallowed this goal it would have caused the biggest controversy of the tournament so far,' he said.

That might surprise some, but you need to understand this – as a referee, a good referee, you have to interpret the *Laws of the Game*, not be a slave to them. As a team we had made the right decision for the good of the game, and it was fair.

Collina was so impressed with our level of detail. He sent the rest of the team out of the room and spoke to me privately.

'You've had a great tournament, Mark. I'm sending some referees home now.'

He poked me in the chest.

'If England lose, you have a chance to go further.'

He never mentioned the final, but I took that as his meaning.

It was England versus Iceland in the last-16 the following day. I had been on a bit of a rollercoaster of emotions the past week or so and I needed to settle down. I booked a table for me and my team at the Irish Bar in the village.

★　　★　　★

UEFA were struggling with their allocation of tickets for Spain versus Italy at Stade de France on the same night as the England game. I had some and offered to give them up. The UEFA guys could not stop thanking me for helping them out. Don't thank me too much, I thought, I would prefer to go to the pub and watch England.

We had a nice dinner and were just settling down in front of the big screen with a beer when some of the UEFA referees committee walked into the bar. Ah, bollocks. Two of the guys came over, Jaap Uilenberg and Bo Karlsson.

'Enjoy the game,' they said, smiling.

England went 1–0 up after four minutes, a Wayne Rooney penalty. One of the committee referees tapped me on the shoulder.

'Unlucky,' he said.

It got my mind racing, they clearly knew something. Iceland equalised straight away and then, after only eighteen minutes, they were 2–1 in front. At this point I was still thinking like an England fan. Of course they'll come back and win, it's only Iceland.

My God, the longer the game went on, the worse England got. I started to think, 'Fuck them, they don't deserve to go through.' For the last half hour we were the only Englishmen in the bar wanting Iceland to win. I was kicking every ball. I never thought I would be so desperate for England to lose like this.

And there it was, the full-time whistle. I leant back in my chair and allowed myself to breathe. Was I angry about England? Yeah, a bit. I am a football fan and I thought they had choked. But my priority now was me and the team, and I was secretly thrilled England were going home. Uilenberg and Karlsson came back over.

'Congratulations,' they said, and smiled again.

We walked back to the hotel and I phoned Claire. I told her everything, from Collina's comments about not being on holiday to what the UEFA guys had said in the bar. The tournament was opening up in front of me, just like it had done in years gone by for other English referees. England underperforming at major tournaments was good news for us. Howard Webb was an incredible referee, but he got the 2010 World Cup Final after England went out to Germany in the last-16. You need that luck.

There was a three-day break now until the quarter-finals and we were told the number of referees would be cut. I think Martin Atkinson expected to stay after England were eliminated. But I came down to breakfast the following morning and his team looked miserable. They were going home. I shook Atkinson's hand and wished him all the best.

But there was one situation that had annoyed me. He was fourth official for Spain versus Italy on the same night as England played Iceland. His two additionals, Michael Oliver and Craig Pawson, were in the hotel with us. I asked them to come to the Irish Bar to watch the game and unwind. It had been an intense few weeks and I thought all the Premier League lads could have a nice night together. Atkinson would not be there and that made it even better.

Except, he had told his team they were not allowed to leave the hotel.

'Are you joking?' I said to them. 'You shouldn't be controlled by this guy. If you want to go for a beer, go for a beer.'

I always told my team, 'Do what you want but be professional. If you get into trouble then don't come crying to me. But if you want to go for a drink or some food, go for it.' They even went to Euro Disney while I was fourth official for a game elsewhere. No problem. Enjoy yourselves.

But Oliver and Pawson were so scared of Atkinson. It was pathetic. I called Michael.

'Come on, don't be daft, come for a beer,' I said.

He was adamant, he was not allowed. Carlsberg were one of the sponsors and I had been given a few bottles, so I took them around for Michael.

'There you go, if you change your mind, you know where we are.'

I did not want to leave them out. Whatever people thought of me, I tried to include everyone.

Atkinson had also moved his team to the other side of the hotel from where we were staying. I joked with the lads, 'Is that to get away from us?' So no, I did not feel sorry for him when he was sent home. Trying to control his team, that was his style – square deal. I always wanted my team to feel relaxed and we did a lot together.

One thing we had not yet done was go to the Fan Zone in Paris, and that looked far too good to miss after seeing the pictures on TV. I wanted us to enjoy that, we just needed an opportunity.

After England went out, the appointments for the quarter-finals were announced. We did not have a game. That was fine, it meant we were in line for a semi-final. Or, in my mind, the final. There was one obstacle remaining, Wales. They were on a brilliant run and were into the last eight. The problem was we could not referee matches involving the Home Nations. Wales played Belgium in their quarter-final on 1 July. This was our chance for a night out in the Fan Zone. I sorted us a car and we headed into Paris. We were in high spirits. Belgium would smash Wales, or so we thought.

Belgium took an early lead. Great. But then it was 1–1, 2–1 to Wales, 3–1. Am I watching the right game here? Is this a horror movie? How the hell are Wales beating Belgium? Full-time. Wales had won 3–1.

I was in a Fan Zone surrounded by thousands of supporters, yet I felt lost in my own thoughts. Everything beyond me was a blur of noise and colour. I was stunned, the sort of feeling that makes you feel hollow inside. My tournament could be over because Wales have got to the semi-finals. Congratulations, yes, but forget about Wales. I am thinking about Mark Clattenburg here. It felt like I had arrived at the Fan Zone with a winning lottery ticket in my hand, only to drop it and see it trampled to pieces.

We got the car back to the hotel. I was looking at Paris from the window, all of the iconic landmarks. It could be the last time I see them this tournament. The next stop could be the airport. I was so close to refereeing the final and it could all be ruined by Chris Coleman and Wales. I like Chris a lot, by the way, and they had some great players who I respected, the likes of Gareth Bale and Aaron Ramsey. But this had shaken me, I did not sleep well at all that night.

I could not train properly, either, in the days leading up to Wales' semi-final against Portugal, I was distracted. Collina then called a meeting of all the officials who were left. From nowhere, he brought up the footage of my coin toss before the penalty shootout between Switzerland and Poland a week earlier. What's going on here?

I knew there had been a law change on the coin toss before penalty shootouts, or at least I thought I knew. It was now heads for the penalties to be taken at one end of the stadium and tails for the other end. I chose that, not the players. You then had a second coin toss and the players chose which team took the first penalty.

Collina then showed footage of the coin toss before the Germany versus Italy penalty shootout in their quarter-final. Referee Viktor Kassai had allowed the players to decide which end of the stadium they were taken, and that was different to what I had done.

Collina turned to the room.

'Come on then, what is right?' he said.

He asked for a show of hands. It was weighted 70–30 in favour of Viktor. He then asked Nicola Rizzoli, the 2014 World Cup Final referee, what would he do? Nicola sided with Viktor. Shit, I've done mine wrong. Collina exploded.

'You don't know the *Laws of the Game*?'

I was sinking in my chair. He then looked at me.

'Mark, tell everyone what the law is.'

I stuck to my guns.

'Exactly!' Collina shouts. 'Why do referees not know the *Laws of the Game*?'

What a relief. I came out of that meeting feeling ten feet tall.

Simple things like that meant a lot to Collina. You can defend a referee when it comes to interpretation, but not when it comes to actually knowing the laws.

The appointments were announced for the semi-finals. I did not have one. This was good news. All of us who were left knew then that, if Wales lost, I was almost certain to get the final.

Wales played Portugal in the first semi in Lyon on 6 July. I am not being nasty but you get one chance at something like this, so of course I wanted Wales to lose. I would want England to lose in the same situation.

I gathered the team in my hotel room to watch the game. It was goalless at half-time. I was pacing around, I could not look when Wales went forward. I had a few of those Carlsbergs left over, but I could not stomach a drink.

Then, five minutes into the second half, Cristiano Ronaldo scored. We went mental. I nearly fell off my balcony! Three minutes later and Nani made it 2–0 to Portugal. I started crying. It was sheer relief. Four weeks' worth of emotion came flooding out in that moment. Where's that Carlsberg?

'This is it,' I thought, 'I am going to referee the final of the European Championship.' I rang Claire and told her to get a dress ready and to book a business-class flight because Mike Riley was paying, as he had promised he would after the Champions League Final.

Collina still had to confirm my appointment, of course. He was away in Marseille at the second semi-final, in which France beat Germany.

He made the announcement via video call the following day. Except, the call was jumpy, it did not come through properly. None of us knew what he had said. He hung up. Are you kidding? What did he say? Did we get it or not? Hugh Dallas stepped in.

'I don't think that came through correctly, but Mark Clattenburg will referee the final.'

Yes, I was expecting the news, but it was still a special moment. We all hugged each other.

Then it sinks in, I actually have to referee this game. But I was in a good place. I was on a high. Nothing was going to faze me, or so I thought.

Sunday 10 July.
France 0 Portugal 1 (after extra-time). Euro 2016 Final.
Stade de France, Saint-Denis.

I spent the day of the final watching Andy Murray win Wimbledon. So much for getting some rest, I was jumping all over my room cheering every point.

There was a problem the day before when we were forced to move from our hotel. A concert was due to take place outside on the day of the game and UEFA did not want us to be disturbed. I could have told them I had no plans to sleep, because there was no way I was missing Murray's match against Milos Raonic. Seeing him win, it gave me another lift.

The excitement I felt was very different to the Champions League Final six weeks earlier. That night in Milan was a one-off. You live in the moment, not wanting it to ever end. The Euros is more relief, like a graduation ceremony. You have been away from home for over a month and are looking forward to the end. That does not detract from the experience, it is just a different emotion.

Driving to the stadium, especially with the host nation being one of the finalists, it was an awesome sight. The banners, flags and whistles. The noise and the colour. The painted faces and smiles on every corner. It was spine-tingling driving through that, knowing you were part of it. I cast my mind back to being a fourth official at the Under-17 European Championship in Durham, fifteen years earlier. I had worn a UEFA tracksuit for the first time and it felt good. I had wondered then what it would be like to be one of the best referees in Europe.

Here I now was, walking into Stade de France about to referee the final of Euro 2016, the eyes of the world on this one match. The enormity of the occasion is all around you, it is inescapable. I casually wandered past the world famous DJ, David Guetta, who was performing during the closing ceremony.

'You've got the easy bit, mate,' I said to him.

I walked out to see the pitch for what should have been a moment of calm, a chance to take it all in and have a few seconds to myself. That, sadly, would not be happening – we had company.

As I left the tunnel, I was met by thousands and thousands

of insects. What the fuck? They were everywhere. In my hair, clinging to my tracksuit, I was spitting them out. They had left the stadium lights on overnight and this swarm of moths had invaded the place. It was all you could concentrate on, swatting them away. The game was never in doubt, we were just praying they would disappear, which they didn't. At least social media saw the funny side – 'Thank God, Lizard Tongue is here, Clattenburg will eat them!'

The game started and I was nervous. I could tell the players were, too. There was a challenge early on, France forward Dimitri Payet on Cristiano Ronaldo. Payet won the ball and I waved play on, but Ronaldo was hurt.

I never had a problem with Payet when he was at West Ham, he was honest. He could not tackle but this seemed like a fair one. Watching it back now, maybe it was a foul, he catches Ronaldo as well as getting the ball. But, at the time, I could not book Payet just because Ronaldo looked injured.

It makes me angry that people later accused Payet of trying to injure Ronaldo to give France the best chance of winning. That is rubbish, he was going for the ball. But I was gutted for Ronaldo. He had lived for this moment, scored in the semi-final, and he was now being forced off after just twenty-five minutes. You could feel a sense of despair among the Portugal players. It felt like someone had died.

I finished the half feeling flat, it had been a poor game. My mood was not helped when the Portuguese started attacking me about the Payet challenge. I got back to the dressing-room and was agitated. Did I get that wrong? I asked my team. No one came back with anything. It would have been nice to have VAR to reassure me that it was not a red card.

We came back out and Portugal were still having a go at me, 'You've missed a red card.' I do not know if they were trying to play a game, trying to get inside my head, but I did not feel one hundred per cent. There was a negative energy around the match after Ronaldo's injury, it was like the air had escaped from a balloon. The game finished goalless after ninety minutes. It had been tense, not much enjoyment for anyone, myself included.

In the first half of extra-time I gave a handball against France defender Laurent Koscielny. It looked obvious and I booked him. Only later did I realise it was actually a handball the other way. I got it wrong but I got lucky when Portugal hit the bar from the free-kick. Imagine the uproar if that had gone in.

At this point, deep down, I wanted a penalty shootout. Like in the Champions League Final, it takes the focus off the referee, they usually cannot blame you for influencing the result if it's decided by penalties.

Then, from nowhere, Portugal scored in the 109th minute. It was a blinding goal by the substitute Eder, twenty-five yards out and drilled into the bottom corner. It was enough to win the game and I reasoned that at least France could not blame me for losing. Portugal would have done because of the Ronaldo incident.

People might wonder, 'Why are you so bothered about

blame?' As a referee, you want to leave the pitch with the story of the game being about the players, not you. A TV camera in your face as you are heading for the tunnel, or a manager waiting for you on the touchline, they are never a good sign. As I walked off at Stade de France I knew it was not about me, and that is always a source of some comfort.

But here is something that does bother me. Months later I spoke to Koscielny. He said that, if I had not incorrectly booked him for the handball, he would have clipped Eder in the transition period before the goal. He would have taken a booking for the team. He said he could not, of course, because he was already on a yellow and did not want to be sent off. I understood exactly what he was saying and it made me regret that decision even more.

When I blew for full-time, honestly, there was sadness. I had given everything during a month of the tournament but, in that moment, I knew it was not my best game. In fact, it was my worst. And those bloody moths were still everywhere. I did not enjoy it.

I saw Collina and he congratulated me. But he knew my feelings, he knew I was down. France manager Didier Deschamps shook my hand and said there were no complaints from them. That reassured me a little bit.

I was called for my medal and Ronaldo tried to grab me by the face as I went up towards the steps. I did not know if he was going to kiss me or cuddle me. I just think he was so happy, it was the second final he had won with me in a matter of months. I brushed him off. I did not want anyone to think I had given special favours. As much as I respect Ronaldo, you have to be wary of things like that, as the incident proved with Sir Alex Ferguson before the FA Cup Final.

I collected my medal and saw Claire as I was coming down the stairs on the other side. That picked me up. To share that moment with her was special. I had been through so much in my career, met with so much opposition, but she was always there for me. Without her, I would not have had that medal in my hand.

Back in the dressing-room everything was upbeat. We had a beer for what must have been the first time ever in front of Collina. Giorgio Marchetti from UEFA came in and he was on a high. For them, it had been an amazing tournament, probably the best ever Euros for refereeing. In that regard, I was happy. But why did I still feel so bad?

We went to a restaurant in Paris that night with Collina and all of our wives. They were half-pissed already. They had stayed in the hospitality lounge during the second half with Laurent, their French bodyguard. He had a gun, much to their excitement. To be fair, they had the right idea given how boring the game was.

But at the restaurant I was forcing myself to look like I was having a good time. I just wanted to go to bed. I hate it when I feel like I have not performed. I am a perfectionist. People used to think I was arrogant, that I always walked off satisfied with myself no matter what. That was not true. It was tough in that restaurant, trying to keep everyone happy, when inside there was frustration eating away at me. I have no shame in admitting that is how I felt.

I invited Mike Riley to the dinner because I thought he was paying for everyone's expenses for the final. He paid for mine but only half for the other guys on my team. I was pissed off about that. He should have stuck to his word. It was such a massive achievement, why shouldn't the PGMOL pay for our guests to come out? We were not just representing ourselves, we were representing the Premier League and our country. But really, I should not have been surprised. That was Riley. That was the PGMOL. I was reaching the end of my tether with them, as time would tell.

We flew back to Newcastle the following day and the only turbulence was in my head. You have been in a bubble for a month, with the same guys around the clock. That transition to home life is weird, much more extreme than what I felt after the Champions League Final. I was not a referee now. I was a dad, a husband. It takes some adjusting to get back home, put your medal on the mantelpiece and then have your wife ask you to nip to the shop for a loaf of bread!

People say, 'What's wrong with you? Why are you so low?' But, in sport, you build yourself up so much, mentally and physically, that the comedown on the other side is like falling off a cliff. I did not speak much for days. I would not say I was depressed, but it is a depression, a period that is hard to drag yourself out of, even though you know you should be so thankful.

We went on holiday to Spain, where a little pick-me-up was waiting in the form of a tattoo parlour. I had the logos of the Champions League and Euro 2016 finals tattooed on my arm, to go with an existing tattoo from the 2012 London Olympics, where I had also refereed the final.

What a storm it caused when the girl who did them posted a picture of her and me with the tattoos on her Instagram page. The media turned it into a negative. I was egotistical, they said, it was all about me. Some people laughed at me, some got angry, some were quite nasty about it.

To all of them, I would say – why do you give a shit? I don't tell anyone else how to dress. So don't tell me what I should and should not be doing. Why shouldn't I celebrate?

I wanted something to remind me of what I had achieved, that I had done all right, a kid from a council background. To have overcome the suspensions, the sackings, the interference and obstruction from people who should have been helping me. I wanted to be able to show everyone – this is what I have done. I am different. That is why, I believe, I went as far as I did. I will always be proud of that.

So you know what, every now and then I do look down at my tattoos and remember those occasions and what it means to have reached that level. It means the world to me. I realise I am very fortunate, but I only got there because of hard work and sacrifice.

But I never forget this, either – thank God for Iceland.

14

THE BOSS

'Is this God?'

PIERLUIGI Collina is the reason I was voted the best referee in the world in 2016. I owe him everything.

He was, for the best part of a decade, the world's number one referee, someone I had idolised from afar. It was not just because of his baldy head that he was so iconic; he genuinely was on a different level to anyone we had ever seen.

He became UEFA's head of referees in 2010 and, with that, my boss. I was happy when I heard the news, but little did I know how much he would do for me over the course of the next six years. He changed my career. He changed my life.

I first came across Collina in 2004, two years after he had taken charge of the World Cup Final. He was refereeing a World Cup qualifier in Zagreb, Croatia. I was there for my first international match, as fourth official to Mike Dean for Croatia Under-21s. I had just been promoted to the Premier League.

When we arrived in Zagreb there was no fuss. When Collina landed everything came to a standstill.

'Is this God?' I asked the others.

What a presence he had, everyone was in awe of him. I was a rookie who had been refereeing in the Northern League five years earlier. Five years before that I was watching Collina on Channel 4's *Football Italia*. I was starstruck.

I later met him through Soccer Aid charity matches and we did a few UEFA courses together, but you were scared to speak to him. You could tell why he had the respect of the players. His aura was intimidating, but also to be admired.

When he became my boss, I did not know him on a personal level. He was fifteen years older than me, so there was always that distance. I soon realised he was a man I should stick to. I made it my mission to absorb every last drop of information and advice.

Not long after Collina took the job, we had a get-together of UEFA's Elite referees and the development group in Antalya, Turkey. He arranged for us to do a new fitness exam, the yo-yo test. All of the Elite referees, of which I was one, passed, but a handful from the development group failed. It was the first time I saw Collina get angry. He laid into them about body fat and why fitness, in the modern game, meant being able to keep up with supreme athletes.

At least his bollocking helped with weight loss, because once Collina does that, you soon lose your appetite! But it planted a seed with me.

I never had a problem with fitness. I could run backwards and pass those tests. But I looked down at my belly and thought, 'I'm too fat here.' I always had a little bit of excess about me. In that moment, because of Collina, I decided to change. I wanted to impress him so badly. I wanted to return and show him that my body fat was down. I was so driven. I looked at everything, from eating and drinking to my training regime, anything I could do differently to get that marginal gain.

Every time I returned for our UEFA courses I was fitter and faster, and less fat. I noticed a difference in how I was able to get around the pitch, my speed and stamina improved and my decision-making became sharper. It makes sense, of course, but sometimes you need that lightbulb moment. Collina gave me that.

As time went on, I noticed how Collina started to take more care with me compared to other referees. He was becoming a father figure. Since my dad died maybe I had been lacking a bit of guidance at times. Mike Riley, my boss at the PGMOL, was never able to be the mentor that I needed. Other referees might have a different view but, from what I saw of him, he did not have the people skills or the ability to recognise talent and encourage it.

The way Riley behaved towards me, it led me to believe he did not want me to improve and be successful. Collina did. He knew I was different to other referees. He recognised that I had a bit of cheek and a spikiness. He did not try to change that. He once said to me, 'Mark, always be yourself.' That stuck with me. He believed that my character, perhaps a bit rough around the edges, lent itself to being a strong referee on the pitch.

Our relationship continued to grow and he appointed me

to the UEFA Super Cup in 2014, in which Real Madrid beat Sevilla 2–0 in Cardiff. We flew from Bristol to Geneva the following day for the UEFA referees summer course. There was me, Collina, Gianni Infantino, the UEFA Secretary General, and Michael Oliver, who had been part of my team for the game.

The air hostess asked Collina what he wanted from the trolley. He ordered a double espresso and downed it in one, cool as you like, typical Italian. The air hostess was looking at him. He was looking at her. It was a bit awkward. Collina always flew first-class. I had to break the ice.

'Boss, this is EasyJet now, man.'

'What? You have to pay?' he said.

'Yeah. I'll get it.'

He was laughing, thankfully. Little opportunities like that you had to take with Collina. He liked it. It was £2.50 well spent!

By now, I was growing in confidence around him. Too many referees, such as Michael, were in awe of him for too long. I had been there as a young referee myself, I knew how that felt. But once he was the boss, I realised you had to impress your personality upon him.

Everything was going well and Collina would always invest time in me whenever the group met. Then, in November 2014, I ballsed it all up. I was refereeing Malmo versus Atletico Madrid in the Champions League group stage. At the time, referees did not go to the matchday briefing on the morning of the game. The referees' observer went along to make sure everything was okay from our perspective. I met him for a coffee afterwards and asked if there were any issues. He did not speak much English.

'No, Mr Mark, all is fine.'

'Great,' I thought. 'I'll have a bit of lunch, an hour's sleep and then get my kit ready.' I had four different coloured jerseys. I put my FIFA badge on the orangey-yellow top and left the others in my room. I thought nothing else of it.

In the tunnel before the game Atletico had their tracksuit tops on. We walked out and lined up on the pitch for the Champions League anthem. No problems. Then, all of a sudden, Atletico's players removed the tracksuits. Oh fuck. I cannot believe this – we are wearing the same colour kit as them!

Peter Kirkup was my fourth official, who I did not like anyway, he was part of Martin Atkinson's clique. I heard his squawky little voice down the headset.

'Mark, Mark, you've got the same colours on.'

'I fucking know that,' I said.

It looked like Atletico had fourteen men on the pitch. I could not walk off, we would look stupid. Kirkup was still on at me, saying how the UEFA director was not happy with the colours. He was doing my head in. The players were also complaining, saying they kept trying to pass to me. I was just trying to hide. All I could do was get through to half-time and try to resolve it.

We got into the dressing-room. Has anyone got a different coloured jersey? Blank faces. We only had one between us. There was no time to go back to the hotel, so I took the one black top we had and wore it for the second half. Atletico won 2–0. 'We might just have got away with this,' I thought. I was wrong.

I was preparing to fly home from Copenhagen the following morning when an email from Collina landed on my phone. He went to town on me.

'This is not what I expect from a top-level referee. It is unprofessional and unacceptable.'

He tore into me, and quite rightly so. I had not done my homework in the first place. Then, on the day of the game, I had not prepared properly by double checking things like potential kit clashes. It was complacency.

I sat on the plane nearly in tears, full of self-loathing and regret. It was such a stupid mistake to make. Little things like that can hurt your career. You think you are on the way up but then you take your eye off the ball and it sets you back. What a dick. I was angry with myself. Why had I allowed this to happen?

I started drafting an email in response. I had to get this right. I apologised and admitted my error. I was to blame, there was no escaping that. But I also outlined what I would do in the future. I would put a system in place where the observer, at the morning meeting, would take pictures of the two kits which the teams would be wearing. He would then send them to me and I would pick my colours accordingly. I apologised again and pressed send. After that, I hoped for the best.

I heard nothing until the next round of Champions League

appointments a couple of weeks later. I thought I would be out in the cold as punishment, and deservedly so. But then the email arrived. Collina had given me a match.

It was clever management, typical of him to think beyond the obvious. He had kicked me from pillar to post but now he wanted a reaction. I thought, 'You know what, I will give you one million per cent.' Every game from that point onwards, I went over and above anything I had ever given before. I pushed harder and harder to be the best, to prove to Collina he was right in backing me.

At our next UEFA referees meeting, there was a moment that made me smile. I had been getting text messages from the other referees about the kit clash, all of them saying, 'Thank God that happened to you first, it could have been any of us.' Collina recognised the flaw in the system and announced that, from now, all referees must get the observer to send them a picture of the two kits to be worn by the respective teams. I was sitting there feeling very pleased with myself, although I resisted the temptation to jump up and tell the room, 'That's my idea!'

Yes, I made a careless error, and that email from Collina still sends a shiver down my spine. But it worked out okay in the end – and I never made the same mistake again.

I loved doing European matches for Collina, far more than I enjoyed the Premier League. Every time I was with him I felt that I returned a better referee. What follows is the best example of how he did that, of how he made me one of the best in the world.

Collina, when he was refereeing, would get inside players' heads. He had so much knowledge of the tricks they would pull that he would stop a lot of fouls and infringements from happening in the first place. Just by him being there it served as a deterrent. Everyone always used to say, 'Nothing ever happens in Collina's games.' That is exactly what you want as a referee. He studied tactics and observed the dark arts that teams and players would employ. He knew what was coming and how to prevent it. I was trying to think like him in that regard.

In May 2015 – six months on from my kit cock-up – he appointed me to the second leg of Bayern Munich versus Barcelona in the Champions League semi-final. Barcelona had won 3–0 in the first leg at the Nou Camp, but you still felt the tie was alive.

I arrived in Munich and Collina was the observer. I was pleased to see him, as ever, but it also meant I could not have a glass of wine with dinner the night before the game. You did not dare when he was around. Before going to bed he asked if we could have a meeting, just the two of us, the following day after lunch. No problem, boss. But what does he want? I certainly could have done with that glass of wine to help me sleep now.

We met the next day in the hotel. He opened his laptop.

'Did you watch the first leg?' he said.

'Of course, six times. I've been over everything,' I said.

'Are you sure you've seen everything?'

'Yes. I'm more than happy.'

'Okay, but I'm going to show you something.'

He played a tactic of Bayern's at set-pieces. Their smallest player was Thiago, the midfielder. He was blocking Barcelona's biggest player, the defender Gerard Pique. It was subtle and allowed the likes of Bayern's Robert Lewandowski and Thomas Muller to attack the space. He showed me six clips of this happening in that one game. Nothing had come of it, so it had gone unnoticed. I certainly had not seen it. Collina was marking my card.

'Mark, you have to be aware of this. But it's up to you to solve it. It's your game, you deal with it. Good luck.'

Bayern scored early to make it 3–1 on aggregate. Game on. The stadium was bouncing. The Allianz Arena is one of the best in the world for atmosphere and during those first ten minutes it was electrifying, they really believed their team could turn the tie around.

Then, in around the thirteenth minute, Bayern won a free-kick. Before it was taken, I pulled Thiago to one side.

'If you block Pique . . . ' I said, gesturing with my whistle to my mouth.

He put his hands in the air, as if butter wouldn't melt. The ball was delivered into the penalty area and, sure enough, Thiago stepped across Pique. I blew for a free-kick. As I ran back into position, I spoke to Thiago.

'Do it again and I'll give another free-kick, it's up to you.'

Luis Enrique, the Barcelona manager, was applauding the decision on the touchline. Pique was looking at me, nodding his head.

In that moment, I knew I had the players on side. I could

have blown for six penalties and everyone would have believed them to be right. That is what Collina had done, he had empowered me.

From that game on, I could sense a change in the attitude of players towards me. They knew I was thinking one step ahead of them, like Collina used to.

I took that level of detail back into the Premier League. I started to think more about tactics, studying corners and free-kicks of teams I would be refereeing. I picked up on things I never would have noticed previously.

Because of that, I was now inside the players' heads rather than them getting inside mine. I was playing mind games with them. Collina had given me that authority. I look back at that Champions League semi-final in Munich and believe it was the moment my career took off in the direction of the very top.

Bayern won 3–2 that night – Barcelona went through 5–3 on aggregate – and afterwards Collina gave me a cuddle, and a little wink. I left Munich thinking, 'Wow. I would die for you.'

Twelve months on and he appointed me to the 2016 Champions League Final. By now I felt more at ease around him, even if he was always 'The Boss'.

Before the final in Milan, between Real Madrid and Atletico Madrid, all of the officials and their guests met in the courtyard of our hotel. Collina had two daughters. I remember the first time I asked after them, trying to be friendly and make conversation, he prodded me in the chest with his finger.

'Mark, you like your refereeing career, don't you?' he said.

Point taken, boss.

One of his daughters was at the hotel. She had been studying at university in London. I was standing with Collina.

'My daughter is over there,' he said. 'With her boyfriend.'

Again, point taken. I went across and introduced myself and we chatted about London. I came back over and Collina thanked me.

'That's fine,' I said. 'It was nice to meet her. She must have got her good looks from her mother.'

He stared at me.

'Mark, I've warned you once about you refereeing career. You either want one, or you don't.'

He was joking, I think!

But that summer, at Euro 2016, he definitely wasn't joking during an incident in the hotel dining hall. It reminded me of the side I had seen in Turkey after the failed fitness tests several years earlier.

We had a sports scientist with us at the Euros, Werner Helsen. He decided to change the menu one day to lighten the mood among the referees. We had been away from home for a few weeks and everyone was getting irritable. Helsen thought it would be a good idea to introduce hot dogs and chips. It was like a fast-food feast.

Collina went up to get his dinner. He froze on the spot, staring at these hot dogs, and then exploded.

'This is a disgrace. This is not what athletes eat,' he was

screaming. 'We're supposed to be professional. We have to prepare properly.'

Was he joking? Was there a punchline? Clearly not. It was awkward. You looked around the room and all these top referees were pushing their plates towards their assistant referees, 'You take that one for the team, pal.'

It did not help that Collina was on a diet. He returned to his table and sat down. You could have heard a chip drop.

One of the additional assistant referees from Sweden was a guy called Markus Strombergsson. He was a great fella, he did not give a fuck. He broke the silence by standing up and walking to the buffet area. He put a hot dog on his plate and went back to his table. You could see that everyone was ready to burst with laughter. Collina would have thought we were taking the piss out of him, there would have been hell to pay. I thought, 'I've just got to get out of here, I'll survive without one dinner.' I got back to my room and fell on the bed laughing. So the sports scientist was right, those hot dogs had lifted the mood!

I have written earlier about Euro 2016, but Collina was incredible with me during that tournament. I refereed the final between France and Portugal and, at the end of that summer, our relationship could not have been in a better place.

But then, in February 2017, I quit the Premier League for Saudi Arabia. Collina did not take it well. Looking back, I think he did not want to lose me. Euro 2016 had been a huge success from a refereeing perspective and Collina won a lot of praise. He still wanted me for the big Champions League games. After I left, mistakes started happening in high-profile matches. Maybe he was thinking, 'Clattenburg would have done that game.' He ended up stepping down from UEFA in 2018. I think refereeing performances had dropped.

But even after leaving for Saudi, I still could have refereed in the Champions League and at the 2018 World Cup, if Collina and UEFA had tried to find a solution. They did not want to. That was sad.

Since then, I have only spoken to Collina on a professional level, never personally. That is sad, too.

I will never forget what he did for me, and how much I owe him.

15

EASTERN PROMISE

'I felt more like Thomas Cook than I did
Mark Clattenburg'

Late afternoon. Thursday 14 December 2017.
Riyadh, Saudi Arabia.

It is rush hour. And we really are in a rush. Our driver, Anas, isn't afraid to put his foot down when he needs to. Chance would be a fine thing. All we can see is brake lights. Kick-off is an hour away, but so is the stadium in this traffic. We had been sent to the wrong venue by the Saudi Football Federation. I should be there by now, I'm the referee. This isn't good enough. Finally, five minutes before the game is due to start, we screech up outside the King Fahd University Stadium in the north of the city. Except, we're on the wrong side. It would take another ten minutes to drive around to the main entrance. Fuck it, let's start running. We grab our bags and head for the nearest entry point. We're in. There's only one thing for it now, we're gonna have to run across the pitch. The players are just finishing their warm-up. What a farce. I've been brought in to make things more professional, to improve standards. But look at us! This is a joke. I feel let down. I'm not sure how much longer I can stick this.

I LANDED in Riyadh for the first time with the city under the cover of darkness, and that feels appropriate on reflection. It would not happen straight away, but gradually I found a light being shone on the reality of living and working in Saudi Arabia.

This was February 2017 and the start of my journey. A new life, one where I was about to be free of the abuse and anxiety that had led me to quit the Premier League earlier that month.

To begin with, all was well. I was in and out of Saudi on an almost weekly basis, returning to England to see out the remaining matches of my Premier League contract. I was staying in a Marriott hotel in Riyadh's Diplomatic Quarter, which was pleasant enough except for the absence of a licensed bar, and I was getting to grips with my new roles as director of refereeing and chairman of the referees' committee. I was also taking charge of matches in the Saudi Professional League, the country's top division.

The president of the Saudi Football Federation demanded that I referee the Crown Prince Cup Final just a week or so after I signed my contract – which meant flying in and out for one day – but if he wants that, you do it. I was also responsible for organising foreign referees when Saudi clubs asked for them, but I always had fourteen days' notice to sort the logistics. It was a gentle introduction to my new surroundings.

I had replaced Howard Webb in the role and, before the

Saudi season ended in May, I moved into his old accommodation. That is when my early enjoyment began to fade. The house was a dive. It was tired and worn and the furniture was older than me. I wore flip-flops everywhere. The Wi-Fi did not work and I had to stand in the corner of an upstairs room to get a phone signal. The Muslim call for prayer on the loudspeakers from the mosques was at 5 a.m. every day and, while I respected that custom, I could never get back to sleep during those first few months, in part because of my concerns. I knew it was up to me to adapt, but I missed things like having a beer to unwind at the end of the day.

It got to the point where I snapped. I rang Claire, crouched in the corner of the room to get a signal.

'I've made a mistake,' I told her. 'I'm coming home. I can't live like this.'

She calmed me down. It was not that I regretted my decision to leave the Premier League, I was relieved to be free of that. But my new world was not what I expected and I was finding it difficult to settle. I had to get out of this house, for starters.

The short-term fix was the Narcissus Hotel in Riyadh. It boosted me – there was a gym, they served breakfast and they showed a bit of Premier League football. I also had WhatsApp again, which might sound trivial, but when it's the only way to see pictures and videos of your children, you realise how much it means to you. For all of that, living in a hotel is never much fun. You want a place you can call home.

My salary was not being paid on time, either. The first

month was fine. After that, it was like bingo which day of the month it would land on. I told the president of the federation on one occasion. He made a couple of calls and it was sorted. But I should not have had to chase my wages. I was learning that Saudi Arabia played by its own rules when it came to business.

I noticed they always scheduled meetings to start at around 11.30 a.m. I soon realised it was because prayer time was fifteen minutes later. They used to say, 'We'll finish the meeting afterwards', but that was the last you saw of them. Getting them to do anything was tedious.

I got through the first season and had a holiday with my family and came back full of enthusiasm in the summer of 2017. I organised a pre-season training camp in Valencia, Spain. It was too hot in Saudi at that time of year and it was exciting for the local referees to get out of the country. Not that they seemed too enthused about punctuality. I would tell them we were starting training at 10 a.m., only for half of them to stroll down at quarter past. I'm trying to help you here! They wanted to start late and finish early.

That camp was my first real chance to pass on my knowledge and give them some tuition. It actually went well, once we started. They were receptive to my ideas. We got back to Saudi and the season began with no refereeing controversies. I felt like I had made a positive impact and people were saying nice things to me. My contentment was short-lived.

In October 2017, Turki Al-Sheikh, the Saudi sports minister, announced there would be no more Saudi referees in the top division. He said all officials would be brought in from abroad. I had to move all of the Saudi referees into the second division and, because there were only two leagues, the referees there were kicked out of football. It did not sit right with me. My problems, however, were only just beginning.

Each round of fixtures had seven matches, meaning I had to bring in seven teams of three officials from abroad. The referees were getting nearly £3,000 per match, so a lot of them wanted to come, and that helped.

But from being the director of refereeing, I quickly became the director of logistics. I felt more like Thomas Cook than I did Mark Clattenburg.

Our travel company did not seem to know the first thing about travel, either. That was a concern. There was one incident when I did not know whether to laugh or cry.

'These flights are wrong,' I told the guy who had booked them for a team of officials due to arrive.

'No, they're fine,' he said.

'You've got them changing in Frankfurt.'

'Yes, what is the problem?'

'Well, their first flight lands in Frankfurt at midday. But their connecting flight to Riyadh leaves half an hour earlier, at 11.30 a.m. Where are they going to exchange, in mid-air? You have to land first!'

This is what I was up against. Physically and mentally I was drained. I was working through the night, doing their job for them.

I was embarrassed at times. Referees, who I had brought in, were ringing me at 2 a.m. saying there was no driver waiting for them at the airport. These guys were being left stranded in the middle of the night and were getting angry with me. I would have been pissed off in their situation. The money was good but they soon got sick of the cock-ups and sub-standard hotels.

I started producing information sheets for every team of officials. They contained all of the names and telephone numbers for the drivers and for where they were staying. I spent hours collating the details. Then, in the first week with my shiny new sheets, the travel company changed half of the drivers and hotels. It was carnage. It did not matter what I tried, it always ended in mayhem. For such a wealthy country, they went about their work in a careless and disorganised manner.

I was still refereeing the odd game, either to keep the Saudi federation happy – they liked my name attached to matches – or simply because I could not organise any foreign officials. Appointing myself to a fixture was often the easiest option.

But I never expected to make international headlines, which is what happened when I stopped play during one match for the call to prayer. That had never been done before. The supporters applauded my gesture and said it was respectful for a foreign official to recognise the Saudi culture. But that does not tell the full story. I will explain.

I had brought in Jake Collin as my assistant director of refereeing. Jake was my assistant referee in the Champions League and European Championship finals of 2016. I have always trusted Jake. We wanted to make a good job of the management role in Saudi, because that is where we saw our future. But, like me, Jake was caught up in the chaos of arranging travel for foreign officials. We were like a couple of holiday reps, only minus the nightclubs and waterparks.

In January 2018, we agreed to take charge of a King's Cup match between Al-Feiha and Al-Fateh. The president wanted me to do the game and for us it was a break from telephoning airlines and hotel reservation desks.

But there was a problem – myself and Jake had arranged to meet our wives in Dubai for a short break. Our flights left from Riyadh at around 9 p.m. The game kicked off at 2.30 p.m., two hours north of Riyadh in Al Majma'ah. It was doable, if we avoided extra-time and penalties.

At 1–0 we were ready for our getaway when Al-Fateh equalised in the second half. Bollocks. It was all Jake and I were talking about down the headsets. We had a driver waiting and, as long as we avoided any more delays and a penalty shootout, we could still make the flights.

At the end of normal time, the match manager pulled me to one side. He said we would have to delay the start of extra-time by ten minutes. What? Why? He explained that prayer time was about to begin. I had to think on my feet.

'You can't do that,' I said. 'The players will cool down. It's not acceptable. We will risk injury.'

The match manager was adamant, but so was I. I told him we were starting on time.

Five or so minutes into extra-time, the call to prayer went out on the loudspeakers in the nearby mosques. I blew my whistle to stop play. This was a better solution than delaying the kick-off. We restarted after a couple of minutes once the call to prayer had finished, and there was some clapping in the stands. I thought nothing else of it.

We were heading for penalties – and about to wave goodbye to our flights – when Al-Feiha scored with three minutes remaining. I felt like joining the celebration!

I blew for full-time and ran for the tunnel. We did not even have a shower. We jumped in the car, stinking of sweat, and yelled to the driver, 'Let's go!' The game had only been finished five minutes and we were on the road flying south to Riyadh.

Jake and I were on different flights, leaving fifteen minutes apart. I got checked in and had my boarding pass. Jake appeared from nowhere, shouting and screaming in Scouse. His desk had already closed and they were refusing to let him on the flight. The guy from my airline told him that, if he stopped making such a racket, he could help him. This fella was like a referee, telling us to calm down! He was good to his word and Jake made his flight.

I landed in Dubai and switched on my phone. I had message after message and a screenful of notifications on social media. Oh God. What have I done? But it was good news. The Saudi people were thanking me for showing respect by stopping the game for the call to prayer.

The president of the federation called me at 3 a.m., which

was typical Saudi, to ask where I was. I could not tell him I was already in Dubai – jumping on a flight to the nearest party city straight after a game was not a good look – so I said I was leaving the next morning. He told me to come to his office as soon as I returned, he wanted to thank me in person for what I had done. He wanted to take photographs and prepare a press release. He had realised the world was talking about this and saw it as an opportunity to show Saudi football in a good light. I did not have the heart to tell him the full story.

But, you know what, we did stop the game. We did not have to. I thought it was the right thing to do, even if it was a compromise that gave us a better chance of catching our flights. We had a great weekend with our wives on the back of it. It was nice to know we would be returning to Saudi for a pat on the back, rather than a kick up the arse.

★   ★   ★

It was still me dishing out the arse-kickings to the travel company as we entered 2018. But at least I had managed to get my own house in order, quite literally.

At Christmas, Jake and I had been invited to a party at a residential compound by one of the Belgian coaches who lived there. Well, it was a party as far as Saudi law allows. There was some home-brewed beer and wine which, when you have not had alcohol for weeks, tastes magic. It was like piss really.

But I fell in love with the place. Just little things made me smile, like the fact they had a Christmas tree! It was modern and clean. I arranged to rent an apartment and, for the first time since arriving nine months earlier, I felt settled. There was a bar area where you could meet people. It was pretty soulless and they did not serve alcohol, but I made some friends, including a couple from Bolton who were teaching in Riyadh. I also had good internet and could use the phone without having to dance around the room for a signal.

I was learning what you needed to survive as a westerner in Saudi. The first time I had been out to a restaurant earlier that year, I was shouted at in Arabic for walking in the wrong door. I had gone in the family entrance. There was another door for men only, where you were separated and could not see any women. The reality of life in Saudi kicks in. I had an app on my phone which alerted me to all of the prayer times, because everything closed. It was shutters down, you're not getting in. You had to plan all of your meals and movements around those times.

The hardest day of the week for me was Sunday. It was a working day in Saudi, while back home Claire and Mia were sending me pictures of their Sunday roast. It always made me homesick.

My first experience of a Saudi banquet was an eye-opener, as well as a stomach-turner. I was invited to the home of the brother of one of the Saudi referees. A whole lamb was on the table on top of a bed of rice. All the guests started tearing into this roasted meat carcass with their hands and scooping up the rice with their fingers. It was their tradition and I respected that, but this was one banquet where I was happy to leave hungry.

My greater concern was the workings of the Saudi federation. Jake and I were taking charge of an Al-Nassr game one early evening in December 2017. I had been in the federation office all day. Our driver, Anas, then took us to the Prince Faisal bin Fahd Stadium in the south of Riyadh, where Al-Nassr usually played their home matches. We were approaching the stadium and something did not feel right, there was not a soul in sight. Anas pulled up and was speaking hurriedly in Arabic to the security guard. All of a sudden he reverses the car, *Dukes of Hazzard* style, and puts his foot to the floor.

What's going on? Anas explained that we were at the wrong stadium. What on earth? I had spent all day at the federation office and no one told me they had changed the venue. We now had to get through rush hour to the north side of the city. Kick-off times matter in Saudi because they are scheduled around prayer time. We arrived with five minutes to spare, albeit on the wrong side of the stadium. We ran across the pitch, got changed and kicked off one minute late. I would have settled for that when we were wheel-spinning out of the wrong stadium an hour earlier.

But this was typical of the problems we were encountering. It was dawning on me that I was fighting a losing battle. It was a struggle to get any money to implement my ideas. I said to myself, 'See out your two years until February 2019 and then take stock.'

In the summer of 2018, after working as a pundit for ITV at the World Cup in Russia, I arranged another training course for the Saudi referees in Granada, Spain. It started badly when the bags did not arrive because of an issue with the airline. One of the referees leaked to the press that it was my fault. Even the Saudi officials thought I was their travel rep!

I should have known there would then be an issue with our hotel. Saudi Arabia had been to the World Cup and, when they arrived in Russia, they discovered their hotel rooms had been given away. They did not understand the European custom of paying a deposit in advance. They would always settle the bill, just on their own terms a few weeks down the line.

Sure enough, the hotel in Granada were refusing to let us check in because the bill had to be paid up front. I had to use €10,000 of my own money to sort it out. Without that, the training camp would not have started. I got the money back a few days later, but could I really be bothered with all of this aggravation?

I was educating the Saudi officials on the use of VAR, which was being brought in for the new season. We spent so much time training them up. The foreign referees would still be taking charge of matches but the Saudis would be operating the video technology. It was like a comedy sketch of how not to do VAR. I had my head in my hands half the time.

They were unplugging the VAR to charge their mobile phone and the system was going off. You would see operators running across the stadium using their mobiles to communicate because the headsets had gone down. Cables were missing or did not work. It was farcical. I was under pressure from IFAB and FIFA to do it properly, but this was embarrassing. It was like Benny Hill does video technology!

Then, a few weeks into the season, the sports minister announced that all VAR operators would now come from abroad. He wanted international officials for everything in the top division, and I had to sort it. I felt like jumping out of the window when I heard the news.

I was trying to organise six foreign officials per game across eight matches every weekend. That was forty-eight people who needed flights, hotels and payment. I wasn't sleeping properly. That 5 a.m. call to prayer was now my alarm for work. The framework just was not in place to deal with this new demand.

In October 2018 I told the president I was stepping down as chairman of the referees' committee. I was honest, I was struggling. I could not juggle all of the roles expected of me. It was an impossible task. I was not educating referees, I was a full-time travel agent.

I felt the federation were just using my name to have it associated with Saudi football. In reality, I was there to do whatever they told me to. They were not interested in me helping the local referees, as I had hoped I would be.

There was a story in England that I had been sacked, but the media had misinterpreted the press release announcing I was no longer chairman. It was nonsense, I was still employed as the director of refereeing and taking charge of matches.

But, by now, I did not feel like a valued part of the

organisation and there was a situation earlier in the year that made me realise I was on the outside.

It was late one evening in May and I was in London waiting for a flight back to Saudi. I was flying from Heathrow into Jeddah to watch the King's Cup Final the following day. It was not exactly the West End but I took the chance to have a few beers in the airport terminal before returning to a diet of fruit juice and water.

The president of the federation called. He needed me to find a foreign referee for the final. Why? What has happened? He would not tell me. He said they would send a private jet wherever I needed to get a referee into the country in time for the game.

I tried but there was no chance, I was giving referees less than 24 hours' notice to drop everything and head to Saudi. I sent the president a message apologising and said I could not sort anyone. He replied, 'Okay, you might have to do it.'

Why had they not given me more notice to prepare properly? I would be arriving in Jeddah at 9 a.m., after a night flight before which I'd had a couple of drinks. It was a big game, there would be 60,000 fans there, and I'd done no physical or tactical preparation.

I woke up to a text message from the president as we landed – I was refereeing the final, there was a driver waiting to take me straight to a hotel.

It was only later I discovered that Fahad Al Mirdasi, who was due to referee the game and was going to the 2018 World

Cup the following month, had been arrested on suspicion of match-fixing. It was the first I had heard, and I was the director of refereeing. What the hell is going on?

I was exhausted and irritated but I refereed the match, which of course went to extra-time. There were no issues and Al-Ittihad beat Al-Faisaly 3–1. Everyone was happy, except me.

Al Mirdasi had been the Saudi pick as their referee for the World Cup, not mine. He was their man. But I thought I had the right to know what was happening on my watch. Instead, they handled the full investigation. No one told me anything, other than to keep out of it and get on with my job. Al Mirdasi confessed to offering to fix the King's Cup Final. He was banned for life and kicked out of the World Cup. I still do not know the full facts. The whole episode made me uneasy. I was having serious doubts about my future in Saudi.

Six months later, in November 2018, I was in Dammam Airport when I took a call from my agent, Rob Segal. It was approaching midnight on a Thursday. I was flying to Dubai for a couple of days for a friend's birthday party. I had refereed a Saudi league game and sent my kit and equipment back to Riyadh with a driver. All I had with me was my dancing shoes and a couple of shirts.

'Can you get to China?' Rob said.

'Why?' I asked, thinking he was winding me up.

'They want you to referee their FA Cup Final on Sunday.'

'Yes, okay. But I'll need a visa, flights, kit and equipment. I can't referee it wearing my boat shoes!'

I also had to clear it with the president of the Saudi federation. I wanted to do the game because, personally, keeping in with the Chinese was a wise move given my state of mind. I told the president it would be good for Saudi to build relations with China, so he gave me permission.

I was at brunch in Dubai with my friends the following day, still thinking something would happen to scupper it, when the flights came through on my phone. It is not often I would give up a weekend with my mates without protest, but I knew this opportunity could prove significant down the line.

I arrived in Beijing at 11 p.m. on the Saturday, and it was minus five degrees celsius. The first thing they gave me was a coat and tracksuit. I wore them the entire time I was there. I think I even kept them on for bed.

The original referee was injured and they were so grateful I had agreed to do the match at short notice. The game went well and I returned to Saudi with a thought stuck in my head, 'China could be my escape.'

My Saudi contract was due to end in February. They wanted me to extend for six months but I was playing a waiting game, giving them a taste of their own medicine when it came to urgency.

Then, in December, Hugh Dallas phoned. He was one of the refereeing officers at UEFA. He said that China had asked him for a recommendation for a foreign referee and he was putting my name forward. I let my agent liaise with the Chinese and, on Christmas Eve, I realised there was a deal to be had.

As long as I was not responsible for referees' travel or group excursions to the Great Wall of China, I was listening.

★   ★   ★

I went on holiday to Spain in February. It had gone quiet on the Chinese front, even though a deal had been agreed in principle.

A Twitter notification flashed up on my phone. 'Mark Clattenburg announced as new referee in Chinese Super League.' That was nice to know, I had not signed the contract yet. The same statement said that Milorad Mazic, the Serbian referee, would also be joining the league. I called him straight away.

'You've kept that quiet,' I said.

'I could say the same about you!' he came back.

It all happened quickly after that. China wanted me there for the start of the new season in March. We agreed a salary similar to what I was earning in Saudi, around £500,000 net, and it was a relief to be leaving behind a job that had turned into a nightmare.

Not that life in China started smoothly. I had originally expected a head of refereeing role with some matches on top, like in Saudi. I wanted more management experience. Instead, I was simply a referee, contracted to do thirty-five games per season.

Ahead of the opening weekend, Claire's dad, Tom, passed away. He was a lovely man and was like a father to me. I probably did not realise how much we meant to each other until after he died. I was at Newcastle Airport a short time later and

I was stopped by a stranger who knew Tom. They had worked together as tilers.

'Your father-in-law never shut up about you,' he said.

It made me smile, I did not have a clue. He never really showed that pride, but he clearly felt it. I flew back from China for his funeral, but it was a difficult time. Tom will always be a huge miss to all of us.

When I finally got around to apartment hunting in Beijing, it was even worse than that first house in Saudi. Nothing felt clean, there were cats and dogs everywhere. I decided to move into a Marriott apartment hotel and ended up staying there permanently. It was cleaned twice a week and had towels, and that was enough for me.

I found life tough at first, on and off the pitch. I had been away from regular refereeing for nearly two years. Milorad Mazic had just refereed the Champions League Final and had been to the World Cup; he was at the top of his game. I definitely wasn't, and I was relying on VAR too much. I never liked to do that. It should be there as a back-up, not a first port of call. I could not get anywhere near the fitness levels of when I was in the Premier League, and that bothered me. I worried about my reputation.

The food was also an issue and I was not fuelling properly before games. Chinese food should be a treat on a Saturday night, not a pre-match meal. I used to send pictures back home to Claire. I would order the duck, a bit of protein, I assumed. They would then put the feet, beak and eyes down in front of you!

I was losing weight, especially as a lot of matches were at

high humidity. I was shedding a kilo during some games, on top of the duck beak diet. I persevered and told myself it would get better with time, which it did.

I was lucky in that the friends I had made in Saudi, the teachers from Bolton, were now in Beijing. I met some of their friends and we would have a few drinks in the German bars where the ex-pats congregated.

But the time difference to the UK was a problem. I was a columnist for the *Daily Mail* and they would ring me at 4 a.m. asking for comment on live Champions League matches. I had to accept that – it wasn't their fault I had moved to China – but I could never get back to sleep after analysing decisions in the middle of the night.

I was also having to wait until 3 p.m. every day to speak to Mia before she went to school and it was after midnight by the time she got home. It felt like they were living in a different world, and that was upsetting.

But Claire and Mia came out for a few weeks and they loved it. We went to see the Great Wall of China. There is so much history to explore. As a country, I grew to like it.

I refereed the Chinese FA Cup Final in December 2019 – like I had twelve months earlier when hot-footing it from Dubai – and I was in talks to extend my contract for another year. The money was good and I had built a life I enjoyed. I was ready to sign. But then along came a virus that would change everyone's world, including mine.

★   ★   ★

I was struggling to breathe. I called Claire, I was panicking, this did not feel right. I was due to come home from China for Christmas, so we arranged for me to have some tests in the UK.

I had been poorly during the early part of December and I flew back from Beijing feeling better, although something was still lingering. The tests on my heart came back normal. Given that my dad died at a young age following heart problems, I was concerned. But the doctors said everything was okay.

We went to Spain for New Year and I suddenly felt worse, as if I was about to stop breathing with this enormous pressure on my chest. My friends were saying it was probably anxiety. I did not know what was wrong with me. I was not ill, at least in that I never had a sore throat, a cough or a cold and was not bed-ridden. But I had no explanation for it and neither did any experts.

Then, in January, news started breaking in China. There was an outbreak of a killer virus, COVID-19. Oh God. Could that have been what I had? It had to be, surely? But I'd had none of the key symptoms, such as the fever or continuous cough.

Gradually, the breathing problems eased. I was not tested until months later, by which time I returned negative, and I still do not know for certain if I contracted coronavirus in China. But even now I am not one hundred per cent within myself. I go for a run and I lose my breath far quicker than I ever used to.

If I did have the virus in China, I must have been beyond the contagious period by the time I returned to the UK, because no one I came into contact with fell ill or tested positive. At least in that sense the first few weeks of me feeling poorly were spent away from home. But it is scary, looking back, thinking of how much worse it could have been.

The Chinese Super League shut down and I remained at home on lockdown in County Durham. I got a message saying that China planned to start the new season in June but that all teams and officials would be in a bubble. I did not feel comfortable about returning. You would basically be in a hotel prison for ninety days, and the virus was still rife. I told them I did not want to go. They responded by cancelling my contract. I was stunned. I assumed they would allow me to return later when the pandemic had eased, that there would be a degree of understanding. Not so. But that's life, you just get on with it. I did not know what the future would hold.

Claire, Mia and I flew out to Spain when it was deemed safe to do so. Hugh Dallas had a villa in the same area as us. I told him I was looking for work and left it at that. A little while later he sent me a text message, 'Good luck.' What did he mean? My next message was from Roberto Rosetti, the Italian who had succeeded Pierluigi Collina as UEFA's chief refereeing officer.

He said there was a job available in Greece, as head of refereeing, but I would need to retire as a referee. That would actually be doing me a favour, as anyone who saw me in China would testify!

A Zoom call was arranged with the presidents of the leading clubs in Greece and, later, I was told they wanted me to take the job. I agreed to it. At the age of forty-five, I had finally blown the whistle on my refereeing career.

16

THE FUTURE

'VAR? Referees are hiding behind it . . .'

I WONDERED at the onset of this book if, come the end, the reader would have changed their perception of me.

The goal was not to be loved, but rather to be understood. I genuinely believe that, before revealing my side on these pages, the real me had never been represented in public.

I was either the referee or, more recently, the pundit. The latter affords you a voice, but it hardly allows for a deep dive into the soul.

This book, I hope, can now serve as a reference point for my take on the controversies and successes of my career. I have shed tears as I picked at some of the scars, reopening old wounds in an attempt to express my true feelings.

But it is a relief to finally have my version out there, to address all that has been said and written about me during the past twenty years or so.

I even recall one social-media post about me buying Tesco's cheaper own-brand beans, instead of Heinz. Well, this is my chance to say – I liked them!

There was another picture on social media of me in Poundland. 'Clattenburg must be struggling,' it said. I'll say this – why buy your batteries anywhere else?

I was able to laugh about them, but they are small examples of how, until now, the portrayal of me has been almost entirely at the mercy of social media and the press.

In an age of mass media, perception is so important. That is not meant to come across as superficial, it is simply a reality of the world in which we live. Once folk turn against you, for right or wrong, it is not easy to reverse such opinion.

Take VAR as an example. At the time of writing, its reputation is in the gutter. But VAR cannot speak out for itself, so I will.

VAR is not the problem – the technology works perfectly fine. Rather, its issues are caused by human interpretation and how the *Laws of the Game* are applied to the technology. Trust me, the game will benefit from video assistant referees. But right now, in the Premier League the process is being undermined by human error.

One of VAR's biggest triumphs is not immediately obvious, and that is a problem when it comes to convincing people of its worth. I am referring to shirt-pulling, blocking and grappling from corners and free-kicks. Five years ago, it dominated every piece of TV analysis, the outrage at defenders not being punished for obstructing attackers. Now, if it does happen, it comes at the expense of a penalty.

But here is the thing – defenders have largely stopped doing it. VAR is the policeman on the bridge. It is the deterrent. More goals are being scored from set-pieces because of an increased freedom of movement inside the penalty area.

Note also, off-the-ball offences such as elbows, head-butts and punches are long gone. Why? VAR means you can no longer get away with it. In general, foul play has been greatly reduced simply by the presence of VAR.

But how do you praise something you cannot see? It is unfortunate for VAR that its positives either go unnoticed or are often taken for granted.

That is not to say VAR is getting a bad deal when it comes to criticism. Absolutely not. In its current form, it has stripped the raw emotion from the game, and that is wrong. That instantaneous release of joy at the sight of your team scoring a goal is the reason we love football. To check that emotion with fear of that goal being disallowed is damaging to all who love the game.

I predicted from the start that marginal offsides and a handball law that needlessly disallows goals would cause havoc, and they have. The advantage has been given to the defending team, and that is not in the spirit of football. We have to remember it's a sport that is meant to entertain and to be enjoyed.

In that regard, the PGMOL has to do away with drawing lines to try and determine if an attacker's upper arm or big toe is offside. They have to listen, because no one wants to see this. Let the assistant referees make the call and VAR can intervene when an obvious error has been made. The current tolerance levels have to change. We saw how that worked well during Euro 2020.

Likewise, we need to get referees back to making decisions.

Right now, in England they are hiding behind VAR. They have become robots. They have lost courage and conviction. I know, I have been there myself during my early months in China. I relied on VAR far too much and lost my confidence. In the end, I said to myself, 'No, I am going to referee this game, I make the decisions.'

VAR should be there to save us from the major mistakes, not to micro-manage a football match. We need to strip it back and say, 'Right, this is what it's going to be used for', and that should not include debate over subjective decisions. Those calls belong to the referee on the pitch, because an official sat in Stockley Park does not sense the smell of the game.

But we must persevere and work together to get it right, to find a balance between helping a referee when they need it and protecting that raw emotion which makes the game so special. Because now, more than ever, referees do need help.

The current group of Premier League officials has never been weaker. There are no leaders. By that, I mean a referee who will take the majority of the big matches. Graham Poll did it when I first joined the Premier League. Later, it was Howard Webb, and then me. That takes the pressure away from the rest of the group. At present, no one is taking ownership of those games, meaning a lot of referees are being exposed to matches beyond their capability.

The PGMOL are also stuck with a lot of average officials. That is a by-product of turning professional, because employment law means it is now harder to get rid of someone who has not performed. In turn, that stops referees coming through from the Football League.

I look at the Championship and below and worry about where the future planning has gone, the pathway I took to the Premier League. There needs to be better management of the development of referees in our country.

At the time of writing, I am employed as head of officiating in Greece. Would I return to a management role within the PGMOL? No.

Mike Riley, the PGMOL general manager, has done a lot of good in structuring the business, and I give him credit for that. But he has lost the experience and expertise of the likes of myself and Howard – more should have been done to retain us and some others. For refereeing standards to improve, Riley needs better people beneath him within the organisation. There are too many jobs for the boys.

But, personally, I could never work for the PGMOL. I think this book explains the reasons as to why. I also want to retire by the age of fifty-five and see the world with my family, as well as work on my golf handicap. Before then, I have a decade or so to give something back to refereeing, and I would not rule out a management role within UEFA or FIFA.

You exist within a bubble when you work in the Premier League. Now, I have experienced football and officiating across Europe and beyond, given my time in Saudi Arabia and China. It has broadened my perspective.

I have no regrets about quitting the Premier League – and

later refereeing – at the times I did. But nor do I have any regrets about the career I chose to pursue.

Yes, it took me to some dark and lonely places in my life, but there was a reason I always fought back. That was my love of refereeing and desire to be the best.

The setbacks made me stronger and I made it to the top when I was named the number one referee in the world in 2016, and that gave me huge pride.

It was proof that, no matter your background, hard work is the key to realising your dreams. That is why I have no regrets – I achieved what I set out to do.

I went after that dream by being different, because I knew that to conform was to settle for mediocrity. The fact I was a daft Geordie electrician from a council estate was a strength, not a weakness, even if it did appear to offend some.

So when I came to reflect following my last international match between Brazil and Australia at the MCG in 2017, I thought to myself, 'Wow, you did it, you proved a lot of people wrong.'

I hope this book has done the same.

ACKNOWLEDGEMENTS

I would like to say a few thank-yous.

To Claire - without your love and support I would not have had the strength to beat the hard times. You are an amazing wife and mother.

To Mam and Dad – you supported me and brought me up in a happy family, and gave me the drive to succeed in life.

To Thomas and Anne Lindley, my wonderful in-laws – I cannot thank you enough for your support and love. We miss you, Tom.

To Pierluigi Collina – you are the man and mentor who changed my career and my life.

To Craig Hope – I could not have told my story without your help and expertise. I will miss our weekly chats, and I definitely owe you a beer.

To everyone at Headline for giving me this opportunity, and to Tom Whiting for his help in editing my story.

To Ian King – a brilliant friend who was always there in the darkest days, for me and my family. You were there during the good times, too, and that meant a lot.

To David Reach – the schoolteacher who put me on the path to refereeing. You made a difference to my life.

To Jake Collin, Simon Beck, Anthony Taylor and Andre Marriner – I had a great team around me in 2016. Without that, I would not have achieved what I did.

To Rob Segal, my agent, who has always been there for me, and to Emma Alexander.

To Phil Dowd – what a laugh we had during my early days in the Premier League. The room-mate who became my best mate in refereeing.

To Keith Hackett – you gave me my chance in the Premier League and I always thought you were fair.

To George Courtney – an inspiration during my early refereeing career.

INDEX

INDEX